AUSTRALIAN
BIRDS

A Concise Photographic Field Guide

This Field Guide *is a pocket version of the authors'*
Australian Birds -Simply Classified *first published as* Australia Land of Birds *in 1987. It is now in its 4th edition and 8th printing, with sales of over 50 000 copies*

Published by
Murray David Publishing
35 Borgnis Street, Davidson, New South Wales, 2085, Australia
Postal Address: P.O. Box 140, Belrose West, New South Wales, 2085
Phone: 61 2 9451 3895 Fax: 61 2 9451 3663
www.m2d.com.au
email: mail@m2d.com.au

Publishing Director: Marion Child
Marketing Director: David Jenkins
Executive Director: David Forsythe

in association with
Gary Allen Pty Ltd
9 Cooper Street, Smithfield, New South Wales, 2164, Australia
Telephone: 61 2 9275 2933   Fax: 61 2 9609 6155
email: customerservice@garyallen.com.au

First edition 2002
Reprinted 2004, 2008

Wholly devised and designed by Donald and Molly Trounson

Copyright © M2D Publishing Pty Ltd 2004
Copyright © photographs: individual photographers as credited

Printed in Indonesia

ISBN 0-9752428-4-9

BIRDS
AUSTRALIAN

A CONCISE PHOTOGRAPHIC FIELD GUIDE

DONALD AND MOLLY TROUNSON

MURRAY DAVID PUBLISHING
in association with
GARY ALLEN

ENGLISH NAMES
NUMBERS

v

HOW TO SEARCH

If you have difficulty in identifying your bird, proceed as follows:

1   Seek the help of the Section Index

2.   Bypass the obviously irrelevent Sections, thereby limiting the area of search.

3.   Choose the most promising Section from its title as your starting point.

4.   Scan the colour plates for a photograph resembling your bird–and, if necessary, repeat the process with other Sections by trial and error.

5.   When successful, check the caption for the size of the species and the distribution map to see that it occurs in your area.

6.   If you remain unsure of your identification, look for corroborating data, (eg voice) in the corresponding Species Note in the latter part of the Guide.

CONTENTS

THE 21 SECTIONS

PHOTOGRAPHS LAND BIRDS
(distribution maps
included)
                Sections 17 to 21

SPECIES NOTES LAND BIRDS
(keyed numerically
with the
photographs)   Sections 17 to 21

*locates an Index

ORGANISATION OF THE GUIDE

In bird guides worldwide, it has long been the the convention to interleave the illustrations with their texts throughout the book. This means that the reader may have to leaf through the entire book to find a picture of a particular bird. It is self-evident that this could become a serious impediment in the field when quick reference is needed. In this Guide, we have adopted a radical solution to the situation by separating the photographs from their texts and transferring them *en bloc* to the front where they become immediately accessible - with the Species Notes following in the same sequence and carrying identical numbers.

INTRODUCTION

The Guide has been developed as a compact companion to our book *Australian Birds - Simply Classified*. It represents the 690 species of birds recorded in Australia as residents or regular visitors and replicates all the 815 photographs and the associated texts of the parent book which directly relate to their identification. Most of the photographs are reproduced in their original size, and the texts, which are unabridged, are printed in easy to read type.

CLASSIFICATION OF THE BIRDS

The Guide inherits the central feature of the parent book which relates to a simpler system of classifying the birds pioneered by us when planning the book during the 1980s. This is independent of the conventions of the established ornithological classifications used in most bird books and is achieved by arranging the 80 bird families into groups by common characteristics and naming them under collective titles in everyday language. The land and water birds are separated, and these are subdivided into 21 Sections which are listed, with the names of the families represented, in the following Section Index. The Sections themselves are in the form of autonomous part works, each individually indexed with the names and photo numbers of the families and species it contains. By these means, bird identification is brought within reach of everyone.

Intact families are used, as far as possible, in the makeup of the Sections, and they can therefore be equated with the established ornithological classifications which are tabulated at the end of the Guide in the *Systematic Index of Orders and Families*. This we have cross-referenced with the relative Section numbers, to provide an alternative means of reference to the Guide's contents.

Of the sections, 12½ represent the 47 non-passerine families, and 8½ the breaking up of the continuous block of the 33 passerine families.

The Sections provide an invaluable choice of distinctive starting points when beginning as search - as indicated in the notes on HOW TO SEARCH on page vi.

THE COLOUR PLATES

The 815 photographs are presented in 103 double page colour plates. These include the distribution maps, and brief captions giving the English name(s) and photo number(s) for each species or races illustrated. Key data relating to size, gender and maturity (if known) is also included.

Layouts Wherever possible, photographs of look-alikes are placed together for comparison, with western and eastern birds placed left and right and the northern and southern birds top and bottom. The photographs are scaled, within the limits available, to a size relationship between the birds on a given page.

Distribution maps These were originally delineated by the late Arnold McGill to accord with *The Atlas of Australian Birds* published by the RAOU in 1984. Some have since been revised on the advice of Graeme Chapman. Stippling, notably in Section 2, represents occasional sightings. Areas identified with letters denote regions where distinctive geographic races occur.

THE SPECIES NOTES

The English and scientific name is given, also the trinomials for all the geographic races where they are indicated in the distribution maps. Texts are in the form of narratives about the species and their lifestyles, and include data relating to food, nesting, breeding periods and endemicity. They conclude with codas, in italics, specifying, sex, maturity, plumage variations and voice. In difficult cases, clues to identification are also given.

Voice Descriptions of voice are limited by space to brief clues. These are based partly on personal experience, onomatopoeia by Ernest Hoskin for the birds of New South Wales, and abbreviations favoured in books such as *A Field Guide to the Birds of Australia* by Graham Pizzey, and Readers Digest's *Complete Book of Australian Birds,* for which acknowledgement is readily given.

English names *The Recommended English Names for Australian Birds* published by the Royal Australasian Ornithologists Union (now Birds Australia) in 1977 are used, as revised in 1994. Popular alternative names are also given in the indexes at the head of each Section and in the Species Notes.

Scientific names These conform to Monograph No. 2 of the RAOU The *Taxonomy of Species of Australia and its Territories* by Leslie Christidis and Walter E Boles (1994).

THE ILLUSTRATIONS AND TEXTS ARE KEYED
TOGETHER THROUGH TWIN NUMBERING

SECTION INDEX

LAND BIRDS

Birds of the bush, forest and desert

PASSERINES (SONGBIRDS)
Sections 9-16 with Sections 4(part) and 5

WATER BIRDS

Birds of the inland waters, shore and ocean

Opposite: Little Corellas (D&M Trounson)

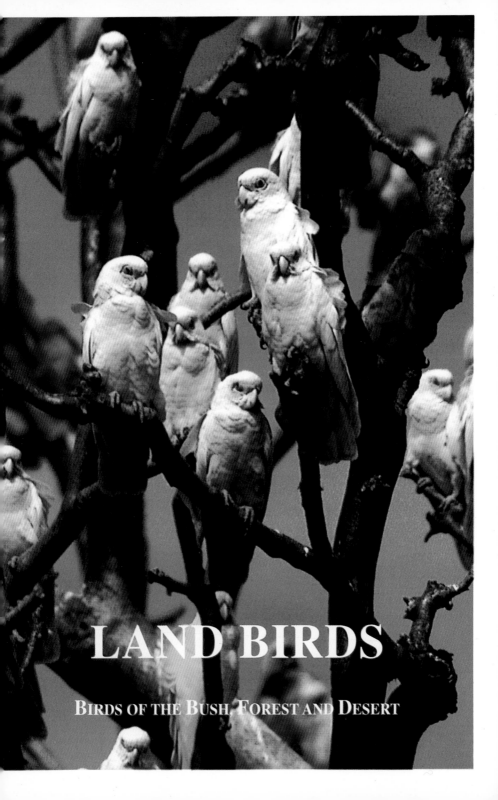

LAND BIRDS

BIRDS OF THE BUSH, FOREST AND DESERT

1 Flightless Birds

1

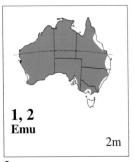

1, 2
Emu

2m

2

2

FAMILY

3, 4
Southern Cassowary
                1.5m

2 Diurnal Birds of Prey

FAMILIES

INDEX

2

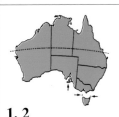

1, 2
Wedge-tailed Eagle
♂90cm ♀100cm

2   1

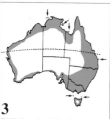

3
White-bellied
Sea-Eagle
Adult

4
Immature
♂75cm ♀85cm

4

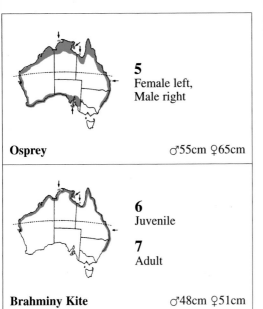

5
Female left,
Male right

Osprey ♂55cm ♀65cm

6
Juvenile

7
Adult

Brahminy Kite ♂48cm ♀51cm

5

6

7

2

8, 9
Little Eagle
Male
Two shots of the same
bird, 8 showing crest

♂48cm ♀55cm

10
**Black-shouldered
Kite**
♂36cm ♀38cm

11
Letter-winged Kite

♂36cm ♀38cm

12
Whistling Kite
♂53cm ♀58cm

13, 14
Black Kite
♂52cm ♀55cm

15
**Black-breasted
Buzzard**

♂52cm ♀60cm

8

10

13

10

9

11

12

14

15

2

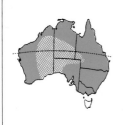

16, 17
Square-tailed Kite

♂53cm ♀56cm

18
Red Goshawk
♂51cm ♀61cm

19
Brown Goshawk
♂45cm ♀55cm

20
Grey form

21
White form

Grey Goshawk   ♂42cm ♀54cm

22
Collared
Sparrowhawk
♂32cm ♀38cm

23
Swamp Harrier
Immature male
♂57cm ♀61cm

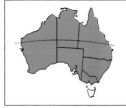

24
Spotted Harrier

♂55cm ♀60cm

16

19

22

17

18

20

21

23

24

25
Light form left,
dark form right

Brown Falcon ♂45cm ♀50cm

25

26
Male

29
Female

Peregrine Falcon ♂42cm ♀50cm

27
Pacific Baza
♂40cm ♀45cm

28
Australian Hobby
♂32cm ♀35cm

27

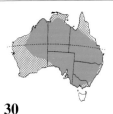 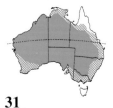

30
Black Falcon
♂50cm ♀55cm

31
Grey Falcon
♂36cm ♀43cm

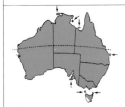

32
Nankeen Kestrel
Male

♂33cm ♀35cm

30

26

8

29

1

32

3 Nocturnal Birds

FAMILIES

INDEX

3

Southern Boobook

Race **B**
Western populations

1
Northern form

2, 5 Race **A**
Eastern populations

4
Southern form

♂23–36cm
♀27–36cm

3
Rufous Owl

50cm

6
Barking Owl
Race **B**

43cm

7
Powerful Owl

♂65cm ♀54cm

8
Race **C**
Tasmania

♂35–42cm
♀43–57cm

9
Race **A**
Mainland

♂33–41cm
♀38–46cm

Masked Owl

1

2

4

7

3

5

6

8

9

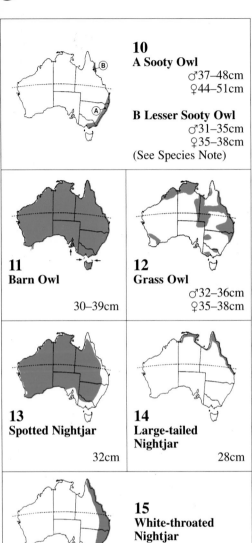

10
A Sooty Owl
♂37–48cm
♀44–51cm

B Lesser Sooty Owl
♂31–35cm
♀35–38cm
(See Species Note)

11
Barn Owl

30–39cm

12
Grass Owl
♂32–36cm
♀35–38cm

13
Spotted Nightjar

32cm

14
Large-tailed Nightjar

28cm

15
White-throated Nightjar

35cm

10

13

11

12

4

15

3

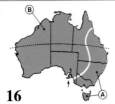 

16
Tawny Frogmouth
Race **B**
Kimberley form

Marbled Frogmouth
Race **A**

19
Race **B**
South-western form
Sizes vary
North/South and
East/West

♂34–53cm
♀35–49cm

17
Night posture

20
Day posture

♂37–41cm

18
**Australian
Owlet-nightjar**
Race **A**
23cm

21
**Papuan
Frogmouth**
Race **A**
50–60cm

16

19

17

18

0

21

4 Ground-frequenting Birds

This Section includes the most notable examples of birds that live on or near the ground in a wide variety of habitat - ranging from sparse vegetation of heath, grasslands, and low scrub in open country to the confines of the forest floor. Represented are 11 of the smaller passerine families, and the 6 families of fowl-like birds.

Examples of ground-frequenting birds to be found in some of the other Sections, including arboreal-living birds that come to the ground to feed or catch prey, are listed overleaf.

FAMILIES

SOME PASSERINES OF THE OPEN COUNTRY, LOW SCRUB AND THE GRASSES

Number

Meliphagidae	CHATS (including GIBBERBIRD)	1-6
(Part with Section 13)		
Motacillidae	PIPIT	10
	YELLOW WAGTAIL	7
Alaudidae	LARKS	8, 9
Sylviidae	SONGLARKS	11, 12
(Part with Section 12 for:	Reed Warbler, Grassbirds, Spinifebird,Cisticolas)	
Cinclosomatidae	QUAIL-THRUSHES	13-21
	WHIPBIRDS	26, 27
	WEDGEBILLS	29, 30
Corcoracidae	APOSTLEBIRD	22
(Part with Section 16 for Chough)		
Pomatostomidae	BABBLERS	23-25, 28

BIRDS OF THE FOREST FLOOR AND HEATH

Orthonychidae	LOGRUNNER	31
	CHOWCHILLA	32
Pardalotidae	PILOTBIRD	33
(Part with Section 12)	BRISTLEBIRDS	34-36
Atrichornithidae	SCRUB-BIRDS	37, 38
Pittidae	PITTAS	39-41

FOWL-LIKE BIRDS

Megapodiidae	MOUND-BUILDERS	42-44
Odontophoridae	CALIFORNIA QUAIL	45
Phasianidae	PHEASANT	58
	PEAFOWL	59
	TRUE QUAILS	46-48
Turnicidae	BUTTON-QUAILS	49-54
Pedionomidae	PLAINS-WANDERER	56, 57
Otididae	BUSTARD	55

4

INDEX

OTHER SECTIONS WHICH INCLUDE GROUND-FREQUENTING LAND BIRDS

SECTION

1	FLIGHTLESS BIRDS
3	GRASS OWL, NIGHTJARS
5	LYREBIRDS
6	THE GROUND-FEEDING PIGEONS AND DOVES
7	GROUND PARROT, NIGHT PARROT, ROCK PARROT, GOLDEN-SHOULDERED PARROT (nests in termite mound)
9	THE KINGFISHERS, BEE-EATER (nests in burrows or termite mound)
10	SCRUB-ROBINS, ROBINS, WILLIE WAGTAIL, SANDSTONE SHRIKE-THRUSH, GROUND THRUSHES
11	WRENS
12	WARBLERS OF THE GRASSES AND REEDS
14	FINCHES, PARDALOTES (most nest in burrows)
15	BOWERBIRDS (during courtship displays)
20	PLOVERS AND PRATINCOLES (these forage and nest in open country often in the vicinity of water)

Arboreal-living birds that are often ground feeders include:

2 & 3	BIRDS OF PREY
7	THE WHITE COCKATOOS AND MANY PARROTS, ESPECIALLY THE SMALL NEOPHEMA GRASS PARROTS
10	SHRIKE-THRUSHES, SONGTHRUSH, BLACKBIRD
12	SOME OF THE THORNBILLS, NOTABLY THE BUFF-AND YELLOW-RUMPED THORNBILLS
16	CROWS, RAVENS, CHOUGHS, MAGPIE-LARKS

4

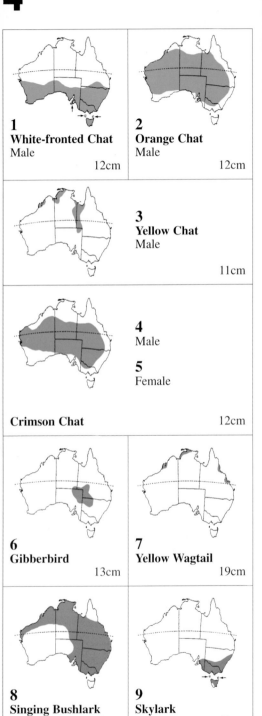

1
White-fronted Chat
Male
12cm

2
Orange Chat
Male
12cm

3
Yellow Chat
Male
11cm

4
Male
5
Female
Crimson Chat
12cm

6
Gibberbird
13cm

7
Yellow Wagtail
19cm

8
Singing Bushlark
13cm

9
Skylark
19cm

1

4

7

2

3

5

6

8

9

4

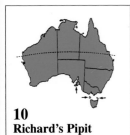

10
Richard's Pipit
17cm

11
Rufous Songlark
18cm

12
Brown Songlark
Male

♂24cm ♀18cm

13
Male

14
Female

**Spotted
Quail-thrush**
26–28cm

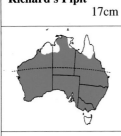

15
Male

18
Female

**Chestnut-breasted
Quail-thrush**
22–24cm

16
Male

17
Female

**Chestnut
Quail-thrush**
23–26cm

10

13

16

1

12

14

15

17

18

4

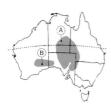

Cinnamon Quail-thrush

Race **B**
Nullarbor form

19
Pair

20
Male

Race **A**
Inland form

21
Male

18–21cm   19–22cm

22
Apostlebird
33cm

23
White-browed
Babbler
20cm

24
Hall's Babbler
23cm

25
Chestnut-crowned
Babbler
22cm

26
Western Whipbird
25cm

27
Eastern Whipbird
28cm

19

22

25

20

21

23

24

26

27

4

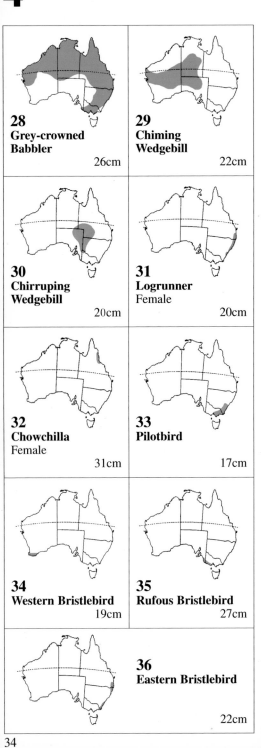

28
Grey-crowned Babbler
26cm

29
Chiming Wedgebill
22cm

30
Chirruping Wedgebill
20cm

31
Logrunner
Female
20cm

32
Chowchilla
Female
31cm

33
Pilotbird
17cm

34
Western Bristlebird
19cm

35
Rufous Bristlebird
27cm

36
Eastern Bristlebird
22cm

28

31

34

29

30

2

33

5

36

4

37
Noisy Scrub-bird
Female
24cm

38
Rufous Scrub-bird
16cm

39
Rainbow Pitta
18cm

40
Red-bellied Pitta
19cm

41
Noisy Pitta
21cm

42
Orange-footed Scrubfowl
40cm

43
Australian Brush-turkey
70cm

44
Malleefowl
60cm

45
California Quail
Male
24cm

37

40

43

38

39

41

42

44

45

4

46
King Quail
Male left, female right
14cm

47
Brown Quail   17cm

48
Stubble Quail
Female left,
male right
18cm

49
**Red-chested
Button-quail**
Male
♂13cm ♀15cm

50
**Painted
Button-quail**
♂17cm ♀20cm

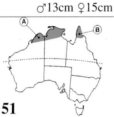

51
**Chestnut-backed
Button-quail**   Race **A**
♂15cm ♀18cm

**Buff-breasted
Button-quail**   Race **B**
(See Species Note)

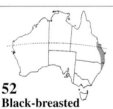

52
**Black-breasted
Button-quail**
Female left, male right
♂16cm ♀18cm

53
**Red-backed
Button-quail**
Female
♂13cm ♀15cm

54
Little Button-quail

♂14cm ♀15cm

46

49

52

47

48

50

51

3

54

4

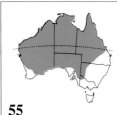

55
Australian Bustard
♂1300cm ♀800cm

Plains-wanderer

56
Male

57
Female

♂16cm ♀18cm

58
Common Pheasant
Male
♂85cm ♀60cm

59
Indian Peafowl
Male
♂2.4m ♀90cm

55

58

57

9

5 Lyrebirds

1

1
Superb Lyrebird
Male
       up to 100cm

2
Female
       86cm

2

FAMILY

3

3
Albert's Lyrebird
Male

90cm

4
Female

65cm

4

6 Pigeons and Doves Cuckoos

FAMILIES

INDEX

CUCKOOS

1

2

1
Diamond Dove
    22cm

2
Peaceful Dove
    23cm

3
Spotted Turtle-Dove

    31cm

3

6

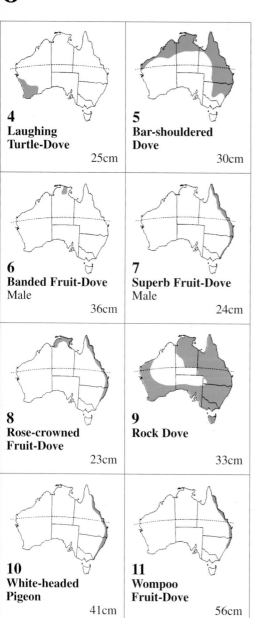

4
Laughing Turtle-Dove
25cm

5
Bar-shouldered Dove
30cm

6
Banded Fruit-Dove
Male
36cm

7
Superb Fruit-Dove
Male
24cm

8
Rose-crowned Fruit-Dove
23cm

9
Rock Dove
33cm

10
White-headed Pigeon
41cm

11
Wompoo Fruit-Dove
56cm

4

7

10

5

6

8

9

11

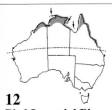

12
Pied Imperial Pigeon

44cm

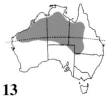

13
Flock Bronzewing
Male

30cm

14
Squatter Pigeon

32cm

15
Race **A** Yellow-eyed

16
Race **B** Red-eyed

Partridge Pigeon 28cm

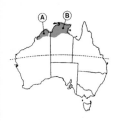

17
Topknot Pigeon

46cm

18
White-quilled Rock Pigeon

30cm

19
Chestnut-quilled Rock Pigeon

32cm

12

17

13

14

15

16

18

19

6

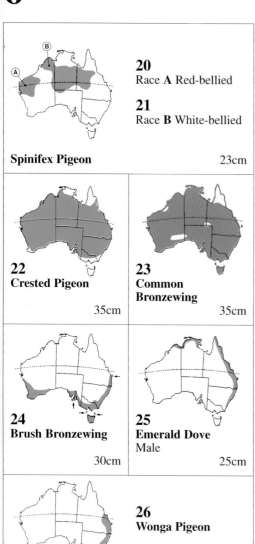

20

23

25

22

24

6

6

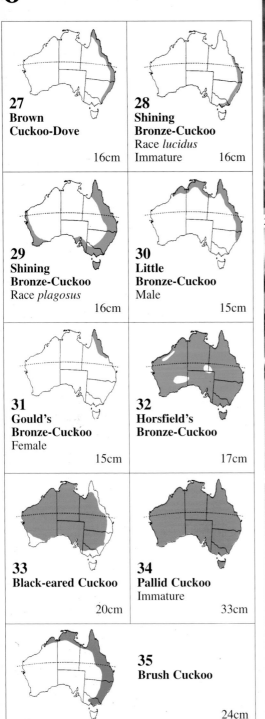

27
Brown
Cuckoo-Dove
16cm

28
Shining
Bronze-Cuckoo
Race *lucidus*
Immature   16cm

29
Shining
Bronze-Cuckoo
Race *plagosus*
16cm

30
Little
Bronze-Cuckoo
Male
15cm

31
Gould's
Bronze-Cuckoo
Female
15cm

32
Horsfield's
Bronze-Cuckoo
17cm

33
Black-eared Cuckoo
20cm

34
Pallid Cuckoo
Immature
33cm

35
Brush Cuckoo
24cm

27

30

33

28

29

31

32

34

35

6

36
Oriental Cuckoo
33cm

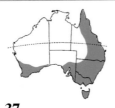

37
Fan-tailed Cuckoo
27cm

38
**Chestnut-breasted
Cuckoo**

23cm

39
Male

40
Immature

Common Koel
46cm

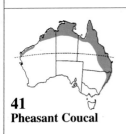

41
Pheasant Coucal

66cm

42
**Channel-billed
Cuckoo**

65cm

36

41

37

38

39

40

42

7 Parrots

FAMILIES

COCKATOOS

PARROTS

INDEX

7

1
**Palm
Cockatoo**

60cm

2
**Glossy
Black-Cockatoo**
Male left,
female right   50cm

3
**Sulphur-crested
Cockatoo**

49cm

4
Male

5
Female

**Red-tailed
Black-Cockatoo**
61cm (north)
52cm (south)

6
**Major
Mitchell's Cockatoo**
Female
36cm

7
**White-tailed
Black-Cockatoo**
Short-billed form
Female   55–60cm

Long-billed form
(See Species Note)

8
**Yellow-tailed
Black-Cockatoo**
Female   69cm

9
Galah
Male

36cm

7

10
Little Corella
38cm
Western Corella
(map above) 42cm

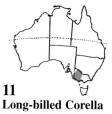
11
Long-billed Corella
38cm

12
Gang-gang Cockatoo
Young male
36cm

14
Male

15
Female

Eclectus Parrot 43cm

13
Cockatiel
Female, male,
juvenile
33cm

16
Red-cheeked Parrot
Female left,
male right 25cm

17
Double-eyed Fig-Parrot
Race **B** Male 16cm

18
Musk Lorikeet
23cm

10

13

16

11

12

14

15

7

18

19

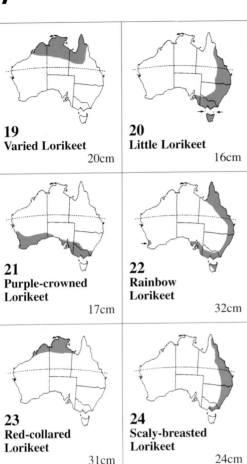

19
Varied Lorikeet
20cm

20
Little Lorikeet
16cm

21
**Purple-crowned
Lorikeet**
17cm

22
**Rainbow
Lorikeet**
32cm

23
**Red-collared
Lorikeet**
31cm

24
**Scaly-breasted
Lorikeet**
24cm

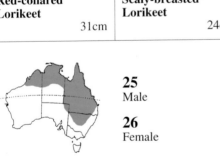

25
Male

26
Female

Red-winged Parrot
33cm

27
**Australian
King Parrot**
Male
44cm

22

25

20

21

23

24

26

27

7

28
Male

29
Female

Superb Parrot 42cm

30
Princess Parrot
Male
46cm

31
Regent Parrot
Male
41cm

32
Crimson Rosella
Yellow form
34cm

33
Crimson Rosella
Adelaide area
36cm

34
Adult

35
Immature

Crimson Rosella 37cm

36
Green Rosella

36cm

28

31

34

9

30

2

33

5

36

7

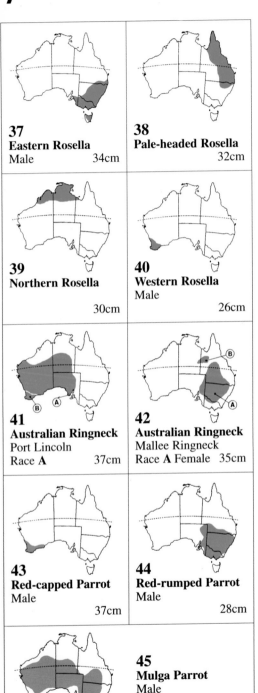

37
Eastern Rosella
Male   34cm

38
Pale-headed Rosella
      32cm

39
Northern Rosella
      30cm

40
Western Rosella
Male   26cm

41
Australian Ringneck
Port Lincoln
Race **A**   37cm

42
Australian Ringneck
Mallee Ringneck
Race **A** Female   35cm

43
Red-capped Parrot
Male
      37cm

44
Red-rumped Parrot
Male
      28cm

45
Mulga Parrot
Male
      30cm

37

40

43

38

39

41

42

44

45

7

46
Paradise Parrot
Historic distribution

30cm

47
Female

48
Male

Golden-shouldered Parrot

27cm

49
Hooded Parrot
Male

27cm

50
Blue Bonnet
Race **B** Male

35cm

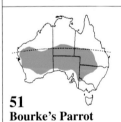

51
Bourke's Parrot
Female

22cm

52
Blue-winged Parrot

23cm

53
Turquoise Parrot
Male

21cm

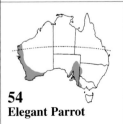

54
Elegant Parrot

24cm

46

49

52

47

48

50

51

53

54

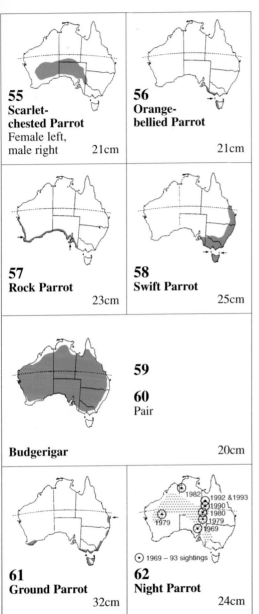

55
Scarlet-chested Parrot
Female left, male right   21cm

56
Orange-bellied Parrot
21cm

57
Rock Parrot
23cm

58
Swift Parrot
25cm

59

60
Pair

Budgerigar
20cm

61
Ground Parrot
32cm

62
Night Parrot
24cm

1982   1992 & 1993
1990
1980
1979   1979
1969

⊙ 1969 – 93 sightings

55

58

6

57

9

60

1

62

8 Kingfishers

FAMILIES

INDEX

1
Forest Kingfisher
Female
23cm

2
Red-backed Kingfisher
24cm

3
Sacred Kingfisher
23cm

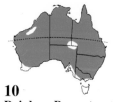

4
Collared Kingfisher

29cm

5
Male

6
Female

Yellow-billed Kingfisher   21cm

7
Buff-breasted Paradise-Kingfisher
36cm

8
Azure Kingfisher

19cm

9
Little Kingfisher

13cm

10
Rainbow Bee-eater
Male

28cm

11
Dollarbird
Immature

30cm

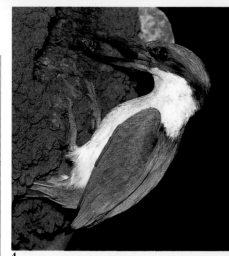

4

7

9

6

8

10   11

12

13

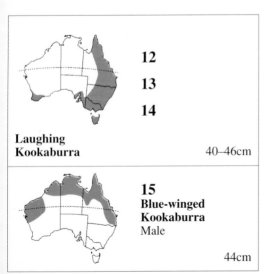

12
13
14

Laughing Kookaburra   40–46cm

15
Blue-winged Kookaburra
Male

44cm

9 Cuckoo-shrikes and Allies Woodswallows, Swallow-like Birds Sittellas and Treecreepers

FAMILIES

INDEX

9

1
**Black-faced
Cuckoo-shrike**
33cm

2
**White-bellied
Cuckoo-shrike**
28cm

3
**Barred
Cuckoo-shrike**
28cm

4
**Ground
Cuckoo-shrike**
36cm

5
Male

6
Female

Varied Triller   18cm

7
Male (breeding)

8
Male (eclipse)

9
Female

White-winged Triller   18 cm

1

4

7

3

6

9

9

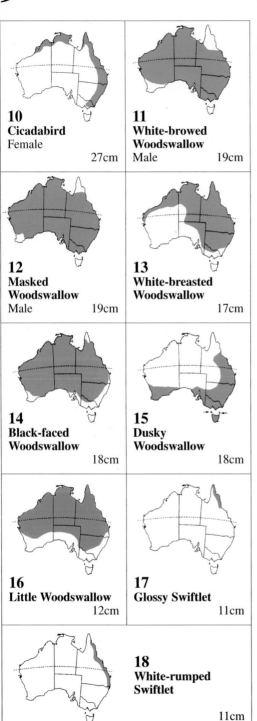

10
Cicadabird
Female
27cm

11
**White-browed
Woodswallow**
Male   19cm

12
**Masked
Woodswallow**
Male   19cm

13
**White-breasted
Woodswallow**
17cm

14
**Black-faced
Woodswallow**
18cm

15
**Dusky
Woodswallow**
18cm

16
Little Woodswallow
12cm

17
Glossy Swiftlet
11cm

18
**White-rumped
Swiftlet**
11cm

10

13

16

12

15

18

19 **Fork-tailed Swift** 19cm	**20** **White-throated Needletail** 20cm
21 **White-backed Swallow** 15cm	**22** **Barn Swallow** 17cm
23 **Welcome Swallow** 13cm	**24** **Tree Martin** 13cm
25 **Fairy Martin** 12cm	**26** **Varied Sittella** Race **A** White-winged 10cm
27 **Varied Sittella** Orange-winged Nominate race 12cm	

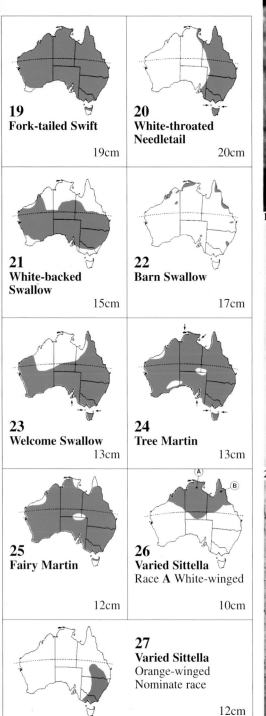

19

20

22

25

21

24

27

9

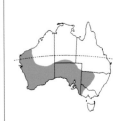

28
Black-capped
Male

29
Female

Varied Sittella   12cm

30
Varied Sittella
White-headed
     12cm

31
**White-throated
Treecreeper**
Female   17cm

32
**Red-browed
Treecreeper**
Male
     15cm

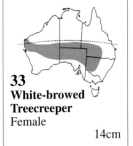

33
**White-browed
Treecreeper**
Female   14cm

34
Rufous Treecreeper
Male
     17cm

35
Brown Treecreeper
Male
     17cm

36
**Black-tailed
Treecreeper**
Race **A**
Male
     20cm

28

31

34

30

10 Robins, Flycatchers, Whistlers and Thrush-like Birds

FAMILIES

INDEX

1

2

1
Male

2
Female

Flame Robin   14cm

3
Dusky Robin

16cm

3

10

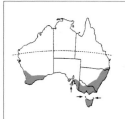

Scarlet Robin

4
Male

7
Female

14cm

Rose Robin

5
Male

8
Female

12cm

Pink Robin

6
Male

9
Female

14cm

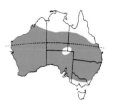

Red-capped Robin

10
Male

11
Female

12cm

12
Mangrove Robin

16cm

4

7

10

6

9

1

12

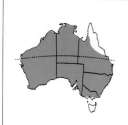

13
Male

14
Female

Hooded Robin 17cm

13

15
White-breasted Robin
14cm

16
Western Yellow Robin
16cm

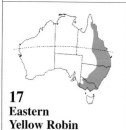

17
Eastern Yellow Robin
17cm

18
Pale-yellow Robin
13cm

16

19
White-faced Robin

12cm

20
Race **B** Buff-sided

21
Race **A** White-sided

White-browed Robin 17cm

19

4

15

7

18

0

21

10

22
Grey-headed Robin
17cm

23
Southern Scrub-robin
23cm

24
Northern Scrub-robin
21cm

25
Yellow-legged Flycatcher
12cm

26
Kimberley form

27
Cape York form

Lemon-bellied Flycatcher
14cm

28
Jacky Winter
14cm

29
Spectacled Monarch
16cm

30
Black-faced Monarch
19cm

22

25

28

23

24

26

27

29

30

10

31
Black-winged Monarch
15cm

32
Yellow-breasted Boatbill
Male   12cm

33
White-eared Monarch
14cm

34
Frilled Monarch
16cm

35
Pied Monarch
Male

16cm

36
Male

39
Female

Satin Flycatcher   17 cm

37
Male

38
Female

Shining Flycatcher   19 cm

96

31

34

37

32

33

36

8

39

40

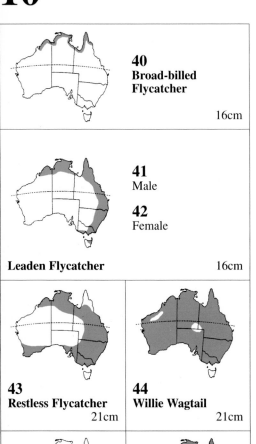

40
Broad-billed
Flycatcher

16cm

41
Male

42
Female

Leaden Flycatcher 16cm

43
Restless Flycatcher
21cm

44
Willie Wagtail
21cm

45
Red-whiskered
Bulbul
23cm

46
Grey Fantail
16cm

47
Northern Fantail
18cm

48
Rufous Fantail
16cm

43

46

1

42

4

45

7

48

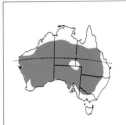

49
Male

50
Female

Crested Bellbird 23cm

51
Crested Shrike-tit
Northern form
Female 16cm

Crested Shrike-tit
Nominate race
Eastern form

53
Crested Shrike-tit
Western form
Female 17 cm

52
Male

54
Female

19cm

55
Male

56
Female

Rufous Whistler 17cm

49

50

52

54

56

10

57
Male

60
Female

**White-breasted
Whistler**   21cm

58
Male

61
Female

Golden Whistler   18cm

59
Male

62
Immature female

**Mangrove Golden
Whistler**   17cm

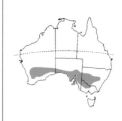

63
Male

64
Female

Gilbert's Whistler   20cm

57

60

63

58

61

64

59

62

10

65
Male

66
Female

Olive Whistler   22cm

67
Red-lored Whistler
Female

21cm

68
Northern Territory
form

69
Cape York form

Grey Whistler   15cm

70
Little Shrike-thrush
Race A

19cm

71
Race *harmonica*
Male

72
Race *rufiventris*
Male

Grey Shrike-thrush   23cm

65

68

71

66

67

69

70

72

73
Bower's
Shrike-thrush
21cm

74
Sandstone
Shrike-thrush
26cm

75 Song Thrush

23cm

76
Bassian Thrush /
29cm

Russet-tailed Thrush
29cm

77
Female

78
Male

Common Blackbird
25cm

73

75

77

74

76

78

11 Wrens

FAMILIES

INDEX

1
Mainland form
Male

2
Female

Superb Fairy-wren 13cm

3
Tasmanian form
Male

14cm

11

4
Male

5
Female

Splendid Fairy-wren   13cm

6
Splendid Fairy-wren
Black-backed race
Male   13cm

7
Splendid Fairy-wren
Turquoise race
Male   14cm

Nominate race

8
Male

9
Female

Variegated
Fairy-wren   14cm

10
Purple-backed race
Male

11
Female

Variegated
Fairy-wren   14cm

12
Variegated
Fairy-wren
Lavender-flanked race
Male
                    14cm

4

7

10

6

9

12

11

13
Male

16
Female

Lovely Fairy-wren   14cm

14
Male

17
Female

**Blue-breasted
Fairy-wren**   14cm

15
Male

18
Female

**Red-backed
Fairy-wren**   13cm

DIRK HARTOG ISLAND
BARROW ISLAND

19
**White-winged
Fairy-wren**
Nominate race
Black-and-white form
Male

20
Blue-and-white form
Male

21
Female

13cm

13

16

19

15

18

21

11

22
Red-winged
Fairy-wren
Male
14cm

23
Purple-crowned Fairy-wren
Male left, female right
16cm

24
Female

25
Male

Southern Emu-wren   20cm

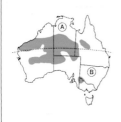

26
Mallee Emu-wren
Male (**B**)

15cm

27
Thick-billed Grasswren
Race **A** Male
18cm

28
White-throated Grasswren
Male
21.5cm

29
Carpentarian Grasswren
Male

17cm

22

24

27

26

29

11

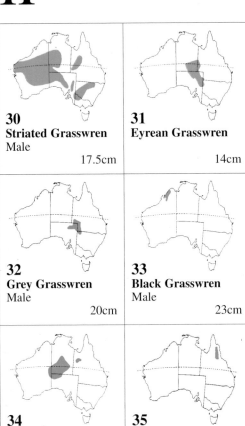

30
Striated Grasswren
Male
17.5cm

31
Eyrean Grasswren
14cm

32
Grey Grasswren
Male
20cm

33
Black Grasswren
Male
23cm

34
Dusky Grasswren
Female
17cm

35
Fernwren
Male
14cm

White-browed Scrubwren

36
Race **D**
Western form

37
Nominate race **A**
South-eastern form
12cm

38
Yellow-throated Scrubwren
Male
14cm

30

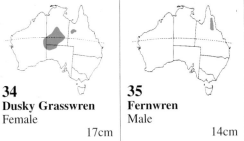

33

36

32

35

38

39

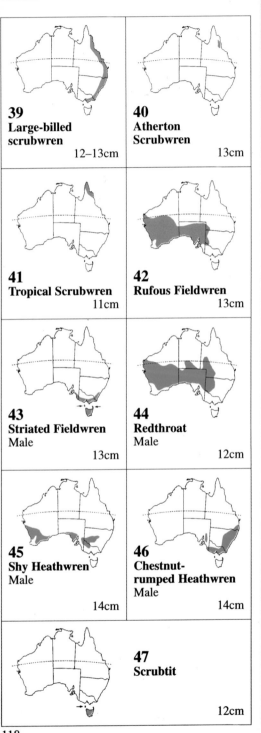

39
Large-billed
scrubwren
12–13cm

40
Atherton
Scrubwren
13cm

41
Tropical Scrubwren
11cm

42
Rufous Fieldwren
13cm

43
Striated Fieldwren
Male
13cm

44
Redthroat
Male
12cm

45
Shy Heathwren
Male
14cm

46
Chestnut-
rumped Heathwren
Male
14cm

47
Scrubtit
12cm

42

45

41

3

44

6

47

12 Warblers

FAMILIES

INDEX

12

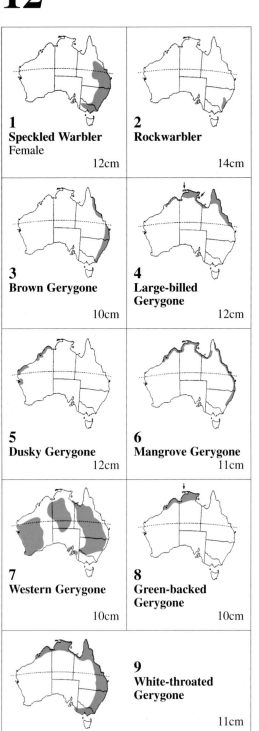

1
Speckled Warbler
Female
12cm

2 **Rockwarbler**
14cm

3
Brown Gerygone
10cm

4
Large-billed Gerygone
12cm

5
Dusky Gerygone
12cm

6
Mangrove Gerygone
11cm

7
Western Gerygone
10cm

8
Green-backed Gerygone
10cm

9
White-throated Gerygone
11cm

1

4

7

3

6

9

12

10
Race **B** Male

Fairy Gerygone   11cm

11
Race **A** Male

12
Race **A** Female

                    11cm   11cm

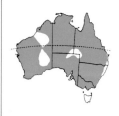

13
Brown form

14
Yellow form

Weebill   8cm

15
Mountain Thornbill
            10cm

16
Brown Thornbill
            10cm

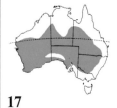

17
Inland Thornbill
            11cm

18
Tasmanian Thornbill
            10cm

10

13

16

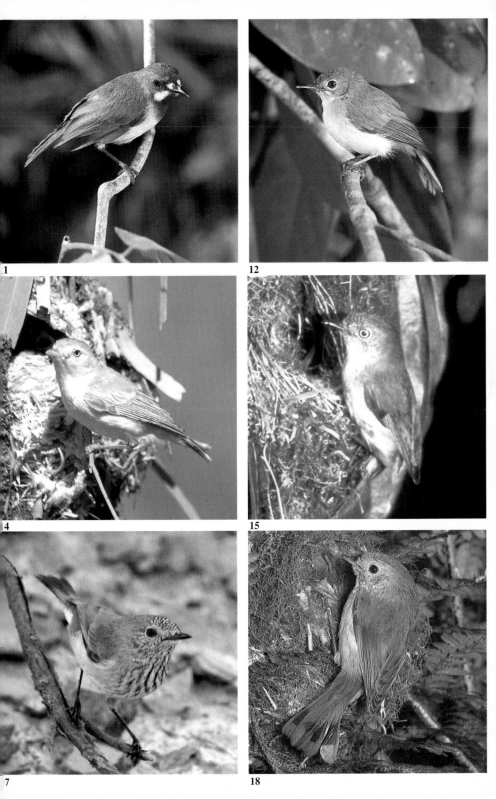

1

12

4

15

7

18

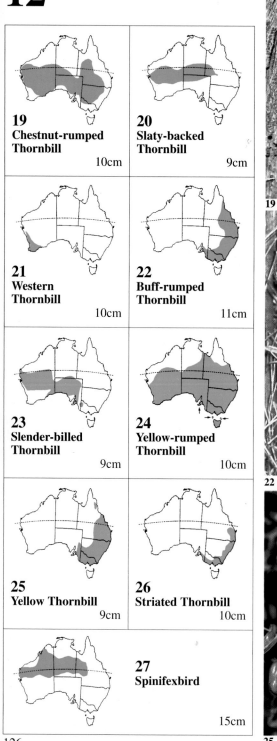

19
**Chestnut-rumped
Thornbill**
10cm

20
**Slaty-backed
Thornbill**
9cm

21
**Western
Thornbill**
10cm

22
**Buff-rumped
Thornbill**
11cm

23
**Slender-billed
Thornbill**
9cm

24
**Yellow-rumped
Thornbill**
10cm

25
Yellow Thornbill
9cm

26
Striated Thornbill
10cm

27
Spinifexbird
15cm

19

22

25

20

21

23

24

26

27

12

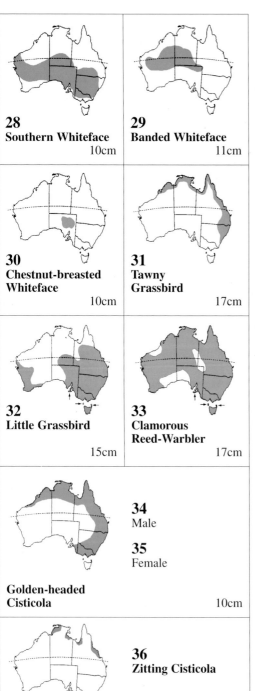

28
Southern Whiteface
10cm

29
Banded Whiteface
11cm

30
Chestnut-breasted Whiteface
10cm

31
Tawny Grassbird
17cm

32
Little Grassbird
15cm

33
Clamorous Reed-Warbler
17cm

34
Male

35
Female

Golden-headed Cisticola
10cm

36
Zitting Cisticola
10cm

28

31

34

9

30

33

5

36

13 Honeyeaters

FAMILY
Meliphagidae

Number

Genera

13

INDEX

13

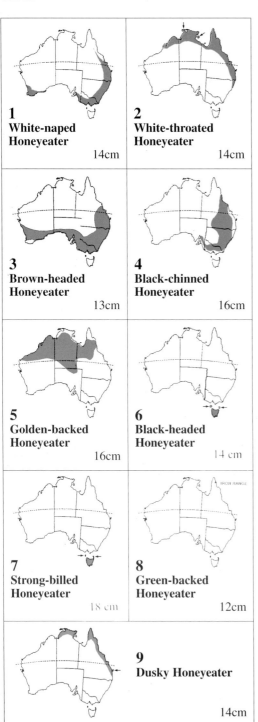

1 White-naped Honeyeater 14cm

2 White-throated Honeyeater 14cm

3 Brown-headed Honeyeater 13cm

4 Black-chinned Honeyeater 16cm

5 Golden-backed Honeyeater 16cm

6 Black-headed Honeyeater 14 cm

7 Strong-billed Honeyeater 18 cm

8 Green-backed Honeyeater 12cm

IRON RANGE

9 Dusky Honeyeater 14cm

4

7

3

6

9

13

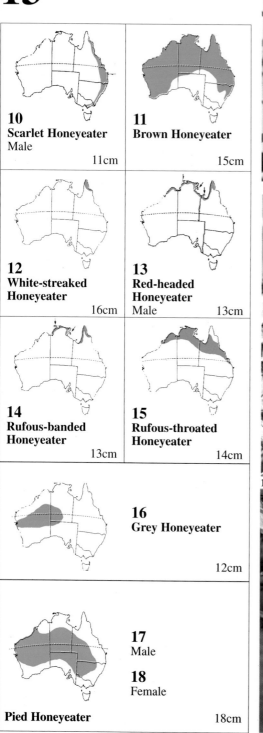

10
Scarlet Honeyeater
Male
11cm

11
Brown Honeyeater
15cm

12
White-streaked
Honeyeater
16cm

13
Red-headed
Honeyeater
Male   13cm

14
Rufous-banded
Honeyeater
13cm

15
Rufous-throated
Honeyeater
14cm

16
Grey Honeyeater
12cm

17
Male

18
Female

Pied Honeyeater   18cm

10

13

16

12

4

15

18

13

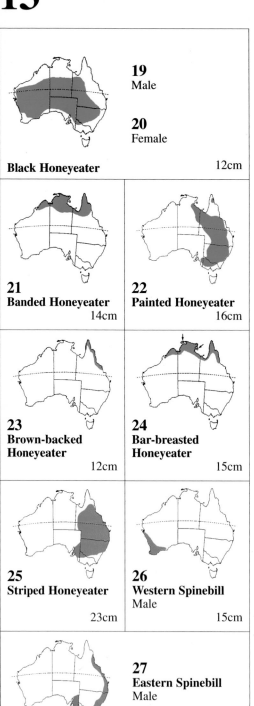

19
Male

20
Female

Black Honeyeater   12cm

21
Banded Honeyeater
14cm

22
Painted Honeyeater
16cm

23
Brown-backed Honeyeater
12cm

24
Bar-breasted Honeyeater
15cm

25
Striped Honeyeater
23cm

26
Western Spinebill
Male   15cm

27
Eastern Spinebill
Male
16cm

19   20

22

25

21

3

24

6

27

13

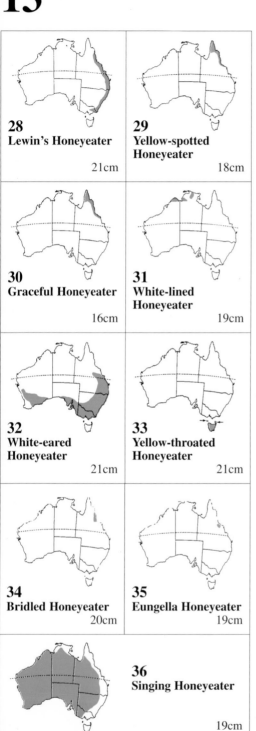

28
Lewin's Honeyeater
21cm

29
Yellow-spotted
Honeyeater
18cm

30
Graceful Honeyeater
16cm

31
White-lined
Honeyeater
19cm

32
White-eared
Honeyeater
21cm

33
Yellow-throated
Honeyeater
21cm

34
Bridled Honeyeater
20cm

35
Eungella Honeyeater
19cm

36
Singing Honeyeater
19cm

28

31

34

9

30

2

33

5

36

13

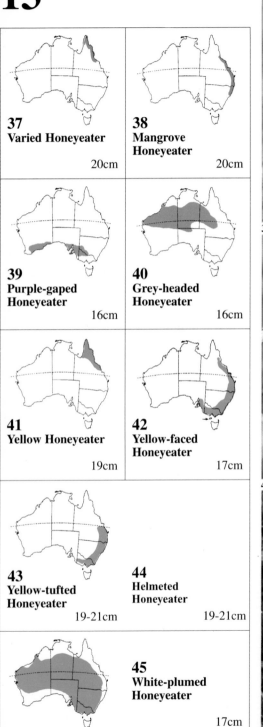

37
Varied Honeyeater
20cm

38
Mangrove Honeyeater
20cm

39
Purple-gaped Honeyeater
16cm

40
Grey-headed Honeyeater
16cm

41
Yellow Honeyeater
19cm

42
Yellow-faced Honeyeater
17cm

43
Yellow-tufted Honeyeater
19-21cm

44
Helmeted Honeyeater
19-21cm

45
White-plumed Honeyeater
17cm

37

40

43

39

42

45

13

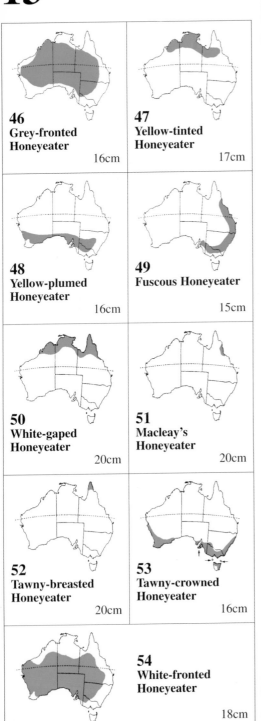

46
Grey-fronted
Honeyeater
16cm

47
Yellow-tinted
Honeyeater
17cm

48
Yellow-plumed
Honeyeater
16cm

49
Fuscous Honeyeater
15cm

50
White-gaped
Honeyeater
20cm

51
Macleay's
Honeyeater
20cm

52
Tawny-breasted
Honeyeater
20cm

53
Tawny-crowned
Honeyeater
16cm

54
White-fronted
Honeyeater
18cm

46

49

52

48

51

54

13

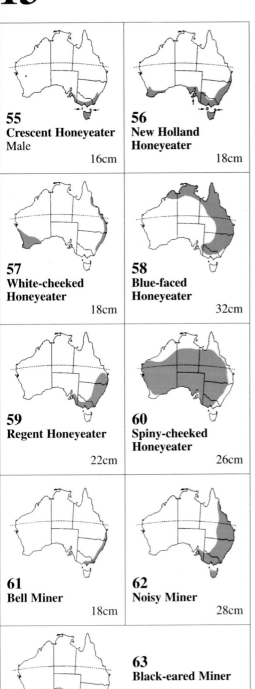

55
Crescent Honeyeater
Male
16cm

56
New Holland Honeyeater
18cm

57
White-cheeked Honeyeater
18cm

58
Blue-faced Honeyeater
32cm

59
Regent Honeyeater
22cm

60
Spiny-cheeked Honeyeater
26cm

61
Bell Miner
18cm

62
Noisy Miner
28cm

63
Black-eared Miner
26cm

55

58

61

57

60

63

13

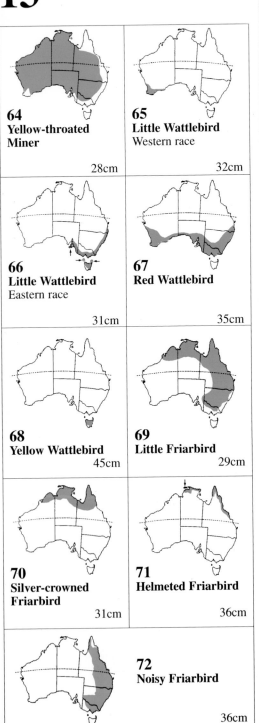

64
Yellow-throated Miner
28cm

65
Little Wattlebird
Western race
32cm

66
Little Wattlebird
Eastern race
31cm

67
Red Wattlebird
35cm

68
Yellow Wattlebird
45cm

69
Little Friarbird
29cm

70
Silver-crowned Friarbird
31cm

71
Helmeted Friarbird
36cm

72
Noisy Friarbird
36cm

64

67

70

66

69

72

14 Finches and Sparrows

FAMILIES

Other Small Brightly-Coloured Birds

INDEX

1
Double-barred Finch
Black-rumped form

11cm

2
White-rumped form

3
Plum-headed Finch
Male

11cm

4
Beautiful Firetail
12cm

5
Red-eared Firetail
12cm

6
Diamond Firetail
11cm

7
Painted Finch
Female left, male right
10cm

8
Red-browed Finch
12cm

9
Star Finch
Male left, female right
12cm

10
Black-bellied form
Male above, female below

11
White-bellied form
Male
14cm

Crimson Finch

12
Zebra Finch
Male left, female right

10cm

4

7

10

6

9

12

14

13
Top End form

14
Cape York form

Masked Finch   12cm

15
Long-tailed Finch

Western (red-billed)
form

                                    15cm

16
**Black-throated
Finch**
White-rumped form
                        10cm

17
Black-rumped form

18
**Blue-faced Parrot-
finch**
                    12cm

19
**Yellow-rumped
Mannikin**
                    10cm

20
Red-headed form

21
Black-headed form
female left, male right
Gouldian Finch   14cm

13

16

19

4

15

17

18

20

21

14

 **22** **Chestnut-breasted Mannikin** 10cm	**23** **Pictorella Mannikin** Female front, male rear 11cm
 **24** **Nutmeg Mannikin** 11cm	**25** **European Greenfinch** Male 15cm
 **26** **European Goldfinch** 13cm	Formerly limited to Murray Bridge, SA -probably died out **27** **Red Bishop** Male (breeding) 11cm
	**28** **House Sparrow** Male 15cm **29** Female
	**30** **Eurasian Tree Sparrow** 15cm

22

25

28

3

24

26

27

29

30

14

31
Silvereye
Western form
12cm

32
Silvereye
Tasmanian form
12cm

33
Silvereye
Eastern race
Race **A**
12cm

34
Yellow White-eye
10cm

35
Pale White-eye
Juveniles
12cm

36
Yellow-bellied Sunbird
Male   12 cm

37
Yellow-bellied Sunbird
Female   12 cm

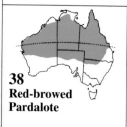

38
Red-browed Pardalote
10cm

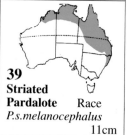

39
Striated Pardalote   Race
P.s.melanocephalus
11cm

31

34

37

33

36

39

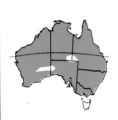

40
Male

43
Female

Mistletoebird   10cm

41
Male

44
Female

Spotted Pardalote   9cm

42
Striated Pardalote
Race *P.s.ornatus*
     11cm

45
Striated Pardalote
Race *P.s.substriatus*
     11 cm

46
Forty-spotted Pardalote

     10cm

47
Spotted Pardalote
Male Yellow-rumped race
     10cm

48
Striated Pardalote
P.striatus striatis
(yellow-tipped)
     11cm

40

43

46

42

45

48

15 Bowerbirds, Orioles, Figbirds and Birds of Paradise

FAMILIES

INDEX

1
Male

4
Female

Satin Bowerbird   27-33cm

2
Male

5
Female

Regent Bowerbird   24-28cm

3
Male

6
Female

Golden Bowerbird   23-35cm

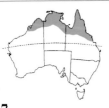

7
Great Bowerbird
32-37cm

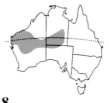

8
Western Bowerbird
25-31cm

9
Spotted Bowerbird

25-31cm

1

4

7

3

6

9

15

10

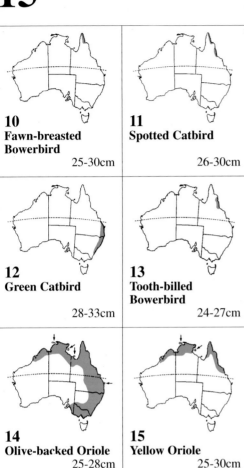

10 **Fawn-breasted Bowerbird** 25-30cm	**11** **Spotted Catbird** 26-30cm
12 **Green Catbird** 28-33cm	**13** **Tooth-billed Bowerbird** 24-27cm
14 **Olive-backed Oriole** 25-28cm	**15** **Yellow Oriole** 25-30cm

13

16
Northern yellow race
Male

17
Immature

Figbird   27-29cm

18
Figbird
Southern green race
Male

27-29cm

16

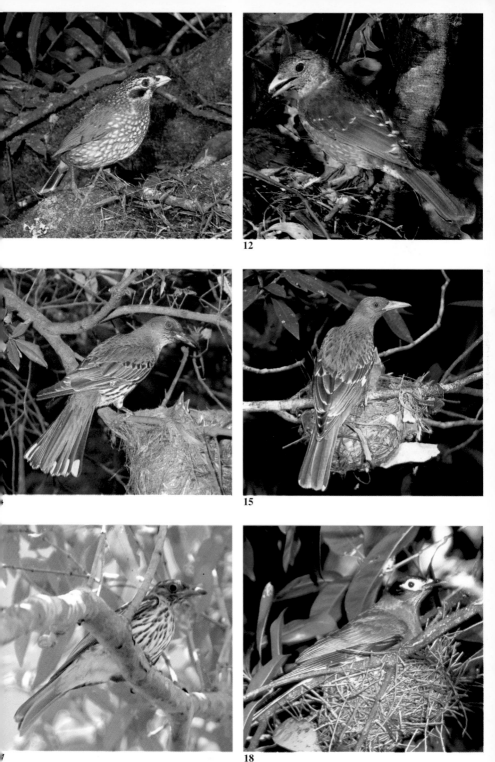

12

15

18

19
Male

22
Female

Victoria's Riflebird   23-25cm

20
Male

23
Female

**Magnificent
Riflebird**   ♂28-33cm ♀26-28cm

21
Paradise Riflebird
Female
                25-30cm

24
Trumpet Manucode
                27-32cm

19

22

16 Mostly Black-and-white Birds

FAMILIES

OTHER BLACK-AND-WHITE BIRDS
SEE SECTIONS, 2, 6, 7, 13 AND AMONG THE WATERBIRDS

INDEX

16

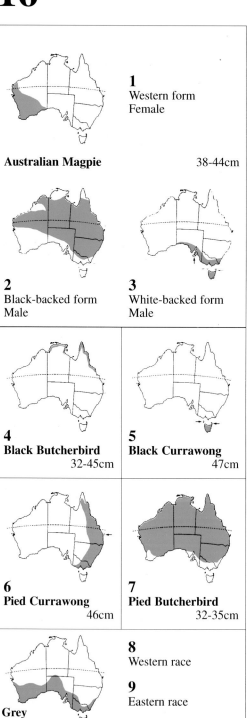

1
Western form
Female

Australian Magpie   38-44cm

2
Black-backed form
Male

3
White-backed form
Male

4
Black Butcherbird
     32-45cm

5
Black Currawong
     47cm

6
Pied Currawong
     46cm

7
Pied Butcherbird
     32-35cm

8
Western race

9
Eastern race

Grey Currawong   50cm

1

4

7

3

6

9

10
Grey Butcherbird
Silver-backed race
28cm

11
Grey Butcherbird
Male
28-32cm

12
Black-backed Butcherbird
25cm

13
Spangled Drongo
30cm

14
Male

15
Female

Magpie-lark
26-30cm

16
Common Myna
24cm

17
Common Starling
21cm

18
Metallic Starling
24cm

10   11

13

16

12

15

18

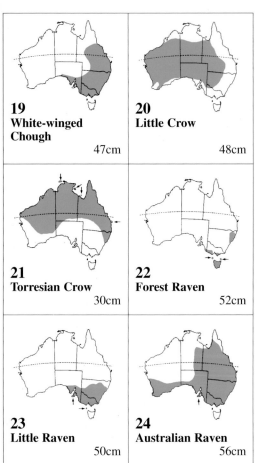

19
White-winged Chough
47cm

20
Little Crow
48cm

21
Torresian Crow
30cm

22
Forest Raven
52cm

23
Little Raven
50cm

24
Australian Raven
56cm

19

22

21

24

Overleaf: Sooty Terns (P.Soleness/APL)

WATER BIRDS

Birds of the Inland Waters, Shore and Ocean

17 Long-legged Waterbirds

FAMILIES

INDEX

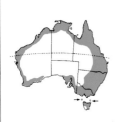

1 Breeding

2 Non-breeding

Cattle Egret 53cm

3
Intermediate Egret
Breeding
63cm

4
Great-billed Heron
1.5m

5
White-necked Heron
Immature
90cm

6
Great Egret
Non-breeding
91cm

1

4

3

6

17

7
Eastern Reef Egret
Grey form
                          61-66cm

8
Eastern Reef Egret
White form
                          61-66cm

9
Little Egret
                          56cm

10
White-faced Heron
                          68cm

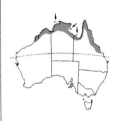

11
Breeding

12
Immature

Pied Heron   48cm

13
Rufous form

14
Grey form

Striated Heron

15
Immature

                          43-51cm

7

10

13

9

12

15

16
Adult

17
Immature

Nankeen Night Heron
56-65cm

18
Australasian Bittern
66-76cm

19
Black Bittern
54-66cm

20
Little Bittern
30cm

21
Glossy Ibis
Immature
52cm

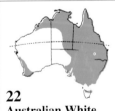

22
Australian White Ibis
70cm

23
Straw-necked Ibis
70cm

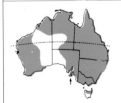

24
Royal Spoonbill
75cm

16

19

22

18

21

24

17

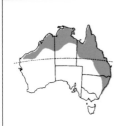

25
Male

28
Female

Black-necked Stork　　　　1.29-1.70cm

26
Yellow-billed
Spoonbill
　　　　89cm

27
Sarus Crane

　　　　1.3-1.4m

29
Beach Stone-curlew
　　　53-58cm

30
Brolga
　　　　1.25m

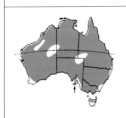

31
Bush Stone-curlew

　　　　50-58cm

25

28

6

9

1

27

30

18 Waterfowl

FAMILIES

INDEX

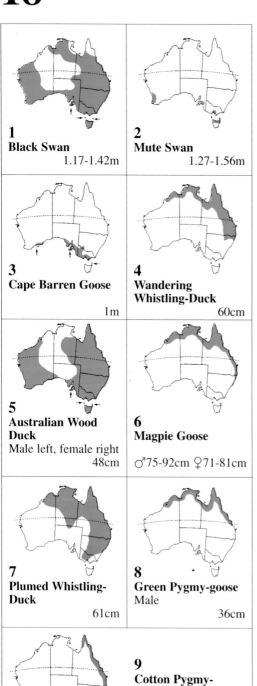

1
Black Swan
1.17-1.42m

2
Mute Swan
1.27-1.56m

3
Cape Barren Goose
1m

4
Wandering Whistling-Duck
60cm

5
Australian Wood Duck
Male left, female right
48cm

6
Magpie Goose
♂75-92cm ♀71-81cm

7
Plumed Whistling-Duck
61cm

8
Green Pygmy-goose
Male
36cm

9
Cotton Pygmy-Goose
Male
38cm

1

4

7

3

6

9

10
Freckled Duck
Breeding male
59cm

11
Radjah Shelduck
55cm

12
Australian Shelduck
Male left, female right
72cm

13
Pacific Black Duck
50-61cm

14
Mallard
Female left, male right
55-68cm

15
Chestnut Teal
Male left, female right
48cm

16
**Australasian
Shoveler**
Female left, male right

45-53cm

10

13

15

12

16

18

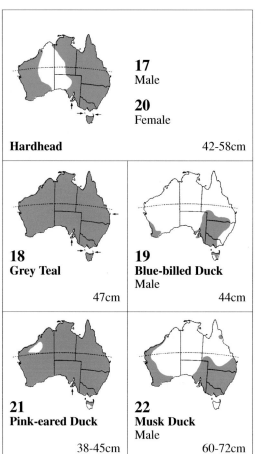

17
Male

20
Female

Hardhead   42-58cm

18
Grey Teal
                    47cm

19
Blue-billed Duck
Male
                    44cm

21
Pink-eared Duck
            38-45cm

22
Musk Duck
Male
                    60-72cm

17

20

19

22

19 Marsh Birds

FAMILIES

INDEX

19

1
Great Crested Grebe
61cm

2
Hoary-headed Grebe
Breeding plumage
31cm

3
Australasian Grebe
26cm

4
Chestnut Rail
52cm

5
Lewin's Rail
23cm

6
Buff-banded Rail
31cm

7
Red-necked Crake
30cm

8
Australian Spotted Crake
Male
20cm

9
Spotless Crake
20cm

2

3

5

6

9

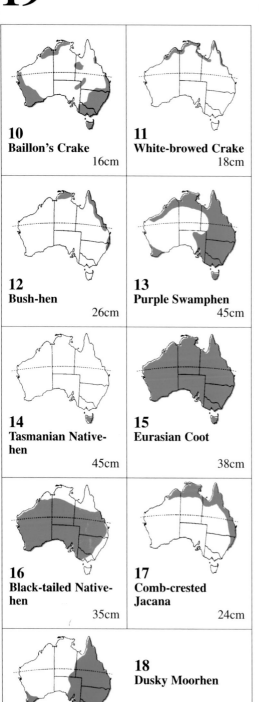

10
Baillon's Crake
16cm

11
White-browed Crake
18cm

12
Bush-hen
26cm

13
Purple Swamphen
45cm

14
Tasmanian Native-hen
45cm

15
Eurasian Coot
38cm

16
Black-tailed Native-hen
35cm

17
Comb-crested Jacana
24cm

18
Dusky Moorhen
38cm

10

13

16

19

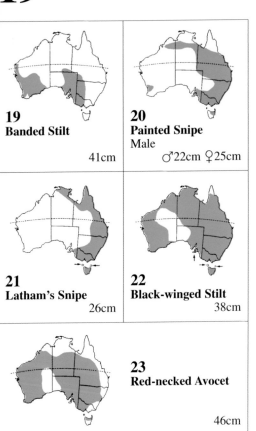

19
Banded Stilt
41cm

20
Painted Snipe
Male
♂22cm ♀25cm

21
Latham's Snipe
26cm

22
Black-winged Stilt
38cm

23
Red-necked Avocet
46cm

19

22

21

23

20 Migratory and Resident Waders

FAMILIES

INDEX

20

Masked Lapwing

1
Race **A** *miles*
(Masked Lapwing)
36cm

4
Race **B** *novaehollandiae*
(Spur-winged Lapwing)
38cm

2
Grey Plover
29cm

5
Banded Lapwing
28cm

Pacific Golden Plover

3
Non-breeding

6
Breeding

25 cm

7
Red-kneed Dotterel
18cm

8
Black-fronted Dotterel
15cm

9
Red-capped Plover
Breeding Male

15cm

1

4

7

3

5

6

9

20

10
Inland Dotterel
20cm

11
Hooded Plover
20cm

12
Oriental Plover
25cm

13
Double-banded Plover
18cm

14
Lesser Sand Plover
Non-breeding
20cm

15
Greater Sand Plover
23cm

16
Ringed Plover
19cm

17
Red-necked Stint
Non-breeding
15cm

18
Long-toed Stint
Non-breeding
14-15cm

10

13

16

12

15

18

20

19
Sanderling
Non-breeding

18cm

20
Non-breeding

21
Breeding

Curlew Sandpiper 21cm

22
Broad-billed
Sandpiper

18cm

23
Sharp-tailed
Sandpiper

23cm

24
Pectoral Sandpiper

23cm

25
Great Knot
Non-breeding

28-30cm

26
Red Knot

25cm

27
Terek Sandpiper
Non-breeding

25cm

19

22

25

21

24

27

20

28

28
Wood Sandpiper
Non-breeding
23cm

29
Marsh Sandpiper
Non-breeding
23cm

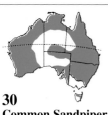

30
Common Sandpiper
20cm

31
Wandering Tattler
Non-breeding
28-29cm

31

32
**Common
Greenshank**
Non-breeding
34cm

33
Grey-tailed Tattler
Non-breeding
26-27cm

34
**Red-necked
Phalarope**
Non-breeding
17-20cm

35
Oriental Pratincole
Non-breeding
23cm

34

36
**Australian
Pratincole**

24cm

30

33

36

37
Eastern Curlew
Non-breeding
60cm

38
Whimbrel
Non-breeding
46cm

39
Little Curlew
35cm

40
Black-tailed Godwit
Non-breeding
36-43cm

41
Non-breeding

42
Breeding Male

Bar-tailed Godwit   ♂38-42cm♀42-45cm

43
Non-breeding

44
Breeding

Ruddy Turnstone   23cm

45
Ruff
Non-breeding
23-30cm

37

40

43

38

39

42

45

21 Seabirds

FAMILIES

INDEX

21

INDEX

Number

1, 2
Black-browed
Albatross
Wingspan c 230cm

83-93cm

3
Shy Albatross
Wingspan c 198-256cm

100cm

3

21

4
Wandering Albatross
Wingspan c 340cm
107-135cm

5
Sooty Albatross
Wingspan c 203cm
84-89cm

6
Light-mantled Sooty Albatross
Wingspan 1.83-2.18m
78-89cm

7
Yellow-nosed Albatross
Wingspan 180-200cm
71-81cm

8
Grey-headed Albatross
Wingspan c 220cm
81cm

9
Northern Giant-Petrel
Wingspan 183-218cm
81-94cm

10, 11
Wingspan 185-205cm

Southern Giant-Petrel
86-99cm

12
White-chinned Petrel
Wingspan c 340cm
51-58cm

4

7

10

220

6

9

12

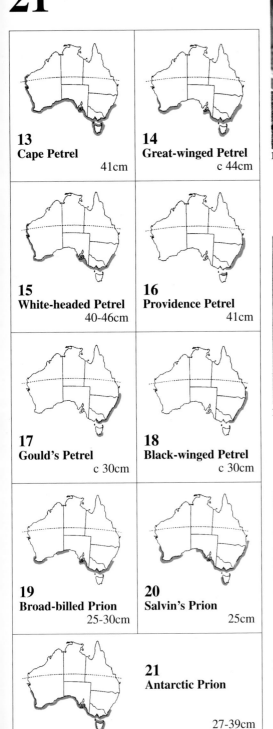

13
Cape Petrel
41cm

14
Great-winged Petrel
c 44cm

15
White-headed Petrel
40-46cm

16
Providence Petrel
41cm

17
Gould's Petrel
c 30cm

18
Black-winged Petrel
c 30cm

19
Broad-billed Prion
25-30cm

20
Salvin's Prion
25cm

21
Antarctic Prion
27-39cm

13

16

19

15

18

21

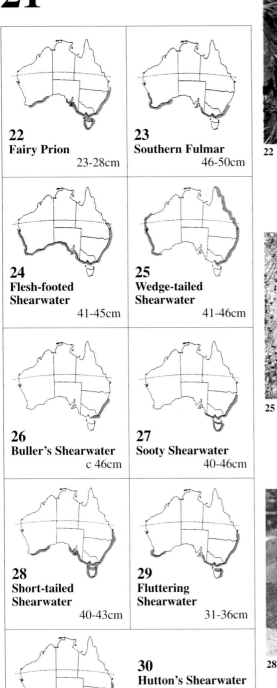

22 **Fairy Prion** 23-28cm	**23** **Southern Fulmar** 46-50cm
24 **Flesh-footed** **Shearwater** 41-45cm	**25** **Wedge-tailed** **Shearwater** 41-46cm
26 **Buller's Shearwater** c 46cm	**27** **Sooty Shearwater** 40-46cm
28 **Short-tailed** **Shearwater** 40-43cm	**29** **Fluttering** **Shearwater** 31-36cm
	30 **Hutton's Shearwater** c 38cm

22

25

28

23

24

27

30

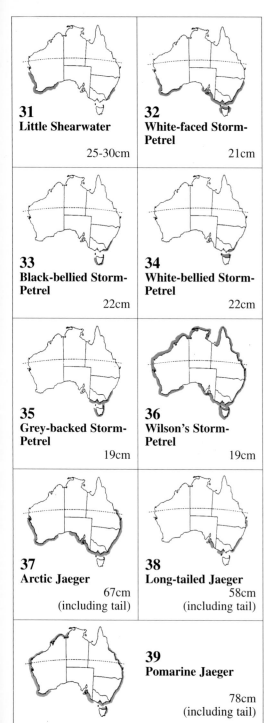

31
Little Shearwater
25-30cm

32
White-faced Storm-Petrel
21cm

33
Black-bellied Storm-Petrel
22cm

34
White-bellied Storm-Petrel
22cm

35
Grey-backed Storm-Petrel
19cm

36
Wilson's Storm-Petrel
19cm

37
Arctic Jaeger
67cm
(including tail)

38
Long-tailed Jaeger
58cm
(including tail)

39
Pomarine Jaeger
78cm
(including tail)

31

34

37

32

33

35

36

38

39

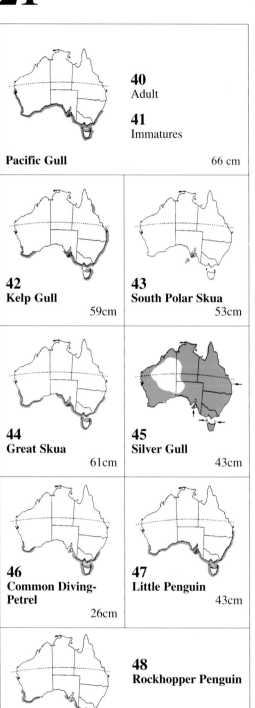

40
Adult

41
Immatures

Pacific Gull 66 cm

42
Kelp Gull 59cm

43
South Polar Skua 53cm

44
Great Skua 61cm

45
Silver Gull 43cm

46
Common Diving-Petrel 26cm

47
Little Penguin 43cm

48
Rockhopper Penguin 60cm

40

43

46

42

45

48

49
Breeding

50
Non-breeding

White-winged Black Tern   23cm

51
Arctic Tern
            38cm

52
Bridled Tern
                42cm

53
Black-naped Tern
            36cm

54
Common Tern
                38cm

55
Caspian Tern
            56cm

56
White-fronted Tern
                42cm

57
Roseate Tern

            41cm

49

52

55

51

54

57

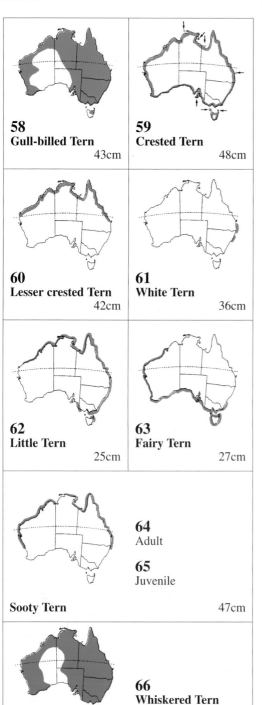

58
Gull-billed Tern
43cm

59
Crested Tern
48cm

60
Lesser crested Tern
42cm

61
White Tern
36cm

62
Little Tern
25cm

63
Fairy Tern
27cm

64
Adult

65
Juvenile

Sooty Tern
47cm

66
Whiskered Tern
26cm

58

61

64

60

63

66

21

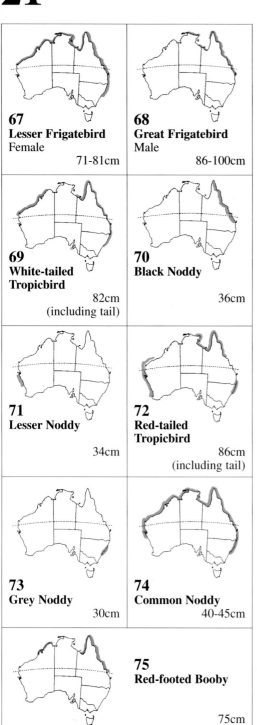

67
Lesser Frigatebird
Female
71-81cm

68
Great Frigatebird
Male
86-100cm

69
White-tailed Tropicbird
82cm
(including tail)

70
Black Noddy
36cm

71
Lesser Noddy
34cm

72
Red-tailed Tropicbird
86cm
(including tail)

73
Grey Noddy
30cm

74
Common Noddy
40-45cm

75
Red-footed Booby
75cm

67

70

73

8

69

71

72

74

75

21

76
Adult

77
Juvenile

Masked Booby   86cm

78
Brown Booby
Chick left, adult
right
            75cm

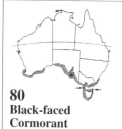

79
Australasian Gannet
            92cm

80
Black-faced
Cormorant
            69cm

81
Little Black
Cormorant
            64cm

82
Little Pied
Cormorant
            64cm

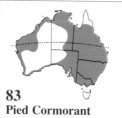

83
Pied Cormorant
            66-81cm

84
Great Cormorant
            92cm

76

79

82

78

80

81

84

21

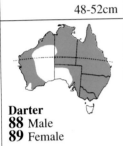

85
Pied Oystercatcher

48-52cm

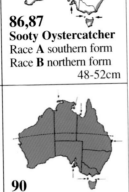

86,87
Sooty Oystercatcher
Race **A** southern form
Race **B** northern form

48-52cm

Darter
88 Male
89 Female

94cm

90
Australian Pelican

190cm

85

88

89

87

LAND BIRDS

BIRDS OF THE BUSH, FOREST AND DESERT

SECTIONS 1 TO 16

1 Flightless Birds

1, 2 EMU *Dromaius novaehollandiae* 2m

The Emu is widespread wherever there is woodland and scrub near water but it avoids settled areas and rainforest. It is highly nomadic, and flocks of up to 500 may migrate over great distances in times of drought. An Emu's strong 3-toed legs can carry it in bursts approaching 50 km/h. It feeds largely on plant food, native fruits, and insects when available especially during grasshopper plagues. It is insatiably curious and, though shy, can be lured by displaying unfamiliar objects. Breeds usually in winter. Nests on ground. Clutches average 5-11 eggs, sometimes as many as 20, but possibly as the result of two females laying in the same nest. Newly-laid eggs have a blue patina but this rubs off during incubation to expose a deep green shell. The chicks can be heard 'cheeping' in their shell within 1 or 2 days of hatching. The male incubates the eggs for about 8 weeks and may lose 4-8kg in weight. It also rears the chicks and may stay with the brood for up to 18 months. Meanwhile, the female may take another mate.

Sexes: *similar but female often larger.*
Immatures: *greyer and paler.*
Voice: *male: guttural grunts; female: resonant drummings.* 1 PK/PLA, 2 HP

3, 4 SOUTHERN CASSOWARY *Casuarius casuarius* 1.5m

In Australia, the Cassowary is confined in two isolated populations in the rainforests at all altitudes of north-east Queensland - with occasional visits to canefields and adjoining parks and gardens. It tends to be solitary and no more than six birds have been seen together. It feeds mainly on fallen native fruits and berries. It raids orchards and will take fruit from people. It is wary and can retreat at prodigious speeds even in thick bush - through which it charges probably using its bony helmet or casque as a battering ram. It sometimes swims. It fights by leaping feet first at an enemy slashing it with the vicious sharp spikes on the inner claw of its 3-toed feet. It has been known to kill people when provoked. The male incubates the eggs and rears the chicks while the female roams in search of another mate, laying a clutch of 3-5 eggs two or three times in a season. Breeds June-October. Nests are lined with a few leaves in a ground scrape and are hard to find.

Female: *larger.*
Immatures: *brown, head and neck duller.*
Voice: *low rumbles, booms, hisses - and loud roars when fighting.* 3 HP, 4 CF

Diurnal Birds of Prey 2

1, 2 WEDGE-TAILED EAGLE *Aquila audax*　　　　　　　　　♂90cm ♀100cm
The Wedge-tailed Eagle is Australia's largest bird of prey, with a wing-span of up to 2.5m. When soaring on upswept 'fingered' wings, it is easily recognised by its distinctive wedge-shaped tail, as illustrated. It is often seen at great heights of 2 000m or more riding thermal currents. Singly, in pairs or loose groups, it frequents a variety of habitats from wooded mountain slopes to treeless plains, and hunts mostly in open areas. Its preferred diet is rabbits, but it also takes young kangaroos, wallabies, reptiles, birds and carrion, including dead lambs. Sedentary; immatures may be nomadic. Breeds May-November. Nests on sometimes huge platform of sticks, usually in a tree, occasionally on a cliff or on the ground.
Sexes: *similar.*
Immatures: *usually paler.*
Voice: *thin, high whistling notes and yelps.*　　　　　　　　　　　1 GS/NPI; 2HP

3, 4 WHITE-BELLIED SEA-EAGLE *Haliaeetus leucogaster*　　　　♂75cm ♀85cm
This fish-eating eagle is seen singly, in pairs or family parties along inland rivers, lagoons, lakes and reservoirs, in coastal areas and on nearby islands. It soars high, its broad rounded wings and short rounded tail giving it a distinctive silhouette. Besides fish, which it snatches from near the surface of water, it will take large birds, turtles, flying foxes and rabbits and eats carrion such as dead lambs. It likes perching on an exposed tree or headland. Mostly sedentary; immatures nomadic. Breeds June-December. Nests in huge stick nest in a tree, on rocks, or on the ground.
Sexes: *similar.*
Immatures: *mottled brown with whitish bulls-eye in wing.*
Voice: *goose-like honks.*　　　　　　　　　　　　　　　　3 M&IM, 4 DB

5 OSPREY *Pandion haliaetus*　　　　　　　　　　　　　　♂55cm ♀65cm
Named after Pandion the mythical king of Athens who was turned into an Osprey. The most specialised for fishing of all raptors, the Osprey has a number of anatomical peculiarities which assist it in grasping its slippery prey. These include a reversible outer toe as in the owls, long needle-sharp talons, and spines on the soles of its feet. A spectacular hunter, it patrols a stretch of water, hovers briefly, then plunges into the water feet first, sometimes disappearing beneath the surface to burst upwards again with a fish in its talons. So vice-like is the bird's grip on a fish that it sometimes has difficulty in releasing it, and there have been a number of instances of an Osprey being dragged under the water and drowned by a fish too heavy to be carried off. In Australia, it frequents the shores, estuaries and islands particularly of the north, singly, in pairs or small family parties, and is occasionally seen inland along large rivers. It has characteristically angled, narrow wings and a conspicuous dark line from its beak through its eyes to its nape. Often perches prominently. Adults sedentary. Breeds April-September. Nests coastally in a sometimes massive stick nest on cliff face, rocky shore, dead tree, or man-made structure.
Sexes: *similar.*
Immatures: *more streaking; heavier chest band.*
Voice: *plaintive whistles.*　　　　　　　　　　　　　　　　　　T&PG

6, 7 BRAHMINY KITE *Haliastur indus*　　　　　　　　　　♂48cm ♀51cm
Formerly known as the Red-backed Sea-Eagle. In Australia this kite frequents northern coastal areas, particularly estuaries, harbours and offshore islands. Often perches conspicuously in a tree. Tolerant of approach. Sometimes flocks with other birds of prey, especially the Whistling Kite. It is a scavenger, congregating to feed on scraps, rubbish and dead fish. It also sweeps low in slow wheeling flight, snatching fish, small animals and crabs; or insects from the air, foliage or the ground. Adults usually sedentary. Breeds April-October. Bulky stick nest in woodland or mangrove tree.
Sexes: *similar.*
Immatures: *mottled brown.*
Voice: *repeated 'pee-ah-h-h'.*　　　　　　　　　　　　　　6 HB, 7 H&JB

8, 9   LITTLE EAGLE *Hieraaetus morphnoides*   ♂48cm ♀55cm
The Little Eagle frequents open forest and woodland, mostly singly or in pairs. It may be distinguished from other similar birds of prey by its flat, broad wings, short square tail, and feathered legs. There are two forms: a light and a dark morph, the former the more common. Small crest sometimes erected. It will, on occasion, eat carrion, but prefers live rabbits and other small animals, birds, reptiles and insects. Sedentary or partly nomadic. Breeds August-December. Nests 5-45m high. Builds its own nest or adds to an old nest of another species.
Sexes: *similar.*
Immatures: *mostly chestnut.*
Voice: *double or treble high-pitched whistle.*   D&MT

10   BLACK-SHOULDERED KITE *Elanus axillaris*   ♂36cm ♀38cm
Frequents open woodland, grassland or cultivated areas, perching conspicuously, singly, in pairs or loose groups. It soars and glides with raised wings but is most often seen hovering waiting to drop swiftly on a mouse, insect or lizard. Mostly nomadic, some seasonal movement, very dependent on mouse numbers. Sometimes breeds twice a year March-May and September-November. Nests often high in thick foliage. Endemic.
Sexes: *alike.*
Immatures: *golden tan streaking on breast, head and back.*
Voice: *harsh 'scree' or 'chip'.*   D&MT

11   LETTER-WINGED KITE *Elanus scriptus*   ♂36cm ♀38cm
The black M or W marking on the underwing gives this kite its name. Distinguished from the Black-shouldered Kite by horn coloured legs and sometimes grey crown. Frequents grasslands and wooded creeks inland and feeds largely on rats and mice. Large flocks are drawn to exploit Long-haired Rat plagues. Nocturnal in habit, its large eyes adapt it for hunting through the night. Often roosts in flocks in daytime and is the only Australian raptor to breed in close colonies. Endemic.
Sexes: *alike.*
Immatures: *heavy golden tan streakings on chest, head and back.*
Voice: *similar to Black-shouldered Kite.*   MW

12   WHISTLING KITE *Haliastur sphenurus*   ♂53cm ♀58cm
A scavenger of carrion, sometimes in large numbers around refuse dumps. May rob feeding water-birds, and hunts low after grass fires, often with other birds. Recognised by somewhat dropped wings and long, round-tipped tail, slow wheeling flight and effortless soaring. Perches alone or in family parties. Quiet and unaggressive. Nomadic during drought. Usually breeds June-November. Bulky stick nest in tall tree.
Sexes: *similar.*
Immatures: *more streaked and spotted.*
Voice: *drawn out descending whistle followed by ascending burst of notes.*   H&JB

13, 14   BLACK KITE *Milvus migrans*   ♂52cm ♀55cm
Formerly known as the Fork-tailed Kite, it inhabits open areas and, as its scientific name suggests, it is a wanderer. Is often seen scavenging in large flocks, sometimes numbering hundreds, around slaughterhouses, refuse tips, stockyards and airfields. It also takes mice, rats and insects (appearing in force when plagues of these pests occur), and nestling birds. It will spiral above bush fires looking for victims. It characteristically twists its forked tail in flight and soars effortlessly. Nomadic. Usually breeds July-November. Nests are flattish and untidy, built in trees lining watercourses.
Sexes: *similar.*
Immatures: *paler.*
Voice: *plaintive mewing or whining.*   13 T&PG, 14 D&MT

2

15   BLACK-BREASTED BUZZARD *Hamirostra melanosternon*   ♂52cm ♀60cm
This bird is identifiable by its large white wing spots and very short tail. Singly, in pairs sometimes in
family groups, it frequents open woodland in the tropical north and timbered watercourses in arid
areas. It soars high and glides effortlessly over the tree-tops. Feeds mainly on live animals, such as
small mammals and birds. Said to drop heavy objects into the nests of emus and bustards to break open
the eggs. Breeds mostly June-December. Nests often on a dead branch near water. Endemic.
Sexes: *similar.*
Immatures: *more chestnut.*
Voice: *hoarse, repeated yelp, harsh whining.*   TH

16, 17   SQUARE-TAILED KITE *Lophoictinia isura*   ♂53cm ♀56cm
Unlike the Black Kite and Whistling Kite, this species is seldom seen in flocks, and is altogether a
rarer and less well-known bird. It inhabits riverine forests and well-wooded areas near open country
and feeds on a wide variety of insects and small animals, especially bird nestlings. It characteristic-
ly soars and glides just above the tree tops with its wings held in a V. Like the Black-breasted Buzzard,
white spots are exhibited under its wings in flight. Seasonal movements and possibly nomadic. Breeds
August-November. Bulky loose nests in high tree. Endemic.
Sexes: *alike.*
Immatures: *more rufous head, less streaked.*
Voice: *hoarse quavering yelp, twitter, soft whistle.*   16 CC, 17 GC

18   RED GOSHAWK *Erthrotriochis radiatus*   ♂51cm ♀61cm
This rare Goshawk was sketched near Sydney by the convict artist Thomas Watling, but is now confined to northern Australia. Singly or in pairs, it frequents coastal rainforest and woodland. It soars
high with 'fingered' wings spread wide. Long conspicuously barred underwing and tail are characteristic features. It preys on birds as large as cockatoos, kookaburras and ducks. Also takes reptiles and
small mammals. Breeds April-November. Nests high in a tree. Endemic.
Sexes: *similar.*
Immatures: *unknown, perhaps more rufous.*
Voice: *high-pitched chatter.*   JC/BOC

19   BROWN GOSHAWK *Accipiter fasciatus*   ♂45cm ♀55cm
This widespread predator, seen singly or in pairs frequents all types of woodland, forest or watercourse
vegetation. On rounded wings, it spirals over tree tops hunting, and takes birds, rabbits, snakes and
large insects. It also dives on victims from tree cover. Northern birds are paler and smaller; south-west
birds more rufous. Breeds June-January. Nests often high in trees..
Sexes: *similar.*
Immatures: *upperparts off white with bold streaking on breast.*
Voice: *high-pitched chatter, more relaxed 'seeep, seeep, seeep'.*   H&JB

20, 21   GREY GOSHAWK *Accipiter novaehollandiae*   ♂42cm ♀54cm
This species can be either grey or white; the latter sometimes with a light grey wash. The two forms interbreed. Northern birds are smaller; only the white form occurs in Tasmania and predominates in the
Kimberley region of WA. The White Goshawk, especially in flight, bears some resemblance to the
Sulphur-crested Cockatoo, and could be confused with it. The species lives in woodland and heavily
forested areas, particularly along watercourse vegetation. It feeds on small to medium sized birds, rabbits
and a variety of insects. It perches in ambush poised to dash suddenly after prey. When soaring, the rounded wings and tail are obvious, the latter somewhat shorter than that of the Brown Goshawk. Adults sedentary; immatures nomadic. Breeds June-December. Nests high in trees.
Sexes: *similar.*
Immatures: *white form - white; grey form - wider barring, slight brown wash. They have yellow eyes*
which deepen to red in adults.
Voice: *loud, piercing 'queet', shrill chatter.*   20 GM, 21JC/BOC

22   COLLARED SPARROWHAWK *Accipiter cirrhocephalus*   ♂32cm   ♀38cm
Attacks at lightning speed, sometimes taking prey larger than itself, but predominantly birds such as finches and sparrows. Singly or in pairs, it frequents forest, woodland, mallee scrub, watercourse margins and even suburban parkland. Distinguishable from the Brown Goshawk by its slighter build and square tail. Sedentary; immatures nomadic. Breeds August-January. Nests usually high in tree.
Sexes: *similar.*
Immatures: *upperparts grey-brown, underparts off white, broad vertical streaks on breast.*
Voice: *shrill chatter.*   GC

23   SWAMP HARRIER *Circus approximans*   ♂57cm ♀61cm
This long-winged species frequents the wetter coastal areas amid swampy grass, reeds and croplands. Wary at its nest. It hunts low often with legs dangling, quartering the ground in search of small animals, eggs and carrion. Usually solitary or in pairs. Roosts with other harriers. Migratory in Tasmania; partially elsewhere. Breeds September-January. Nest mainly on ground. **Recognition:** *adults have a distinctive white rump.*
Female: *slightly browner.*
Immatures: *darker.*
Voice: *high-pitched 'see-ah' and descending 'kee-aa'.*   T&PG

24   SPOTTED HARRIER *Circus assimilis*   ♂55cm ♀60cm
A bird of the inland plains, usually seen singly or in pairs. It is found mainly in the more arid areas in grassland, lightly timbered country, and cropland; only occasionally in wetter areas. It weaves over the ground, often with legs trailing, hunting a wide variety of small mammals, reptiles and ground birds, rarely eating carrion. Nomadic and partially migratory. Breeds June-November. Nests in low-medium trees (the only harrier to nest in trees). Also nests occasionally on telephone poles.
Sexes: *similar.*
Immatures: *rufous brown.*
Voice: *'kikiki' in nest defence.*   T&PG

25   BROWN FALCON *Falco berigora*   ♂45cm ♀50cm
Sometimes known as the 'Cackling Hawk' because of its call and noisy habits. One of the few Australian birds where an Aboriginal name, berigora, forms part of the scientific name. Perhaps the most common and widespread of the falcons in Australia. Its plumage is variable in colour from light to dark and sometimes red, even in the same area. It frequents mostly lightly timbered country but is found almost anywhere except in closed forest. On upswept wings, it soars high, occasionally hovering before dropping onto prey. It is a generalist, eating reptiles, mice, young rabbits, small birds, insects and carrion. Adults sedentary, immatures nomadic, sometimes in loose groups when prey is abundant. Breeds June-November. Mainly uses stick nests of other species, especially corvids, very occasionally a broken off tree stump.
Sexes: *similar.*
Immatures: *buff collar and edges to feathers, legs blue-grey.*
Voice: *raucous cackles and squawks.*   D&MT

26, 29   PEREGRINE FALCON *Falco peregrinus*   ♂42cm ♀50cm
Its remarkable speed is legendary and it is said to exceed 250km/h when stooping at prey. Victims are usually birds taken in mid-air. Its very presence causes universal panic among other birds. Favoured habitat is rocky hills, mountains and cliffs, but it may appear almost anywhere, even in urban areas. Sedentary; immatures nomadic. Breeds July-December. Nests on ledges, in tree hollows or stick nests of other birds. The Peregrine Falcon has suffered grievously from the effects of pesticides, some of which cause a thinning of the eggshell and a serious decline in breeding success.
Female: *heavier beak and thicker legs and toes.*
Immature: *browner than adults with dense black vertical streaking on underparts and sandy brown edges to feathers.*
Voice: *loud screaming chatters 'kek-kek-kek' and whines.*   26 JP, 29 P&JO

27   **PACIFIC BAZA** *Aviceda subcristata*   ♂40cm ♀45cm
Previously known as the Crested Hawk. The only prominently crested hawk in Australia. Seen alone, in pairs, family parties or flocks, it lives quietly and unobtrusively in well-wooded areas. It soars just above the tree tops and occasionally indulges in impressive tumbling display flights. Feeds on frogs, insects and small reptiles often gleaned or flushed from foliage. Sedentary and nomadic. Breeds September-December. Nests usually in a high tree.
Sexes: *alike.*
Immatures: *browner.*
Voice: *mellow 'wee-choo', 'toc-toc-toc', other whistles and trills.*   CC

28   **AUSTRALIAN HOBBY** *Falco longipennis*   ♂32cm ♀35cm
Previously known as the Little Falcon. Hobbies look like miniature Peregrines and are noted for their extraordinary aerobatics and remarkable speed in level flight. Small birds, bats and insects are taken on the wing. They live in open wooded country, parks and gardens. Scarce in Tasmania. Populations in the inland arid areas are paler. Breeds September-January. Nests in high tree or pylon.
Sexes: *similar.*
Immatures: *upper parts browner*
Voice: *high-pitched chatter 'kekekek' and twitters.*   GC

30   **BLACK FALCON** *Falco subniger*   ♂50cm ♀55cm
Comparatively little known, it can be mistaken for the dark form of the Brown Falcon but, unlike the latter, which often carries its more rounded wings at a slight upward angle in flight, it glides with more pointed wings held horizontally. It prefers dry open country and only breeds there. A feared predator, it feeds on rabbits and ground birds, and will strike prey like galahs in the air. Quail are also part of its diet and it follows their movement. Breeds in spring. Usually re-uses nests of crows or other hawks. Endemic.
Sexes: *similar.*
Immatures: *legs, cere and eye ring blue-grey.*
Voice: *'gak-gak'.*   DH

31   **GREY FALCON** *Falco hypoleucos*   ♂36cm ♀43cm
This rare falcon is a bird of the vast plains of the arid interior, where it frequents open scrub and timber, especially tree-lined watercourses. It occasionally appears in the more humid areas. It soars high to drop on prey, or makes low-level dashes at its mainly bird prey. Sedentary; seasonal movement or nomadic. Breeds June-November. Nests in structures of other hawks and corvids. Endemic.
Sexes: *similar.*
Immatures: *upperparts darker, underparts more streaked.*
Voice: *similar to Peregrine Falcon.*   JC/BOC

32   **NANKEEN KESTREL** *Falco cenchroides*   ♂33cm ♀35cm
Traditionally called 'Nankeen' from the colour of a buff-brown cloth once imported from Nanking. This small falcon mainly hunts by patiently hovering in mid-air ready to drop on an unsuspecting mouse, small bird or insect. Singly, in pairs or family parties, it frequents most habitats, particularly open woodland and cultivated areas. Scarce in Tasmania. Breeds August-November. Nests variously on cliffs, buildings and hollow trees.
Female: *tail and head chestnut.*
Immatures: *like adult female.*
Voice: *chatters, whines.*   KI

3 Nocturnal Birds

1, 2, 4, 5 SOUTHERN BOOBOOK *Ninox novaeseelandiae*   ♂23-36cm ♀27-36cm

The Australian populations of the Boobook, smallest and most familiar of the owls in Australia, vary greatly in plumage and size both geographically and ecologically. As many as 10 races were recognised in earlier days, but Schodde and Mason, in their *Nocturnal Birds of Australia (1980)* , reduced them to four, comprising two main populations extending over the continent divided on a line following the western footslopes of the Great Dividing Range with the nominate race *boobook* (A) to the east and race *ocellata* (B) to the west. They note that the western birds are of a more sandy red hue than the eastern birds living in similar country; also that the western birds are smaller and paler in the north (in accordance with Bergmann's Rule), while the trend in the east is reversed. However, an isolated population is identified in the dark and humid rainforest of the high country of north-eastern Queensland, race *lurida* (C), which is smaller. It is also darker (in accordance with Glober's Rule). The Tasmanian birds, race *leucopsis* (D), are even smaller and conspicuously spotted. They have golden-yellow eyes and pale yellow toes like their New Zealand cousins, and some migrate to the mainland as far as Sydney to winter. The Boobook lives in a wide variety of habitat but is particularly partial to eucalypt forest and woodlands. It hunts mostly at nightfall and before dawn, and preys on mice, sparrows and other small birds. It can sometimes be seen diving after moths and beetles under street lights in suburban areas. It draws in its feathers under threat and turns sideways to present a thin profile. Small birds will mob a Boobook unmercifully if it becomes conspicuous during its daytime roost. It may attack passers-by when caring for young, but can also be playful. Breeds August/September-December/January. Nests in the hollow of a dead tree 3-25m above ground.
Sexes: *females slightly larger and more richly coloured.*
Immatures: *paler than adults.*
Voice: *its leisurely two-syllable call which, though soft in tone, can carry for several kilometres, has been variously described as 'mo-poke', 'buk-buk', 'wook-wook', and 'moop-oop'.*
Illustrations: Race (A) 2 taken in Victoria, (H&JB) and 5 taken in NSW (AT); Race (B) 1 taken in the Kimberley (LR) and 4 taken further south (B&BW). [Races (C) and (D) not illustrated].

3   RUFOUS OWL *Ninox rufa*   50cm

The Rufous Owl is uncommon in Australia and restricted to the tropical north. Size and plumage tonings vary slightly, the northern birds being the palest. All live in rainforest and its fringes. Sometimes seen in the quieter garden suburbs of Darwin. It is a wary unobtrusive bird, roosting by day singly or in pairs in its 'home' tree, and feeding on tree-dwelling mammals such as flying foxes, sugar gliders, small birds and insects. Sedentary. Breeds winter and spring. Nests in tree hollows 8-40m high.
Female: *slightly smaller and darker.*
Immatures: *like adults.*
Voice: *soft low 'woo-hoo'.*   JF

6   BARKING OWL *Ninox connivens*   43cm

(A) race *connivens* is the darker; (B) race *peninsularis* is more variable. The most hawklike of Australian owls, relying almost wholly on sight for hunting. Frequents woodland and open forest. Prey includes mammals, quite large birds, and insects taken on the wing. Pairs and family parties use several established roosting trees. Sedentary. Breeds July-October. Nests in tree hollow to 30m high.
Sexes: *similar.*
Immatures: *like adults.*
Voice: *loud barking 'wook-wook'; and blood-curdling 'screaming woman' calls.*   EZ

7   POWERFUL OWL *Ninox strenua*   ♂65cm ♀54cm

Australia's largest owl, with a wingspan of over 1m. Its favoured habitat is the dense eucalypt forests. It uses a series of roosting trees within a selected area in which it hunts. It preys on possums, gliders, quite large birds such as kookaburras and currawongs, and a large variety of other mainly arboreal creatures. Most hunting is by evening and dawn light. It lives in the same territory year after year. Breeds in winter from May. Nests in a tree hole above 15m. Endemic.
Sexes: *similar.*
Immatures: *back paler, smaller chevrons on breast.*
Voice: *drawn-out double-note 'whooooo-hoooo'.*   EZ

8, 9   MASKED OWL *Tyto novaehollandiae*
Mainland races: ♂33-41cm ♀38-46cm
Tasmanian race: ♂35-42cm ♀43-57cm
(A) race *novaehollandiae;* (B) race *kimberli;* (C) race *castanops;* (D) race *melvillensis.* The Masked Owl
is the largest and most powerful representative of the genus Tyto in Australia and the female of the
Tasmanian race is the largest in the world. The dark Tasmanian birds are still reasonably common, but
their mainland relatives have declined alarmingly. In general, the northern race is the palest but there are
also plumage variations from dark, through intermediate to pale within each race. The Masked Owl feeds
mainly on terrestrial mammals up to the size of rabbits. The giant Tasmanian bird has a voracious
appetite, and throws out huge pellets. When on the defensive, it spreads its wings downwards, rocks from
side to side, snaps its beak, and hisses, making a truly fearsome spectacle. The Melville Island birds are
very small. The hybrid of Lord Howe Island is from introductions of the Tasmanian and mainland races.
Breeds variably, mostly March-May and October-November. Nests in tree hollow or cave.
Sexes: *similar apart from size.*
Immatures: *like adults.*
Voice: *drawn-out, rasping or hissing screech.*   D&MT

10   (A) SOOTY OWL *Tyto tenebricosa* (illustrated)   ♂37-48cm ♀44-51cm
These elusive owls have the largest eyes of any masked owl. They live in dense gloomy habitats, and
are on the wing at dusk hunting for terrestrial and arboreal prey, including small birds. They breed
opportunistically and nest very high in tree hollows.
Sexes: *feet and bill of (A)'s female larger, plumages similar.*
Immatures: *similar to adults, but paler below.*
Voices: *weird swooping whistles - northern birds higher pitch.*   H&JB
        (B) LESSER SOOTY OWL *Tyto multipuncata*   ♂31-35cm ♀35-38cm
Distinguished by its silvery masked face. (Not illustrated)

11   BARN OWL *Tyto alba*   30-39cm
This pale owl is closely associated with man through its traditional use in the Old World of barn lofts
and church steeples as nesting sites. It hunts harrier-like for ground-dwelling prey during the hours of
darkness, using its remarkable gifts of hearing rather than sight. It is highly nomadic and populations
fluctuate dramatically during periods of mice plagues. It can eat over 1 000 mice a year. By day it
roosts unobtrusively in secluded places. Breeds variably. Nests in tree hollow, cave or old building.
Sexes: *similar.*
Immatures: *spotted below.*
Voice: *eerie drawn-out screeching.*   H&JB

12   GRASS OWL *Tyto capensis*   ♂32-36cm ♀35-38cm
This rarely seen long-legged owl lives out its whole life on the ground and frequents grassland,
swampy heath, canegrass or reeds. It feeds mainly on terrestrial rodents. Coastal birds are sedentary,
but their distribution inland varies greatly with food supply - especially when there are plagues of
native rats. Normally abroad at dusk, but will hunt by day when food is scarce. Breeds mostly March-
June. Nests under dense deep tussocks.
Sexes: *similar apart from size.*
Immatures: *similar to adults.*
Voice: *like Barn owl but softer, deeper and less vocal.*   JF

13   SPOTTED NIGHTJAR *Eurostopodus argus*   32cm
Where the range of the White-throated Nightjar ends west of the Dividing Range, this widespread and
paler nightjar takes over. It frequents a variety of habitat including the sparse vegetation of the arid inland.
Its roosts by day on ground which blends with its plumage and squats in shade motionless except for turn-
ing its back constantly towards the sun. It hawks for flying insects after dark in bat-like flight. Possibly
migratory. Breeds from September to January (south) and to December (north). Nests on the ground.
Sexes: *alike.*
Immatures: *redder.*
Voice: *musical 'caw-caw-caw-gobble-gobble-gobble'.*   T&PG

3

14   LARGE-TAILED NIGHTJAR *Caprimulgus macrurus*   28cm
Utters bouts of axe-like 'chops' between catching insects, varying from a few to maybe 100. Stories of wagers being placed on the next number of 'chops' by bushmen are legendary - hence the popular name 'Betting Bird'. It lives along edges of humid rainforest and dense monsoon scrub. It hunts exclusively on the wing, early in the evening and before dawn, scooping flying insects into its huge mouth while weaving amongst the trees like a large moth. Breeds August-January. Nests amongst ground litter.
Recognition: *white in tail.*
Sexes: *alike.*
Immatures: *slightly duller.*
Voice: *a succession of 'chops'.*   H&JB

15   WHITE-THROATED NIGHTJAR *Eurostopodus mystacalis*   35cm
One of the world's largest nightjars and the biggest in Australia. It frequents woodlands and stony ridges in the south-east and the fringes of rainforest in the north wherever there is ample dry leaf litter in which to roost by day and nest. It feeds exclusively on nocturnal flying insects, mostly moths. Seasonally migratory from south to north. Breeds September-November in the north and later in the south. Nests on ground.
Sexes: *alike.*
Immatures: *duller and redder.*
Voice: *weird ascending musical whistles and laughter.*   EZ

16, 19   TAWNY FROGMOUTH
          (A) Race *Podargus strigoides strigoides* (nominate Eastern form including Tasmania)
          (B) Race *P.s.phalaenoides* (illustrated)(Western form)
Sizes vary greatly from north to south and east to west with males ranging from 34-40cm to 45-55cm and females from 35-40cm to 45-49cm - accompanied by a bewildering degree of plumage variation. The two populations integrate at the Great Dividing Range. East of the Range, the birds are larger and more boldly marked than the greyer birds (as illustrated at 19) of the west. Those of the inland are small and rufous. The northern birds (as illustrated at 16) are paler and can be half the size of their southern relatives. There are also sexual and phase differences to add to the confusion. The species frequents a widely varied habitat, including forests, woodlands and inland mulga. It becomes active soon after sundown and scouts for prey from a low vantage point - ready to glide silently to ground to snatch terrestrial prey, including beetles, grasshoppers, scorpions, snails and sometimes small mammals and birds. When sleeping by day, it makes no attempt to hide like the owls, but sits motionless with feathers tightly compressed to merge with the tree. It also sleeps on the ground in shade. It is often seen in family groups. Sedentary. Breeds August-December. Nests 2-10m high on bare horizontal branch. Endemic.
Male: *heavier bill and darker.*
Immatures: *like adults.*
Voice: *bursts of low ventriloquial 'ooms' and 'oods' and a variety of other sounds including growling like a dog when threatened.*   16LR, 19JF

17, 20   MARBLED FROGMOUTH *Podargus ocellatus*   (A) 37-41cm (B) 44-48cm
(A) race *marmoratus* (illustrated); (B) race *plumiferus*. In Australia, race *marmoratus* lives in the rainforests of Cape York. The once widespread southerly race *plumiferus,* known as the Plumed Frogmouth, has suffered grievously from over exploitation of its habitat, and is found in small widely separated patches of coastal forest in northern NSW and southern Queensland. Marbled Frogmouths are active from dusk into mid-evening and towards dawn and prey on ground-dwelling insects from low perches. When threatened, they elongate and stiffen their bodies drawing their feathers closely in to present a thin profile in a cryptic pose. (The photographs are of the same bird and are eloquent of the change in attitude that takes place). Breeds August-October. Nests on horizontal branch 3-15m high.
Female: *plainer and more chestnut.*
Immatures: *like adults.*
Voice: *'koo-loo' repeated in short bursts, also descending cackling call ending with a loud bill clap*   D&MT

18 **AUSTRALIAN OWLET-NIGHTJAR** *Aegotheles cristatus* 23cm
(A) race *cristatus;* (B) race *tasmanicus.* This diminutive and agile 'monkey-faced' bird lives in all
types of timbered country. It hunts after dark on the wing for flying insects, or pounces from a perch
for ground insects when aerial prey is scarce. By day it hides in bolt holes in trees or cliffs. Plumage
becomes paler inland and northwards. The Tasmanian race is darker and smaller. Breeds August-
December. Nests at bottom of tree hollow or cliff hole.
Sexes: *alike.*
Immatures: *like adults.*
Voice: *high-pitched rattling 'churrs'.* T&PG

21 **PAPUAN FROGMOUTH** *Podargus papuensis* 50-60cm
(A) race *rogersi;* (B) race *baileyi.* The Papuan Frogmouth, whose stronghold is New Guinea, has an
enormous bill, and is the largest frogmouth in Australia. Race *rogersi* is the larger and darker of the
two Australian populations. The species frequents the edges of tropical rainforest, dense woodland and
mangrove. It is most active during early evening and the last hours before dawn, and takes larger prey
than the other frogmouths. This includes mainly large beetles, grasshoppers and other terrestrial and
arboreal insects which it hunts from low vantage points - gliding down on silent wings. During the day
it retires within the forest to roost, often in small family groups, usually on high bare branches over-
hung with dense foliage. It 'freezes' in typical frogmouth fashion when approached. Sedentary. Breeds
August-January. Nests in tree 6-12m high.
Sexes: *male heavier and darker.*
Immatures: *paler, eye yellow.*
Voice: *mainly drumming low booming 'woos' and 'uums';*
sometimes ghostly laughing sounds. D&MT

4 Ground-frequenting Birds

1   WHITE-FRONTED CHAT *Ephthianura albifrons*   12cm
The most commonly seen chat in southern Australia and Tasmania's only chat. In pairs and small parties, sometimes in large flocks during the non-breeding season, it frequents low dense cover, heath and moist vegetation near water. It is partially nomadic according to season. Like most chats, it perches on the tops of low bushes and tussocks. Its diet consists of insects, possibly also nectar. Breeds July-January. Nests near ground in low scrub such as samphire. Endemic.
Female: *duller, more brown.*
Immatures: *like females.*
Voice: *metallic sounds like 'tang'.*   T&PG

2   ORANGE CHAT *Ephthianura aurifrons*   12cm
A bird of the saltbush plains, the range of the Orange Chat roughly corresponds with that of the Crimson Chat, but it is more thinly spread except for the arid inland where it is very much at home. In general, the habits of the two species are similar, but the Orange Chat is less nomadic and feeds only on insects. Breeds August-September. Nests in low cover in colonies, often in areas shared with the Crimson Chat. Endemic.
Female: *lacks black on face (can be confused with Gibberbird but yellow rump of Orange Chat is distinctive).*
Immatures: *like females.*
Voice: *repeated musical notes in flight.*   GC

3   YELLOW CHAT *Ephthianura crocea*   11cm
This little known chat is found only in isolated colonies of up to 50 birds. It mostly inhabits swamps, often related to bore drains, and frequents dense vegetation such as lignum and sedge. Less terrestrial than the Crimson and Orange Chats, feeding also in bushes and trees. Diet is mainly flies and other insects. Breeds November-January. Nests near ground in thick cover. Endemic.
Female: *paler and lacks black breastband.*
Immatures: *grey-brown above.*
Voice: *pretty three-note call.*   GC

4, 5   CRIMSON CHAT *Ephthianura tricolor*   12cm
Widespread west of the Great Dividing Range. Has adapted well to desert conditions through its highly nomadic movements and its versatile diet, which includes nectar, such as from Sturt's Desert Pea, as well as its main diet of insects. In pairs and loose flocks, sometimes with other chats, it frequents a wide variety of habitat including grasslands, the low vegetation of open plains, scrub and tree savannah. Breeds mainly August-October; variably in north. Nests close to ground. Males may lapse into eclipse plumage after breeding. Endemic.
Immatures: *like females.*
Voice: *repeated high-pitched tinkling notes.*   JF

6   GIBBERBIRD *Ashbyia lovensis*   13cm
The Gibberbird lives only among the sparse vegetation of the arid stony gibber plains. It is seen singly and in pairs, sometimes in small flocks. It has an erect stance and long legs and perches on stones rather than bushes. Possibly nomadic. During the breeding season it performs a song flight unique among chats. Rising almost vertically to over 30m in stages it utters a piercing weet weet weet at each step, then plummets almost to its point of departure. Breeds generally May-October but may vary with conditions. Nests in a ground depression. Endemic.
Sexes: *similar.*
Immatures: *browner.*
Voice: *musical chatter.*   BM

7 YELLOW WAGTAIL *Motacilla flava*   19cm
Unrelated to Australia's Willie Wagtail, which is a flycatcher. This species, which is a regular visitor from Siberia and Alaska, arrives in northern Australia from November to February. Occasionally strays southwards and has been recorded as far south as the Hawkesbury River area in NSW. Terrestrial. Singly or in small parties, it walks with long steps, head rocking back and forth, and pumping its tail up and down. Feeds on insects and leaps into air for prey.
Sexes: *alike.*
Immatures: *browner.*
Voice: *shrill 'tsweep' or brief trill.*   E&DH

8 SINGING BUSHLARK *Mirafra javanica*   13cm
A bird of open country including pastures. It is seen singly and in small groups, occasionally in large flocks. Feeds mostly on seed, also insects. Its plumage varies with the colour of the soil where it lives. Like its introduced relative the Skylark, it sings as it soars aloft, not so loudly but with a more varied song. Also sings from ground on perch by day and night. Breeds September-January in south; with onset of the wet in north. Nests among tussocks.
Sexes: *alike.*
Immatures: *paler.*
Voice: *sweet melodious notes reminiscent of Skylark; accomplished mimic.*   B&BW

9 SKYLARK *Alauda arvensis*   19cm
The Skylark was introduced to Australia progressively from the 1850s. Well established in the south-east and is spreading slowly. Famous for its remarkable song flight, it rises vertically from ground cover pouring out its song while soaring and hovering, then plummets silently to ground on closed wings. Singly or in parties, it lives in heath and other open country. Feeds on seeds, shoots and insects. Breeds September-January. Nests under tussocks. **Recognition:** *bigger than Singing Bushlark, small crest and does not bob tail.*
Sexes: *alike.*
Immatures: *paler.*
Voice: *continuous joyous song.*   GC

10 RICHARD'S PIPIT *Anthus novaeseelandiae*   17cm
There are many plumage variations in Australia of this common species. It runs rapidly in short spurts and characteristically bobs its tail. Singly, in pairs or loose flocks, it mostly frequents open country and cleared land. Usually seen on ground, but also uses low perches such as stumps, rocks or fences. Eats seeds and insects. Breeds August-January. Nests in depression under tussocks.
Sexes: *alike.*
Immatures: *like adults.*
Voice: *rasping 'shreep'; male in display flight, repetitious trills.*   D&MT

11 RUFOUS SONGLARK *Cincloramphus mathewsi*   18cm
The southern population of this widespread endemic species is migratory, arriving in the south to breed in the spring and departing to overwinter in the north in autumn. Sings continuously during the breeding season from conspicuous high perch and in display flight and is one of Australia's most vocal birds. Singly and small parties, it frequents grassy woodlands and open scrub. Feeds on ground on insects and seeds. Breeds September-February. Nests on ground in well hidden hollows.
Sexes: *alike, but female smaller.*
Immatures: *paler.*
Voice: *loud 'witchy-weedle' monotonously repeated.*   D&MT

4

12   BROWN SONGLARK *Cincloramphus cruralis*   ♂24cm ♀18cm

This endemic species is more often seen on treeless plains than the Rufous Songlark. Carries its long tail cocked and sits upright when perching. The male takes off singing on its fluttering nuptial display flight with legs dangling and drops back to the same spot. Southern birds migrate northwards or inland after breeding. Singly and in loose groups, it is a ground feeder taking insects and seeds. Breeds mainly September-February. Nests on ground under tussocks.

Female: *resembles Rufous Songlark but lacks rufous rump.*
Immatures: *like females.*
Voice: *distinctive metallic 'skit-scot-a-wheeler' often repeated.*   GC

13, 14   SPOTTED QUAIL-THRUSH *Cinclosoma punctatum*   26-28cm

This, the largest of the quail-thrushes, lives in the eucalypt forests of south-eastern Australia and is Tasmania's only quail-thrush. No other quail-thrush is found east of the Great Dividing Range. It favours stony hills and ridges afforested with dry eucalypt with a ground cover of litter, or an understorey of shrubs and other vegetation at lower altitudes. It is very wary and elusive, and takes off in explosive quail-like flight when alarmed. Singly, in pairs and family parties, it feeds on seeds and a variety of insects, caterpillars and sometimes small lizards. The male defends a breeding territory by singing from a prominent perch. Its double whistles distinguish it from other quail-thrushes. Breeds July-February. Nests in ground depression under cover. Endemic.

Immatures: *like females.*
Voice: *sibilant high-pitched notes and series of musical double whistles.*   PG

15, 18   CHESTNUT-BREASTED QUAIL-THRUSH *Cinclosoma castaneothorax* 22-24cm

Western race *marginatum;* Eastern race *castaneothorax* (illustrated).Although widely separated by the Simpson and Strezelecki Deserts, the two populations are very alike both in appearance and behaviour. The chestnut breast of the western male is, however, paler and it has a deeper black frontal band. Both species live in dense mulga in stony hilly country. Where their ranges meet with the Cinnamon Quail-thrush, distinct identities are maintained, with few reports of hybridisation. Though fairly common, the bird is rather shy and difficult to see. If approached, it will disappear under a bush or run away to cover, flicking its tail. When flushed, it will break cover in a quail-like burst and fly off in a flurry of wings. Singly, in pairs or small parties, it wanders on the ground foraging for seeds, insects and spiders - sometimes turning over stones. Males sometimes call soon after sunrise from a dead branch or other vantage point with two or three other males often replying. Breeds July-September and almost any time after good rain. Nests on ground well hidden under cover. Endemic.

Immatures: *like females but duller with dusky flecks.*
Voice: *thin, high-pitched whistle.*   15GC, 18CC

16, 17   CHESTNUT QUAIL-THRUSH *Cinclosoma castanotus*   23-26cm

The Chestnut Quail-thrush is the most widely spread of the quail-thrushes and is found in a variety of habitat ranging from the timbered areas of semi-arid southern Australia to the spinifex and other low scrub of the sandy inland desert. Its range extensively overlaps that of the western population of the Chestnut-breasted Quail-thrush, but they tend to separate into their preferred habitats. There is some evidence of interbreeding between them. The chestnut on the back is more extensive and brighter in the desert birds. It rambles in pairs and small families, searching for insects and seeds and is probably nomadic in the desert. It is wary and takes off with whirring wings to a safe distance when alarmed. Breeds mainly July-September, but August-December in the desert areas or following rain. Nests in a scrape under cover. Endemic.

Immatures: *like females.*
Voice: *repeated high-pitched sibilant whistles, especially at dawn.*   16GC, 17JP

19, 20 CINNAMON QUAIL-THRUSH/NULLARBOR QUAIL-THRUSH

Cinclosoma cinnamomeum (B) Race *alisteri* (Nullarbor Quail-thrush)   18-21cm

This very rare and elusive small quail-thrush lives exclusively in the vast stony Nullarbor Plain under extremely harsh conditions where the spare vegetation is almost limited to saltbush and bluebush and the temperature can rise to well over 40°C. It is one of only a few birds to live in this desolate area. Recorded sightings are few, and all in a limited area straddling the border between Western and South Australia. As with its eastern relative, it is elusive and wary and hides if approached. If alarmed, it bursts from cover like a quail. It flicks its tail when walking and wanders sometimes in pairs or small scattered parties. Possibly nomadic following rain. It lives on insects and seeds, often turning over stones with its bill. Breeds July-September, and nests among rocks. Endemic.

Immatures: *like females.*

Voice: *very high-pitched and faint. Wells (see below) describes it as resembling the morse code for the letter 'Y' (dash-dot-dash-dash).*

The photographs   These unique shots were taken in September 1991 in a 'donga' (a shallow depression of richer vegetation) by Bert and Babs Wells. They were the only birds seen during a month-long exploration of the Seemore Downs. (Their fascinating story is published in Geo Vol.14 No. 3 1992).

21   CINNAMON QUAIL-THRUSH *Cinclosoma cinnamomeum*

(A) Race *cinnamomeum* (Inland form)   19-22cm

Fairly numerous in the Lake Eyre basin, it lives in acacia scrub, saltbush or spinifex in stony country. Avoids sandy areas. It interbreeds with the Chestnut-breasted Quail-thrush in some areas where their ranges meet. Habits like those of Nullarbor Quail-thrush. Breeds any time after rain, but mainly July-September. Nests in a ground scrape under a bush. Endemic.

Female: *plainer, no black on underparts.*

Immatures: *like females.*

Voice: *repeated very high-pitched thin whistles. Note: this photograph of a male taken by Graeme Chapman at Lyndhurst (south of Lake Eyre) shows marked plumage differences from the Nullarbor bird.*

22   APOSTLEBIRD *Struthidea cinerea*   33cm

A highly sociable species which lives in close-knit groups of from 6-20 birds - often in twelves as suggested by the name. In the non-breeding season, flocks of hundreds may be seen. Never far from water in open woodland and scrub; also near country homesteads where it is relatively tame. Jumps around in restless groups making a great commotion, often with tails cocked. Feeds on the ground on insects and seeds. Will catch and kill house mice during plagues. Breeds August-February. Nest is a large bowl made of mud and grass. Endemic.

Sexes: *alike.*

Immatures: *smaller.*

Voice: *continuous harsh chattering.*   GW

23   WHITE-BROWED BABBLER *Pomatostomus superciliosus*   20cm

The White-browed Babbler is common in the dry shrublands and semi-desert country of southern Australia, and keeps together in restless groups of from 3-10 birds. Intrusion sets parties off in an indignant chorus of scolding notes. Feeds mostly on the ground foraging for seeds and insects. Breeds July-December. Nests communally in clusters of domed-shaped nests with spout-like entrances. These structures also serve as dormitories for roosting. Endemic.

Sexes: *alike.*

Immatures: *almost similar.*

Voice: *range of loud chattering notes and whistles.*   B&BW

24   HALL'S BABBLER *Pomatostomus halli*   23cm
Until 1964, when a small babbler collected on the Harold Hall Expedition the previous year was found
to differ from the widespread White-browed Babbler, this bird had not been recognised as a separate
species - although the late Monty Schrader knew that babblers like this, long familiar to him at Eulo,
Qld, were different. It lives in lightly timbered mulga through which it moves constantly in noisy chat-
tering groups. A ground feeder. Breeds communally September-June. Nests up to 10m high. Endemic.
Recognition: *small white bib; dark breast and belly.*
Sexes: *similar.*
Voice: *chuckles, growls and liquid notes.*   DD

25   CHESTNUT-CROWNED BABBLER *Pomatostomus ruficeps*   22cm
In its relatively restricted inland range, this babbler is fairly common. It frequents open scrub and wood-
lands and keeps together in groups of from 12-15 birds. Specific sites are selected for socialising and for
use as playgrounds. Here they will chase each other around a bush so often in an apparent game of fol-
low-my-leader that they make well defined circular tracks. Shy and elusive. Retreats noisily if disturbed.
Feeds on insects and seeds. Breeds July-December. Nests 5-10m high in a tree. Endemic.
Sexes: *alike.*
Immatures: *duller.*
Voice: *penetrating whistles and chattering.*   D&MT

26   WESTERN WHIPBIRD *Psophodes nigrogularis*   25cm
This rare bird is now restricted to five small and isolated populations in coastal sandhills, heath and mallee
scrub. Being strongly territorial it is very vulnerable to loss of habitat, and its former range has shrunk
alarmingly. The eastern birds are paler. Excessively shy, it lives in dense cover where it forages for insects
and small invertebrates. Breeds July-November. Nests in dense scrub within 1m of ground. Endemic.
Sexes: *similar.*
Immatures: *white and black throat markings absent.*
Voice: *male four syllable 'lets-scratch-teacher' answered by female 'pick-it-up'.*   RayG

27   EASTERN WHIPBIRD *Psophodes olivaceus*   28cm
A bird of the gullies and wetter wooded areas east of the Great Dividing Range. An isolated northerly population has brown not white undertail tips. Solitary and in small parties, it hops chuckling
through thick undergrowth grubbing for insects and small invertebrates under litter. Also probes fall-
en logs for prey. Shy but inquisitive. Sedentary. Breeds July-January. Nests near ground up to 3m in
thick undergrowth. Endemic.
Sexes: *female smaller.*
Immatures: *white on throat and neck absent.*
Voice: *male's swelling note ending in explosive whip-crack often answered immediately by*
'choo-choo' from female.   D&MT

28   GREY-CROWNED BABBLER *Pomatostomus temporalis*   26cm
The largest and most widespread of the babblers, but becoming quite rare in Victoria. It frequents a variety
of woodland in groups of from 5-10 birds. Feeds mostly on the ground for insects, spiders and even lizards.
Plumage and size varies geographically e.g. some western birds have a pale rufous breast; southern birds
are larger and darker. Breeds July-February. Nests 3-6m high in shrub or sapling; nest is dome shaped.
Recognition: *chestnut wing patch in flight.*
Sexes: *similar.*
Immatures: *slightly paler.*
Voice: *clear 'yahoo'.*   B&BW

29   CHIMING WEDGEBILL *Psophodes occidentalis*   22cm
The Chiming Wedgebill is almost identical in appearance to the Chirruping Wedgebill of the east, but differs markedly in voice and some habits. In pairs and parties of 10-20 birds, it is common to the west of its range and lives in thickets of low scrub and arid tree savannah. Feeds on ground on insects and seeds. Wary and runs quickly to cover when approached. Breeds variably depending on rains. Nests low in thick bushes. Endemic.
Sexes: *alike.*
Immatures: *like adults but bill pinkish and legs paler.*
Voice: *descending chiming sweet tomes 'did-you-get-drunk' repeated monotonously, sometimes by moonlight.*   GC

30   CHIRRUPING WEDGEBILL *Psophodes cristatus*   20cm
The range of the two wedgebills meet in the Simpson Desert and both species have been heard near Oodnadatta. The Chirruping Wedgebill mainly lives in lignum swamps and spinifex of semi-desert country and feeds on insects and seeds. Gregarious, sometimes in quite large parties. Less shy than its relative and more often seen. Breeds March-November, except mid-winter. Nests below 3m in low shrub. Endemic. **Recognition:** *faintly streaked on breast (the Chiming Wedgebill's is plain).*
Sexes: *alike.*
Immatures: *crest undeveloped.*
Voice: *creaky song; female answers male's 'chip-chip-cheroo' with 'chin-up'.*   BL

31   LOGRUNNER *Orthonyx temminckii*   20cm
A bird of the dank deep shades of semi-tropical and temperate rainforest. In pairs and small parties, it runs and hops over fallen debris, seldom flying. Rakes litter and leaf mould with its strong legs, using its stiff spine-shafted tail as a prop. Circular scrapings of about 15cm indicate where it has been feeding. Breeds April-August. Domed nest on ground against rock or tree. Several races in New Guinea.
Male: *white throat.*
Immatures: *like females but plainer.*
Voice: *excited bursts of 'kweek-kweek-kweek'.*   T&PG

32   CHOWCHILLA *Orthonyx spaldingii*   31cm
This logrunner is common in the Atherton Tablelands. Its remarkable voice, reflected in its name, rings through the tropical rainforest at dawn and dominates the early morning chorus. Stopping suddenly, it remains relatively silent during the day. In pairs and small parties, it runs and hops over fallen debris and rarely takes wing. Rakes floor litter for insects and grubs with its strong legs. Breeds May-November. Domed nest up to 4m from ground. Endemic.
Male: *throat and foreneck white*
Immatures: *cinnamon-brown.*
Voice: *resonant repeated 'chow-chowchilla'.*   LR

33   PILOTBIRD *Pycnoptilus floccosus*   17cm
This unique small bird lives in moist eucalypt forest and woodland. It sometimes accompanies the Superb Lyrebird as it fossicks in ground litter taking insects, earthworms and other small invertebrates disturbed by its large companion - hence its name. Solitary and fearless. A weak flier, it hops briskly and runs rapidly when alarmed; tail often carried high and flicked. Breeds August-January. Domed nest on or near ground. Endemic.
Sexes and immatures: *similar.*
Voice: *strong, sweet and varied; includes call of 'guinea-a-week'.*   NC

34   WESTERN BRISTLEBIRD *Dasyornis longirostris*   19cm

This small bristlebird has become one of Australia's rarest birds. Once distributed throughout the dwarf heathlands of the far south-west of WA, it is now confined to an area in and around Two Peoples Bay Reserve near Albany and the Fitzgerald River National Park. It lives in deep dense heath, is remarkably shy and rarely shows itself, even singing hidden from view. Runs swiftly; feeble flight. Breeds September-January. Domed nest near ground. Endemic.

Sexes: *alike.*
Immatures: *undescribed.*
Voice: *variable, including male's 'chip-pee' answered by female's 'quick-more-beer'.*   GC

35   RUFOUS BRISTLEBIRD *Dasyornis broadbenti*   27cm

This, the largest of the bristlebirds, lives in heavy scrub and coastal thickets. Usually in pairs, it is a ground feeder on grubs, insects, seeds and berries. With raised and spread longish tail, it runs swiftly through undergrowth and seldom flies. Shy and elusive. Coorong, SA birds are pale grey on chin and centre of belly. A race formerly of the south-west corner of WA was last reliably reported in 1940 and is believed extinct. Breeds August-December. Domed nest up to 2m from ground. Endemic.

Sexes: *similar.*
Immatures: *undescribed.*
Voice: *penetrating and squeaky calls with responses from female.*   JP

36   EASTERN BRISTLEBIRD *Dasyornis brachypterus*   22cm

Restricted to a series of isolated pockets in coastal and mountain areas from southeast Queensland to Victoria, the Eastern Bristlebird has become rare following the impact of settlement. It skulks in rank, dense undergrowth where it feeds on insects and seeds. It is reluctant to fly and runs with tail partly cocked and sometimes fanned. Solitary and shy. Sings from bushes and is easy to locate from its loud distinctive calls. Breeds August-December. Domed nest on or near ground. Endemic.

Sexes: *alike.*
Immatures: *undescribed.*
Voice: *melodious, penetrating and variable, including 'it-wood-weet-sip'.*   JP

37   NOISY SCRUB-BIRD *Atrichornis clamosus*   24cm

The small surviving colony of Noisy Scrub-birds discovered in the Two Peoples Bay/Mt Gardner area in 1961 and those released on Mt Many Peaks in 1983 live mainly in deep and densely vegetated mountain gullies. Shy and very difficult to see. Feeds among ground litter on insects and small invertebrates. Strong legs carry it swiftly through undergrowth. Winter breeder May-September. Nest spherical with side entrance usually low near running water. Endemic.

Male: *black chest markings.*
Immatures: *like females.*
Voice: *very loud piercing staccato notes.*   HW/NPI

38   RUFOUS SCRUB-BIRD *Atrichornis rufescens*   16cm

The species lives in isolated pockets on the highlands of the Great Dividing Range among deep tangled understorey in moist forest. Rarely flying, it runs fast with tail cocked, and wriggles through litter more like a mouse than a bird. The male has one of the loudest voices in the bush; it is also ventriloquial and a gifted mimic. The female is mostly silent, also the male when not breeding. Breeds September-January. Domed ground nest lined with 'card-board' of chewed wood. Endemic.

Sexes: *similar, but male has dark breast mark.*
Immatures: *underparts chestnut.*
Voice: *repeated loud 'chipping' phrases.*   M&IM

39   RAINBOW PITTA *Pitta iris*   18cm
This strikingly marked pitta of the Kimberley and the Northern Territory lives in a varied habitat of
monsoon rainforest, bamboo thickets and mangrove, and hops among moist ground litter like the
Noisy Pitta. It eats insects, grubs and small snails, breaking their shells on any hard object. Solitary,
shy and retiring. Breeds December-March. Nests vary from partly open in the Kimberley to the char-
acteristic domed construction in the monsoon forests of the far north. Endemic.
Sexes: *alike.*
Immatures: *unrecorded.*
Voice: *loud and clear 'want-a-whip'.*   JE

40   RED-BELLIED PITTA *Pitta erythrogaster*   19cm
Formerly known as the Blue-breasted Pitta. This breeding migrant from New Guinea arrives in the
rainforests of Cape York Peninsula from October and returns March-April. Like the Noisy Pitta, it
smashes snails on an 'anvil'. Hops about when feeding and flies erratically from one foraging spot to
another. Often calls from trees up to 25m from ground.
Sexes: *similar, but chin, upper half of throat and cheeks of female sooty brown.*
Immatures: *duller.*
Voice: *mournful whistling notes.*   BP

41   NOISY PITTA *Pitta versicolor*   21cm
A stocky brightly-coloured dweller of tropical and semi-tropical rainforest. Fossicks for grubs and
insects; also eats berries and large forest snails whose shells are smashed on an 'anvil' of stone or
wood. These are sometimes worn smooth with constant use and heaps of broken shells betray their
location. Hops with upright stance, tail flicking, and flies swiftly. Shy. Breeds mainly October-January.
Bulky domed nest on or near ground with 'doormat' of mammal dung.
Sexes: *alike.*
Immatures: *duller.*
Voice: *resonant notes including 'walk to work'; also at night.*   T&PG

42   ORANGE-FOOTED SCRUBFOWL *Megapodius reinwardt*   40cm
This Scrubfowl is found in Australia mostly in the dense wet coastal rainforests of the tropics. Solitary
and in scattered colonies, fossicks for seeds, roots and grubs on the forest floor. It flies heavily to trees
when disturbed. Sedentary. Its incubating mounds of soil and rotting litter are usually 3m wide and
1.5m high, but they can become enormous, growing even to 15m wide and 4m high. Up to 15 eggs are
laid in holes to 2m deep, then sealed. Breeds August-March.
Sexes: *alike.*
Chicks: *downy.*
Voice: *clucking and squawking like Domestic Fowl.*   H&JB

43   AUSTRALIAN BRUSH-TURKEY *Alectura lathami*   70cm
Endemic to Australia, this mound-builder lives in coastal rainforest and the drier high country scrub.
Mainly a ground feeder on native fruits, seeds and insects. Sedentary. The egg-incubating mound, usu-
ally about 4m wide and 1.5m high, is built by the male, who also controls the mound's temperature at
33°C during the 50-day incubation period. The female lays her 18-24 eggs in holes at intervals accord-
ing to conditions. Cape York birds have bluish-white wattles. Breeds August-December.
Sexes: *alike except for male's breeding wattles.*
Voice: *loud clucking and grunting.*   D&MT

4

44   MALLEEFOWL *Leipoa ocellata*   60cm
Malleefowls usually excavate their mounds in poor sandy soil in mallee scrub and open woodland.
Mounds can grow to 4m across and 1.5m high and their construction and maintenance of the egg
chamber at 33°C involves shifting tonnes of soil and fermenting vegetable matter in a season. From 5-
33 eggs are laid one at a time over 2-17 days with the male preparing the cavity to the female's satis-
faction on each occasion. The species is wary. Food includes buds, flowers, fruits and spilled grain.
Breeds September-April. Endemic.
Sexes: *alike.*
Chicks: *downy with wing feathers.*
Voice: *loud booming and grunts.*   T&PG

45   CALIFORNIA QUAIL *Callipepla californica*   24cm
A large quail species with a waving crest plume. Introduced to Australia from North America around
1860, it failed then to survive, but a further batch introduced to King Island in the 1930's, there pro-
tected from hunters, has become established. Coveys inhabit wooded country and scrub with open
spaces, moving into pasture to feed on plants and insects. Roosts off the ground. Breeds usually
September-January. Nests in a depression under cover.
Female: *lacks black throat, duller, crest shorter.*
Immatures: *like females.*
Voice: *many calls including triple notes, the middle one highest and loudest.*   DA/A

46   KING QUAIL *Coturnix chinensis*   14cm
The King Quail is particularly shy and elusive. In Australia, it keeps mainly to rank vegetation, swamps,
heath and crops such as lucerne and feeds on seeds and insects. If disturbed, it squats but, if forced to fly, it
does so feebly and briefly, quickly dropping back to cover. Usually in pairs or coveys of 5 or 6, sometimes
larger. Numbers fluctuate according to conditions. Breeds most months. Builds nest in ground hollow.
Immatures: *like females.*
Voice: *plaintive 3-note whistle; also calls at dusk and after dark.*   D&MT

47   BROWN QUAIL *Coturnix ypsilophora*   17cm
The Brown Quail, lives in grassland, marshes and scrub. The Tasmanian form (illustrated) - known as
the Swamp Quail - is larger and paler and lives almost exclusively in the wet places. When flushed
they characteristically scatter in a whirr of wings. Breeds from spring in south and January-March in
tropical north. Nests on ground under dense cover.
Sexes: *female larger and more boldly marked.*
Immatures: *like adult females*
Voice: *loud rising whistling 'eyou wheee'; 'be-quick, be-quick' in Tasmania.*   D&MT

48   STUBBLE QUAIL *Coturnix pectoralis*   18cm
The widely spread Stubble Quail lives in all types of country, commonly occurring in grassland,
swamp margins and crop stubble. It has multiplied in some areas following agricultural development.
Partial to seeds of weeds, plants and fallen grain, also takes insects. Companies fluctuate in size and
roam widely; sometimes covering 1 000 km or more. When flushed, runs rather than flies; when
pressed, breaks cover with a whirr of wings in low, short and rapid flight. Breeds mainly October-
February. Nests in ground scrape. Endemic.
Immatures: *like females.*
Voice: *'two-to-weep'.*   AP

49   RED-CHESTED BUTTON-QUAIL *Turnix pyrrhothorax*   ♂13cm ♀15cm
Distribution of this quail is patchy and thin across the north of its range. Some seasonal movement and
can turn up anywhere. Singly, in pairs and small variable coveys, it frequents grasslands and open timbered country with good cover. Feeds on seeds and insects. If flushed, it flies low and straight over
short distance. Breeds October-March. Nests on ground under cover. Endemic. Recognition: easily
confused with Little Button-Quail but darker above.
Female: *brighter; no black markings on neck or breast.*
Immatures: *like adult male, darker eye.*
Voice: *repeated 'ooms'; gurgles.*   IMcC/ANT

50   PAINTED BUTTON-QUAIL *Turnix varia*   ♂ 17cm ♀20cm
This bright-plumaged quail occurs in several isolated populations and certain offshore islands. Its varied habitat includes grassy woodlands and rocky hillsides with open timber or scrub. Birds of the Abrolhos Islands are smaller and paler. Pairs and family parties forage in leaf litter for insects, plant food and seeds, leaving small circular scrapes. Erratic nomadic movements. Breeds September-March south; variably north. Nests in ground depression. Endemic.
Male: *smaller, duller.*
Immatures: *duller, eye brown.*
Voice: *low repeated ventriloquial 'oom'.*   LR

51   (A) CHESTNUT-BACKED BUTTON-QUAIL *Turnix castanota*   ♂ 15cm ♀18cm
 (B) BUFF-BREASTED BUTTON-QUAIL *Turnix olivii*   ♂ 18cm ♀20cm (not illustrated)
T. castanota (illustrated) lives in poorly grassed areas in dry savannah woodland, especially on rocky sandy ridges. *T. olivii* the similar small isolated population found near the coast - has a plain buff breast, and lives in wet open areas with heath-like vegetation fringing rainforest. Both breed December-March, and nest on ground under shelter. Endemic.
Sexes: *similar; female brighter.*
Immatures: *like adults, darker eyes.*
Voice: *repeated low moaning calls.*   JE

52   BLACK-BREASTED BUTTON-QUAIL *Turnix melanogaster*   ♂16cm ♀18cm
This rare quail lives in the thick tangled lantana and vine undergrowth of dry sub-tropical and tropical rainforest. Solitary, or in small coveys, it moves slowly fossicking in leaf litter for seeds and insects, leaving scratched out bare circular depressions along its trail. A reluctant and clumsy flier, it prefers running. Probably sedentary. Breeds variably, but not during colder periods. Nests in ground depression. Endemic.
Immatures: *like adult males, eye dark, legs grey.*
Voice: *female, repeated low booming; male clucks.*   AF

53   RED-BACKED BUTTON-QUAIL *Turnix maculosa*   ♂13cm ♀15cm
So named from the rufous upper back of the female. In Australia the species is found on the margins of wet and swampy areas, rainforest and cleared country. Some plumage variation across its range. In pairs and small coveys, it feeds on the ground on seeds and insects. Shy and elusive and not often seen. Breeds October-July. Nests under cover in ground depression.
Male: *smaller, lacks rufous on upper back.*
Immatures: *like adult males; dark eye.*
Voice: *rapidly-repeated 'oom'.*   FL

54   LITTLE BUTTON-QUAIL *Turnix velox*   ♂14cm ♀15cm
Widespread and more abundant than other quails, it is also the least coloured. It lives in a wide variety of habitat ranging from open woodlands and grassy plains to spinifex in the arid inland. It feeds mainly on seeds and is highly nomadic, moving to areas where rain has provided good growth. Usually seen in small flocks, but these can be in thousands in good seasons. Breeds most months, according to rain. Nests on ground in shelter of grass tussocks. Endemic.
Sexes: *similar except for size.*
Immatures: *like adult male, eye dark.*
Voice: *moaning 'oop', squeaky alarm call.*   JP

55   AUSTRALIAN BUSTARD *Ardeotis australis*   ♂1300cm ♀800cm
Now common only in remote unsettled areas, this elegant and stately bird is a resident of open country with low bushes and scattered trees. In large flocks at times, but more usually seen singly or in pairs. It feeds on insects, small animals and vegetable matter. When disturbed, it freezes then walks casually away with head upstretched, taking to flight only if pressed. Probably nomadic in response to rain. Breeds variably. Nests on ground under tussock or bush. Moves to and from New Guinea.
Sexes and immatures: *alike but female smaller.*
Voice: *low booming but mainly silent.*   D&MT

4

56, 57   PLAINS-WANDERER *Pedionomus torquatus*   ♂16cm ♀18cm

The female of this rare strange quail-like bird is larger and brighter than the male and is polyandrous (it mates with more than one male). To this extent it is like the button-quails, but, unlike them, it has the hind toe of the typical quails. While its instinct is to freeze with the approach of danger and its crouching head-down run is quail-like, it is unlike quails in its quaint habit of standing on tip-toe to survey the land and in its weak uncertain flight. Also unlike quails, it is said to be reluctant to take flight from danger and can even be caught by hand in broad daylight. Because of these unique characteristics, taxonomists have thought it best to leave it on a twig of its own on the evolutionary tree. The spread of agriculture into its natural habitat of lightly grassed flat open plains has led to its alarming decline, although there is some evidence of it adapting to cereal crops and ungrazed paddocks. Usually solitary, also in pairs and small parties, it forages for seeds and insects. Breeds June-January. Nests in scrape under cover. Endemic.

Immatures: *like adults, more heavily scalloped on breast.*

Voice: *repeated mournful 'moo'.*   ES

58   COMMON PHEASANT Phasianus colchicus   ♂85cm ♀60cm

Legend has it that the original stock of this pheasant came from the river Phasis (now Rioni) in the ancient province of Colchis on the Black Sea, and that it was brought from there by the Argonauts on returning from their quest for the Golden Fleece. The scientific name perpetuates this belief. There are many hybrid forms from continuous interbreeding of this famous game bird. Only small feral populations have survived from introductions in Australia - in the south-east and south-west of the continent, in Tasmania and some of the offshore islands.

Female: *mottled brown.*

Voice: *explosive 'karrk-kock'.*   E&DH

59   INDIAN PEAFOWL Pavo cristatus   ♂2.4m ♀90cm

The fabled Peafowl is most often seen in zoos, parks and large estates. A native of India and Sri Lanka, it has been famous throughout history. The Old Testament tells us that Solomon (ninth century BC) imported peacocks with other riches to adorn his temple (I Kings X:22 and 2 Chronicles IX:21). Introduced to Australia, it exists in the wild only in a very few areas, such as Rottnest Island where releases were made in 1912 and 1917. The Peacock is polygamous and may breed throughout the year. Nests in a scrape in the ground.

Female: *smaller, duller and lacks the striking train.*

Voice: *strident screech.*   D&MT

Lyrebirds 5

1, 2   SUPERB LYREBIRD *Menura novaehollandiae*   ♂ up to 100cm ♀86cm

The elusive Superb Lyrebird lives in dark gullies in wet eucalypt forests. Here it grubs among fallen litter for beetle, worms and crustaceans; it also probes for insects under bark of rotting logs. The birds are most in evidence during the colder months when mating takes place and when their displays and wonderful voices are at their peak. The famous display rituals of the polygamous male are usually performed on a special platform, several of which may be prepared in readiness for the mating season. These average about a metre in diameter and are about 15cm high. A series of platforms may be used in a day. After the chick has fledged, the male moults its tail and falls silent for up to six weeks. New tails become progressively longer for up to ten years. The song is constantly improved through practice and the young birds are schooled by their elders. Roosts are often chosen in tree tops, perhaps as high as 40 metres. Breeds April-September.

Immatures: *like female.*

Voice: *'ca-luck, ca-luck', 'pellick, pellick', integrated with mimicry of other birds.*   1H&JB, 2R&DK

3, 4   ALBERT'S LYREBIRD *Menura alberti*   ♂90cm ♀65cm

The Albert's Lyrebird is smaller and more rufous than the Superb Lyrebird. It is restricted to the dense rainforest of the rugged McPherson Range on the Queensland/New South Wales border, and lives in an almost impenetrable habitat of vines and other sub-tropical ground cover where it is exceedingly difficult to find. It is even shyer than the Superb Lyrebird. The Albert's Lyrebird behaves much like its southern relative, except for its display platform which is simply a flat trampled arena of vines and leaves. It is partial to the very large snails that abound in its area. Breeds June-July. Nests on rocky ledge, tree stump or buttress, and sometimes on a high branch.

Immatures: *like female.*

Voice: *perhaps less variable than that of the Superb Lyrebird and much different territorial call.*   3WL, 4ECS

6 Pigeons and Doves

1   DIAMOND DOVE *Geopelia cuneata*   22cm
Australia's smallest pigeon is a bird mostly of the inland, and is nomadic as the climatic conditions dictate. It is highly gregarious, congregating in large flocks at water, flying and roosting in flocks, always at least in pairs and groups. It feeds entirely on the ground on seeds, taking some buds and insects, with an amusing toddling run. Flight is direct and swooping. Breeds all the year round in response to rain. Nests low in trees or bushes or on ground. Endemic.
Sexes: *alike but female has duller and browner foreparts.*
Immatures: *black-grey striping on upper parts.*
Voice: *soft 'poor-pa-poor-papa'.*   D&MT

2   PEACEFUL DOVE *Geopelia striata*   23cm
This dainty native pigeon frequents open forest and scrubby woodland near water, roadsides, parks and gardens. It feeds terrestrially on a wide variety of seeds, in pairs and groups, or in loose feeding and drinking flocks. At other times it roosts quietly in trees; in the breeding season it reacts aggressively to other birds. The species is still reasonably common but may lose out in competition with introduced doves. Sedentary. Probably breeds year round. Nests in trees 6-20m high. Also in coastal islands to the north and north-west.
Sexes: *alike.*
Immatures: *paler and more brown.*
Voice: *'doodle-do' and low churring.*   H&JB

3   SPOTTED TURTLE DOVE *Streptopelia chinensis*   31cm
A native of India and a number of other countries of South-East Asia, it was introduced to Melbourne in the 1860s and has since spread much further afield. It is very common in urban areas and scrubby thickets. In pairs and groups it feeds on bread, grain and seeds. In some areas it seems to be replacing native doves. Relatively tame, it flushes easily with a noisy burst. Breeds all year round. Nests in trees, ledges, or on the ground.
Sexes: *alike.*
Immatures: *no chequered patch.*
Voice: *persistent gentle cooing.*   D&MT

4   LAUGHING TURTLE-DOVE *Streptopelia senegalensis*   25cm
Native of Africa, countries of the Middle East and India, the species was released in Western Australia nearly a hundred years ago. Also called Senegal Dove. It frequents city and suburban areas, farms and silos and is seen in pairs, or small to large flocks where food is plentiful, feeding on the ground or taking seeds and buds from low bushes. It copes well with dry conditions. Probably breeds the year round. Nests in dense foliage.
Sexes: *similar but female duller.*
Immatures: *no speckling, no blue-grey on wing.*
Voice: *long drawn-out cooing with a laughing quality.*   GC

5   BAR-SHOULDERED DOVE *Geopelia humeralis*   30cm
The Bar-shouldered Dove frequents habitat near water including woodland, scrub and mangrove. In recent years there has been a gradual extension of range southwards; on the other hand it may have given ground to introduced species where the latter have established themselves. In pairs and groups, sometimes large loose flocks, it feeds on the ground close to cover, on seeds, preferring those growing in swampy areas. Sedentary. Breeds most months of the year. Nests low to 6m high.
Sexes: *alike.*
Immatures: *hind neck and upper mantle brown.*
Voice: *rollicking 'cook-a-wook'.*   CW

6   BANDED FRUIT-DOVE *Ptilinopus cinctus*   36cm
Living in a very restricted range of pockets of forest amongst sandstone cliffs and gorges in west
Arnhem Land, this pigeon's habitat may be endangered by uranium mining. It feeds quietly and incon-
spicuously on native fruits, and gathers in the tree canopy in pairs or very small groups, or singly, fly-
ing from tree to tree and perching with a forward flip of the tail. Breeds in the dry season May-
November. Nests 2-5m high.
Sexes: *similar.*
Immatures: *grey replaces the white parts of adults.*
Voice: *deep booming, soft 'coo'.*   TH

7   SUPERB FRUIT-DOVE *Ptilinopus superbus*   24cm
This fruit-eating pigeon, widespread in territories to the north, occurs in Australia from Cape York
southward in rainforest and mangroves. Difficult to detect in the canopy, it can betray its presence by
falling fruit pieces when feeding. Nomadic. Breeds June-February. Nests in trees to 10m high.
Recognition: *white underside and flanks of the male.*
Female: *small crown patch, blue instead of purple, lacks dark breastband.*
Immatures: *like females, breast finely scalloped yellow.*
Voice: *low 'oom' exploding into 'woops'.*   H&JB

8   ROSE-CROWNED FRUIT-DOVE *Ptilinopus regina*   23cm
Somewhat similar in distribution and habitat to its close relative the Superb Fruit-Dove, but found also
in northern Australia. It seems to be totally arboreal, even taking water from foliage, and is seen in
pairs or small parties. Nomadic or partially migratory. Breeds variably October-March. nests low in
trees to 30m high. **Recognition:** *lacks the white underparts of the Superb Fruit-Dove.*
Sexes: *alike, but female duller.*
Immatures: *mostly green above.*
Voice: *loud cooing that makes the forest 'throb'. Rapidly accelerating 'woop woop woop woop....'*
descending the scale.   H&JB

9   ROCK DOVE *Columba livia*   33cm
Descended from the wild Rock Dove of Europe. Also known as the Domestic Pigeon. Some occur in their
original state in the north of the British Isles and a few other parts of the world, including Australia, and are
now found wherever there is a city, town or village, in many agricultural areas, and even at isolated homesteads in the interior. Breeds year around almost anywhere including crevices in cliffs and on the ground.
Sexes and immatures: *alike.*
Voice: *cooing.*   D&MT

10   WHITE-HEADED PIGEON *Columba leucomela*   41cm
A large mainly arboreal fruit pigeon which is seen in tropical and subtropical rainforests and scrubs.
Its numbers have declined as a result of white settlement but in some areas it has adapted to thrive on
camphor laurel. Wary and elusive, it lives silently in lower tree branches, occasionally feeding on the
ground in pairs and small groups. It bursts noisily out of cover when a flock suddenly departs.
Nomadic. Breeds most months. Nests in branch or vine tangle up to 18m high. Endemic.
Sexes: *similar but female duller.*
Immatures: *greyer.*
Voice: *low ventriloquial 'oom' or 'oom-coo'.*   H&JB

11   WOMPOO FRUIT-DOVE *Ptilinopus magnificus*   ·   56cm
In tropical and sub-tropical rainforest this large fruit-pigeon feeds agilely, hanging upside down from
frail branches to reach fruit and berries. It spends most of its time in the tree canopy and brilliantly-
plumaged as it is, it is difficult to see unless the yellow undertail catches the eye. Southern populations
are threatened by rainforest clearance. Locally nomadic depending on the fruit supply. Breeds June-
January. Nests high.
Sexes: *alike.*
Immatures: *green patches on purple breast.*
Voice: *loud and deep bubbling 'whompoo'.*   EZ

12   PIED IMPERIAL PIGEON *Ducula bicolor*   44cm
This pigeon is a breeding migrant from New Guinea, and is also known as the Torres Strait Pigeon. It arrives in the Northern Territory and Queensland in great numbers from August and during March and April. The Queensland birds disperse to the offshore islands of the Great Barrier Reef where they set up breeding colonies sometimes consisting of several thousand birds. They eat all sorts of large native fruits, including that of the nutmeg tree, for which they have to cross to the mainland daily, sometimes involving a round trip of sixty or so kilometres. In former times, these daily crossings were of staggering proportions. E.J.Banfield (1908) estimated that 'fully 100 000 come and go evening and morning' over Dunk Island in processions of two miles wide, and that this company was 'small compared with the myriads' of the past. Even now, H.J.Frith (1982) describes these crossings as 'one of the great ornithological experiences of the tropics', but it is now necessary to go north of Cairns to witness this phenomenon, though on a lesser scale. Nests low in mangroves.
Sexes: *alike.*
Immatures: *grey wash over white parts.*
Voice: *loud 'coo-woo'.*   PG

13   FLOCK BRONZEWING *Phaps histrionica*   30cm
Now abundant on the vast open grass plains of the north. Competition for its food source from grazing cattle from the 1870s progressively reduced its numbers and it nearly died out following the disastrous drought of 1893-1902. It is highly nomadic throughout its range with its present stronghold centred in the Northern Territory. Breeds variably. Endemic.
Female and immatures: *head markings are brown instead of black.*
Voice: *relatively silent, single-note murmuring when feeding, throaty 'coo'*
during breeding display.   GC

14   SQUATTER PIGEON *Geophaps scripta*   32cm
The skin around the eye of the Squatter pigeon of Cape York Peninsula is bright red, while it is blue further south. As a result of pastoral development it has become very rare in the southern part of its range, though it has fared rather better in cattle country of the north. Singles or small parties frequent grassy plains or open woodland to forage for seeds of grasses, herbs, trees and shrubs. When flushed, they either explode out of cover or squat to avoid detection. Locally nomadic. Breeds year round. Nests in scrape on ground. Endemic.
Sexes: *alike.*
Immatures: *markings less distinct.*
Voice: *low 'coo-cwoop'.*   T&PG

15, 16   PARTRIDGE PIGEON *Geophaps smithii*   28cm
(A) Race *blaauwi* (Yellow-eyed form); (B) Race *smithii* (Red-eyed form). The yellow-eyed form has chrome-yellow bare skin around its eyes and is found only in the Kimberley region of Western Australia where it lives in open woodland in gorges and among rocks in sandstone country. The red-eyed form has bright red bare skin around its eyes and is particularly associated with the escarpment country of Arnhem Land. The red turns to the same yellow as its relative in museum specimens and the two become indistinguishable. The species is similar in habits and habitat to the Squatter Pigeon, and also freezes or squats in cover. In pairs or coveys of from 15 to 20 birds, sometimes larger, it forages for grass seed in open tropical woodland. Flight is in partridge-like bursts close to the ground. Breeds March-October. Nests in a scrape on the ground. Endemic.
Sexes: *alike.*
Immatures: *upper parts flecked chestnut.*
Voice: *'coo'.*   15GC, 16T&PG

17   TOPKNOT PIGEON *Lopholaimus antarcticus*   46cm
During the early days of white settlement, immense flocks offered a ready supply of fresh food, but today the species is fully protected. However, the decline in size of contemporary flocks is probably due mostly to the clearance of their rainforest and adjacent woodland habitat. It is completely arboreal and even gets most of its moisture from foliage dew and raindrops, as well as its diet of native fruits. Nomadic, following fruiting trees and palms. Breeds June-December. Nests high. Endemic.
Sexes: *alike.*
Immatures: *like adults, bill red-brown.*
Voice: *single low 'coo'.*   AF

18   WHITE-QUILLED ROCK PIGEON *Petrophassa albipennis*   30cm
Though closely related to the Chestnut-quilled Rock Pigeon it lives quite separately in an area extending into the Kimberley region, where it is found on the sandstone escarpments among spinifex and stunted trees. It is sedentary and is seen singly or in small flocks foraging for grass seed and herbaceous plants. Probably breeds April-November. Nests in a loose arrangement of sticks on a rocky ledge. Endemic.
Sexes: *alike.*
Immatures: *less white on throat.*
Voice: *various cooing notes.*   GC

19   CHESTNUT-QUILLED ROCK PIGEON *Petrophassa rufipennis*   32cm
This species occurs in the rocky fastnesses of the Arnhem Land plateau and escarpments, and frequents sandstone, rainforest, woodland or spinifex. Commonly seen in small groups. In the wet season, parties move out from the protection of rocks into nearby woodland, while in the heat of summer, they shelter in cool places under rocks and in caves. The species feeds on the ground and its diet includes wattle, herb and grass seeds. Breeds perhaps February-November. nests in rock crevices. Endemic.
Sexes: *alike.*
Immatures: *duller.*
Voice: *call of 'kukarook'.*   GC

20, 21   SPINIFEX PIGEON *Geophaps plumifera*   23cm
(A) Race *ferruginea* (Red-bellied form), popularly known as the Red-plumed Pigeon, (B) Race *plumifera* (White-bellied form), popularly known as the Plumed Pigeon. The southern birds of (B) have white lower breasts and abdomens and are sometimes recognised as a separate race. These endemic birds of erect bearing live in small flocks or coveys of 50 or more near water, and are seed-eaters. They are sedentary with only minor local movement even in drought seasons. They breed most months, especially after rain and nest in a scrape in the ground. Endemic.
Sexes: *alike.*
Immatures: *lack black and white on face and throat.*
Voice: *repeated 'cu-woo'.*   20 Race (A) B&BW; 21 race (B) H&JB

22   CRESTED PIGEON *Ocyphaps lophotes*   35cm
Widely known by the misnomer 'Topknot Pigeon'. Land clearance and the provision of drinking facilities for stock has actually helped this adaptable native pigeon to extend its range and, except for the sandy deserts, there are few places where this bird is absent. It feeds entirely on the ground mainly on seed, especially Paterson's Curse, but also eats vegetable plant material and insects. It takes off with whistling wings and tilts its tail on landing. Sedentary. Breeds variably. Nests in cover in bush or tree at varying heights up to 18m. Endemic.
Sexes: *alike.*
Immatures: *duller.*
Voice: *single and double 'coo' or rising 'coo-oo'.*   D&MT

6

23   COMMON BRONZEWING *Phaps chalcoptera*   35cm
The abundance of this bird provided the early settlers all over the continent with a welcome change of
diet. It is the most widespread of Australia's pigeons and is found in forests, woodlands and scrubs, in
all but the wettest of areas. Singly or in pairs it feeds on the ground mostly on seeds, grain and native
plants. Large numbers gather at watering places, especially at dusk. Extremely wary and alert.
Sedentary or locally nomadic. Breeds variably. Nests on the ground or in trees, sometimes high.
Endemic.
Sexes: *similar but female duller.*
Immatures: *much duller.*
Voice: *low resonant mournful ventriloquial 'oom'.*   GC

24   BRUSH BRONZEWING *Phaps elegans*   30cm
The Brush Bronzewing prefers denser cover than the Common Bronzewing and is even more secretive and guarded. Its feeding habits are similar. It is seen singly or in pairs and usually runs swiftly
rather than taking to flight. Numbers have declined from interference with habitat and from the depre-
dations of foxes and feral cats. Locally nomadic. Breeds throughout the year. Nests on the ground or
low. Endemic. Recognition: smaller and redder than the Common Bronzewing.
Sexes: *similar but female less chestnut.*
Immatures: *like females.*
Voice: *repeated low cooing.*   PK

25   EMERALD DOVE *Chalcophaps indica*   25cm
Also known as the Green-winged Pigeon. This small but colourful bird is often encountered at close
range in rainforest quietly picking its way through the ground litter of forests, mangroves or lantana
thickets. Unobtrusive and mostly solitary, it may also be seen sometimes in pairs and parties, feeding
on seeds, fruits and berries in clearings. If disturbed it rises silently before going off to cover, from
where it watches alertly. Breeds most months. Nests 4-11m high.
Female: *white shoulder patch of male replaced with grey.*
Immatures: *less green.*
Voice: *extended cooing.*   CW

26   WONGA PIGEON *Leucosarcia melanoleuca*   43cm
This large ground-frequenting pigeon inhabits mostly coastal rainforest and scrub, sometimes on the
fringes of settled areas. Solitary, in pairs only during the breeding season, it forages sedately for seeds
and berries on low bushes and fallen fruit. Exceptionally alert, if disturbed it freezes or flies up with
noisy wing flapping to become near-invisible in foliage. Sedentary. Breeds October-January. nests to
10m high.
Sexes: *alike.*
Immatures: *brownish rather than grey.*
Voice: *Loud continuous and monotonous cooing 'wonk' which can be heard from afar.*   T&PG

27   BROWN CUCKOO-DOVE *Macropygia amboinensis*   16cm
The Brown Cuckoo-Dove, frequents the rainforests of the eastern states. Sometimes referred to as a
cuckoo-dove or the Pheasant Pigeon because of its long graceful tail. It is seen singly or in pairs and
is reasonably common. Tamer than most rainforest pigeons. Breeds most months. Nests at varying
heights in vine tangle or tree.
Sexes: *similar but female less pink and duller.*
Immatures: *black-barred upper breast.*
Voice: *repeated 'cuckoo-whup', soft clucking 'coo'.*   RG

28   SHINING BRONZE-CUCKOO *Chrysococcyx lucidus lucidus*   16cm
This New Zealand breeding race visits the coastal belt of eastern Australia in autumn and occasionally in spring as a passage migrant to and from the Solomon Islands. Recognition: barring bronze-green; greenish sheen on crown and back of neck; male has white line on forehead.
Sexes: *similar but female lacks white line on forehead.*
Immatures: *upper parts bright green.*
Voice: *said to be indistinguishable from the Golden Bronze-Cuckoo.*   AF

29   SHINING BRONZE-CUCKOO *Chrysococcyx lucidus plagosus*   16cm
Also known as the Golden Bronze-Cuckoo. The Australian breeding race is widespread in the Australasian region. It migrates northwards to winter, some birds also reaching the Solomon Islands. Frequents forests, woodlands and suburban areas. Breeds August-January and especially favours fairy warblers and fantails among its 60 hosts. The pale-bronze pigmentation of the egg rubs off.
Recognition: *barring bronze-brown.*
Sexes: *alike.*
Immatures: *grey-brown washed bronze-green.*
Voice: *repeated high pitched ascending 'pee' likened to a person whistling up a dog, fading slightly.*   GC

30   LITTLE BRONZE-CUCKOO *Chrysococcyx minutillus*   15cm
This small cuckoo is an Australian breeding race of a species widespread in areas extending to south-East Asia including New Guinea. It migrates northwards to winter. Solitary, it frequents tropical forests, woodlands and mangroves. It breeds October-January and lays its greenish-olive egg mainly in nests of warblers. **Recognition:** *no rufous, dark blue-tinged bronze-green crown and back of head, contrasting with black.*
Sexes: *eye and eye ring - male bright red, female brown.*
Immatures: *upperparts dull green.*
Voice: *faint piping, a tremulous sigh and four-note call.*   GC

31   GOULD'S BRONZE-CUCKOO *Chrysococcyx russatus*   15cm
The range of this small cuckoo overlaps that of the Cape York part of the Little Bronze-Cuckoo and their habits have much in common. It is a race of a species shared with New Guinea which extends to Borneo and Malaysia. It breeds September-January and lays its dark brown freckled egg in nests of warblers and sun-birds. Recognition: upper breast and tail feathers rufous; upper parts rufous bronze-green.
Sexes: *eye and eye-ring - male bright red, female brown.*
Immatures: *no rufous on breast.*
Voice: *grasshopper-like repeated trill.*   D&MT

32   HORSFIELD'S BRONZE-CUCKOO *Chrysococcyx basalis*   17cm
A widespread endemic breeding species which mainly frequents timber, scrub and open country. Sometimes seen in built-up areas singing on overhead wires. Some birds move inland to winter and others migrate northwards as far afield as Malaysia and Borneo. Breeds June-December. Its whitish speckled egg is laid in the nests of over 60 host species including fairy wrens. **Recognition:** *streaked throat (not barred); broad whitish streak over the eye.*
Sexes: *alike.*
Immatures: *duller.*
Voice: *a descending repeated 'see-you' whistled sorrowfully; also a sparrow-like call.*   GC

6

33   BLACK-EARED CUCKOO *Chrysococcyx osculans*   20cm

An endemic breeding species, though with some migration to the Aru Islands and the Moluccas to winter. It occurs mostly west of the Great Dividing Range in the drier kinds of habitat. Breeds August-January and chooses the nests of birds which lay brownish eggs similar to its own - the Speckled Warbler and the Redthroat being favoured hosts. The pigmentation of its egg rubs off.
Recognition: *no barring on underparts.*
Sexes: *similar.*
Immatures: *brownish-green above, pale eyebrow.*
Voice: *repeated plaintive descending whistle; alternatively it calls 'peer-o-wit-pee-o-weer'.*   T&PG

34   PALLID CUCKOO *Cuculus pallidus*   33cm

A widespread Australian-breeding cuckoo found in all timbered areas. Singly or in pairs, it feeds on large insects including caterpillars and grasshoppers. It moves seasonally in complex migratory patterns, occasionally as far as the Moluccas, and populations fluctuate greatly. Breeds September-January. It has parasitised the nests of over 80 species, including many honeyeaters.
Adults: *alike, female browner. Lack mottling of the immatures.*
Voice: *sometimes called the 'Brainfever Bird' because of the male's frantic courting calls.*
Also repeated 8 or more rising notes, and at night.   GC

35   BRUSH CUCKOO *Cacomantis variolosus*   24cm

A race of a species which extends to Malaysia and the Solomon Islands, and a winter migrant northwards, including to New Guinea. Frequenting forests and mangroves, it perches unobtrusively often alone, feeding on insects and caterpillars. It favours open cup-shaped nests to lay its faintly marked whitish egg, and some 35 hosts have been recorded, including robins, wrens and wood-swallows.
Recognition: *square tail.*
Sexes: *alike.*
Immatures: *brown mottling on upperparts.*
 Voice: *6 or 7 mournful descending notes increasing in volume; also feverish accelerating crescendo of 3 ascending notes continually repeated.*   GC

36   ORIENTAL CUCKOO *Cuculus saturatus*   33cm

This bird, rare in Australia, is a non-breeding migrant from Asia, and is seen from November to April in the forests and woodlands of northern and eastern Australia. Singly, in pairs or small groups, it perches quietly on dead tree limbs or hidden in dense foliage and feeds on insects and their larvae taken from foliage or on the ground. It has a swift falcon-like flight.
Sexes: *alike.*
Immatures: *upperparts red-brown rather than grey.*
Voice: *'kak-ak-ak-aak', like the Dollarbird, also a low subdued trill.*   EZ

37   FAN-TAILED CUCKOO *Cacomantis flabelliformis*   27cm

A race extending to the Aru Islands of a species ranging to New Guinea and New Caledonia. It frequents forest and woodlands, but is absent from the drier inland areas. While mainly arboreal, it often feeds on the ground and is partial to caterpillars. Characteristically, it fans and tilts its tail when alighting. Breeds August-September. Chooses dome nests, such as thornbills or occasionally the open nests of honeyeaters to place its egg. Nomadic or migratory.
Sexes: *alike.*
Immatures: *upperparts and head brown.*
Voice: *a mournful trembling cascade of falling notes; also swelling two-note*
upwards syllables.   D&MT

38   CHESTNUT-BREASTED CUCKOO *Cacomantis castaneiventris*   23cm
This attractively-plumaged cuckoo, abundant in New Guinea, is found only in the remote rainforests of Cape York Peninsula as a small breeding population - though some migration to over-winter in New Guinea is probable. From a low perch, it watches for caterpillars, insects and their larvae, and darts to seize them.
Sexes: *alike.*
Immatures: *upperparts cinnamon brown.*
Voice: *descending trembling and other notes similar to Fan-tailed Cuckoo.*   D&MT

39, 40   COMMON KOEL *Eudynamys scolopacea*   46cm
The Koel, a race of a species ranging to India and China, is a regular breeding migrant from New Guinea, where it is widespread. Birds begin their southward movement in August and most have moved north by April. It is seen singly in pairs or small groups, at times with other birds in fruiting trees. The female is quieter and less obtrusive than the male. Breeds November-January. The female lays her marbled salmon-pink egg or eggs in the nest of one of a number of hosts such as Friarbirds or other large honeyeaters, often choosing a foster parent whose eggs resemble her own.
Female: *mottled and barred like immature illustrated but crown, throat and nape black, eye dark brown.*
Voice: *monotonous endlessly repeated 'koo-eel' rising in a feverish accelerating crescendo. Also at night.*   39D&MT; 40RG

41   PHEASANT COUCAL *Centropus phasianinus*   66cm
The Pheasant Coucal is a sedentary species which extends to New Guinea. Its long broad tail makes up more than half its length and seems to encumber its laboured ungainly flight. The complexly-patterned plumage, predominantly black during breeding, becomes red-brown at other times. It lives in rank vegetation in damp locations, feeding on small animals and insects. Solitary. Breeds August-February sometimes twice in quick succession. Chicks are truly 'ugly ducklings' when hatched, with black bodies covered with developing feathers that look like white threads. The only Australian cuckoo not to parasitise the nests of other birds. It builds its own nest with open canopy on ground or up to 2m in sugar-cane, pandanus etc.
Sexes: *alike.*
Immatures: *mottled.*
Voice: *a series of 'woof' or 'hoop' booming notes with a short pause after the first two, then gradually quickening and descending in volume and tone.*   PG

42   CHANNEL-BILLED CUCKOO *Scythrops novaehollandiae*   65cm
A very large cuckoo which migrates to Australia to breed from territories ranging from New Guinea to Sulawesi. It begins arriving in September with the onset of the wet season in the north and it is usually absent by March. It is sometimes called the Stormbird or Rainbird because its call often presages wet weather. It favours tall timber and feeds on figs and native fruits. It is sometimes seen in flocks of up to fifty birds. Breeds October-December. The blotched eggs vary enormously in colour from off-white to yellowish to red-brown and are placed (sometimes 2 or more) in the nests of crows, currawongs and other large birds.
Sexes: *alike.*
Immatures: *buff head and tips to feathers; lack red eye ring.*
Voice: *very loud raucous screaming 'quork' repeated 6 or more times, including at night and in flight.*   H&JB

7 Parrots

1   PALM COCKATOO *Probosciger aterrimus*   60cm
This cockatoo, widespread in New Guinea, is found in Australia only in the tropical rainforests of the north on Cape York Peninsula. It has a beak strong enough to bend fencing wire and to crack open the hard pandanus nuts which it favours. Under stress, its bare facial patches flush crimson. They roost at night in the topmost branches of tall trees and gather by day in small playful parties in a favoured big tree in open country. Sedentary. Breeds August-February. Nests in trunk hollows 8-12m high.
Female: *small face patch.*
Immatures: *yellow markings.*
Voice: *very loud whistles, wails and screeches.*   D&MT

2   GLOSSY BLACK-COCKATOO *Calyptorhynchus lathami*   50cm
Differing from most other cockatoos by the absence of a crest, this small cockatoo has duller plumage than its name implies. Rather uncommon, it is seen in pairs and small parties in woodland, especially casuarina stands in the south-east, and on Kangaroo Island. It feeds mainly on casuarina seeds and on larvae. It is tame and approachable and its flight has a floating quality. Nomadic. Breeds March-August. Endemic.
Sexes: *similar but female has yellow patches on head and neck.*
Immatures: *like females but wings spotted with yellow.*
Voice: *resembles a filing or sawing sound; also a lugubrious single note, softer than*
Red-tailed Black Cockatoo.   D&MT

3   SULPHUR-CRESTED COCKATOO *Cacatua galerita*   49cm
The 'white cocky' is a familiar sight in the Australian bush in varied habitats of forest, woodland and open country. Often in large flocks, it forages on the ground for seed, grain, roots and nuts while look-outs in the trees stand on sentry duty. It is extremely wary and raises its spectacular sulphur-yellow crest when alarmed or angry. Clamorous and conspicuous, especially in the roosting trees at dawn and dusk. Breeds May-August (north), August-January (south). Also in New Guinea and Indonesia. Introduced in WA.
Sexes: *male - dark brown eye, female - dark red eye.*
Immatures: *faint grey markings.*
Voice: *raucous screeches.*   D&MT

4, 5   RED-TAILED BLACK-COCKATOO *Calyptorhynchus banksii*   61cm (north) 52cm (south)
This bird occurs in flocks of up to 200 in the north but in the south-east it is less numerous. In the wheat belt of SW Australia huge flocks of 1 000 or more gather to feed on 'double-gee' an introduced burr. Birds are smaller in the south-west and in the interior. Ranging through forest and woodland, it is partial to nuts, fruit, casuarina and acacia seeds, and to the destructive longicorn beetle. Wary and difficult to approach. Nomadic. Breeds April-October. Nests in large tree hole. Endemic.
Immatures: *like females.*
Voice: *harsh grating shrieks and loud mournful single notes.*   D&MT

6   MAJOR MITCHELL'S COCKATOO *Cacatua leadbeateri*   36cm
In 1838 the explorer Sir Thomas Mitchell wrote in praise of this 'beautiful species', rhapsodising over its 'pink-coloured wings and glowing crest' and it is named after him. Wary. Usually seen in pairs or small flocks, and uncommon in most areas, it inhabits the arid scrublands of the interior where it feeds on seeds, roots, berries, nuts and wood boring grubs. Breeds August-October. Nests in tree hollows 5-20m high. Endemic.
Male: *eye - dark brown, abdomen - salmon pink.* **Female:** *eye - red, abdomen - white, crest - yellow band may be broader.*
Immatures: *paler than adults and eye light brown in females.*
Voice: *crotchety screams.*   H&JB

7 THE WHITE-TAILED BLACK-COCKATOOS

(A) SHORT-BILLED FORM *Calyptorhynchus latirostris* 55-60cm

Frequents the drier inland areas of WA where it feeds on banksias, grevilleas etc. It breeds in the wandoo and salmon gum forests in the east of its range and returns to the higher rainfall areas towards the coast after breeding.

Male: *cheek patch smaller and dull white, bill grey-black.*
Immatures: *similar to adult female.*
Voice: *high-pitched drawn-out whistle 'whee-la'.* GC

(B) LONG-BILLED FORM *Calyptorhynchus baudinii* 55-60cm

Confined to the heavy timber of the south-west corner, it feeds mainly on gumnuts of the tall marri eucalypts which it is able to extract with its long specially-adapted bill. In the non-breeding season, it may be seen in company with its short-billed relative. The two forms do not however interbreed. Breeds August-December and nests in large tree hollows. Endemic. (Not illustrated)

8 YELLOW-TAILED BLACK-COCKATOO *Calyptorhynchus funereus* 69cm

This large cockatoo is characterised by its long tail - about half its total length. Usually seen in small flocks, but these can sometimes be quite large, perhaps of 200 birds or more. It is nomadic and seen in most types of timbered country. It feeds mostly on the seeds of forest trees and also uses its strong bill to strip bark and probe deeply into the timber for the larvae of wood borers. Breeds March-April (north) July-January (south), and is dependent on finding old trees with large hollows for nesting sites. Endemic.

Sexes: *Males: face patches small and less pronounced; bills dark grey; eyes dark brown; eye rings pink. Females: bills bone; eye rings dark grey.*
Immatures: *like females.*
Voice: *noisy and their wailing 'wee-yu' or 'wy-la' is often heard before birds come into view.* D&MT

9 GALAH *Cacatua roseicapilla* 36cm

One of the most numerous and ubiquitous of the parrots, found in all types of open country, feeding on seeds, grains, fruits, blossoms and shoots as well as insects and their larvae. Adults sedentary, immatures nomadic. Breeds July-December. Nests 4-20m high. Endemic.

Sexes: *similar but male's eye is dark brown, female's pink.*
Immatures: *duller.*
Voice: *extremely varied, loud whistles, strident shrieks and screams.* SP

10 LITTLE CORELLA *Cacatua sanguinea* 38cm

Characterised by its bare eye patch and stiff erectile crown feathers, it sometimes gathers in enormous flocks - as many as 60 000 - 70 000 have been seen at a time in the north-west. It frequents a variety of habitats, including open woodland, scrub, grasslands and suburban trees. Feeds on seed of cereal crops, weeds and insect larvae. It invariably roosts near water. Nomadic. Breeds June-October or variably. Nests in tree hollows or occasionally cliff holes and anthills.

Sexes and immatures: *similar.*
Voice: *a range of raucous calls and screeches.* D&MT

WESTERN CORELLA *(Long-billed) Cacatua pastinator* 42cm

Resembles the Little Corella, but is larger and has an exceptionally long upper mandible - used for digging up corms and roots, its main food. Plumage is often stained in the process. Common in woodland and northern half of the wheat belt of Western Australia - with a small isolated population of bigger birds in the extreme south-west. Its range partially overlaps that of the Little Corella, but the two species apparently do not interbreed. Breeds August-October. (Not illustrated)

11   LONG-BILLED CORELLA *Cacatua tenuirostris*   38cm
Although now uncommon to rare in many of its former haunts, the Long-billed Corella is still occasionally seen in very large flocks, frequenting woodland and adjacent grasslands, seldom far from water. Sentinels are posted when flocks are feeding or drinking. Immatures are nomadic. Breeds August-December. nests in tree hollows. Endemic.
Sexes: *similar.*
Immatures: *shorter mandibles.*
Voice: *a range of raucous calls and screeches.*   GC

12   GANG-GANG COCKATOO *Callocephalon fimbriatum*   36cm
Is often seen in city parks and suburban gardens in search of seeds and berries when, in summer, it descends from mountain forests to lower valleys and coastal regions. It is almost entirely arboreal and becomes so immersed in feeding as to be indifferent to the approach of humans. Breeds October-January. Nests very high in tree hole. Endemic.
Sexes: *Male: crest and head bright red. Female: crest and head grey.*
Immatures: *like females, with underside of tail barred grey.*
Voice: *two or three grinding notes which can almost be reproduced by rubbing the thumb over an inflated balloon.*   D&MT

13   COCKATIEL *Nymphicus hollandicus*   33cm
Also known as the Quarrion, it is seen abundantly in pairs and small flocks in open or lightly timbered country near water. It forages mainly on the ground for grass seed, grain, fruits and berries. Sometimes it effaces itself by perching lengthwise along the branch of a dead tree. Flight is straight and swift. Highly nomadic in the north, seasonally migratory in the south. Breeds April-August (north), August-December (south). Nests in tree hollow. Endemic.
Voice: *soft but far-carrying warbling 'queel-queel'.*   D&MT

14, 15   ECLECTUS PARROT *Eclectus roratus*   43cm
The remarkable feature of this species is that the female has the more brilliantly-coloured plumage. As this is the reverse of normal in the bird world, it was for many years believed that the male and female were different species. The parrot is widely distributed in New Guinea and other islands to the north but, in Australia, it is confined to the rainforests of Cape York Peninsula, where it was discovered in 1913. It is usually seen in pairs and parties foraging in the tree canopy for berries, fruit, nuts and seeds and its strident cries are a characteristic of the forest. Family groups of up to eight birds are supportive in rearing the nestlings. At night they gather to roost together in screeching commotion. Sedentary. Breeds July-February. Nests in a high tree hollow near water.
Immatures: *similar to adults of each sex.*
Voice: *male utters note resembling 'quork'; female has a screeching whistle. Also resonant clanging, wailing.*   D&MT

16   RED-CHEEKED PARROT *Geoffroyus geoffroyi*   25cm
The dense tropical jungle of the Iron Range area on Cape York Peninsula is the only haunt in Australia of the Red-cheeked Parrot, where it was discovered in 1913, although it had been widely known in New Guinea and Indonesia. Plentiful within its restricted range, pairs or family parties gather in favoured trees to feed on seeds and fruit. Not easily seen amidst dense foliage, its flight between trees is distinctive, with quick shallow wingbeats and no undulating or gliding. Sedentary. Breeds August-November. Nests high.
Immatures: *like females.*
Voice: *loud screeching, metallic chattering.*   RM

17   DOUBLE-EYED FIG-PARROT *Cyclopsitta diophthalma*   16cm
(A) Race *marshalli* (Marshall's)
(B) Race *macleayana* (Red-browed) illustrated
(C) Race *coxeni* (Blue-browed)
Widespread in New Guinea, this, the smallest parrot in Australia, occurs in the rainforests of eastern Australia as three isolated races, of which the race coxeni is now exceedingly rare. It feeds silently in a tree, mainly on native figs, betraying its presence by dropping a steady stream of fruit particles from above. Breeds August-October. Nests in decaying tree branches.
Female: *less red on face.*
Immatures: *like females.*
Voice: *high-pitched 'tseet'.*
                                                                  H&JB

18   MUSK LORIKEET *Glossopsitta concinna*   23cm
Acquiring its name from a musky smell said to be associated with it, this is an extremely noisy bird which betrays its presence by high-pitched chattering and screeching when it is engrossed in feeding high among flowering eucalypts and other blossom or fruit trees. It also eats insects and their larvae. It lives in open timbered country, farmland or gardens, forming strongly bonded pairs. Sometimes it joins flocks of mixed lorikeets. Seasonally nomadic. Breeds August-January. Nests high in tree hollows. Endemic.
Sexes: *alike.*
Immatures: *duller; eye brown, bill dark brown.*
Voice: *brassy screeches, chattering.*
                                                                  D&MT

19   VARIED LORIKEET *Psitteuteles versicolor*   20cm
The Varied Lorikeet is usually seen in large flocks feasting voraciously and messily on the nectar and pollen of flowering gums and paperbarks. Berries, seeds and insects are also taken. Noisy, numerous and truculent, it may chase off other species competing for food, although it is often in the company of Rainbow Lorikeets. Nomadic. Breeds mainly April-August. Nests high in a tree hollow. Endemic.
Sexes: *alike.*
Immatures: *crown dull green showing some red.*
Voice: *very shrill screeching and chattering, softer twittering.*
                                                                  K&BR

20   LITTLE LORIKEET *Glossopsitta pusilla*   16cm
Similar in habits to the Musk Lorikeet, the noisy Little Lorikeet is fearless and approachable when it is absorbed in feeding. It is seen in flocks which frequent flowering eucalypts and other blossom and fruit-bearing trees, often in company with other lorikeets. Nomadic. Breeds August-January. Nests in tree holes above 6m, often near water. Endemic. **Recognition:** differentiated in flight from the Purple-crowned Lorikeet by yellow-green underwings instead of red.
Sexes: *alike.*
Immatures: *face duller, bill and eye brown.*
Voice: *shrill 'ssit', twittering.*
                                                                  D&MT

21   PURPLE-CROWNED LORIKEET *Glossopsitta porphyrocephala*   17cm
Widely distributed along the southern fringes of the continent, it is the south-west's only endemic lorikeet. Its chief haunts are mallee and drier forests, where it is abundant, but it also lives close to the coast. In smaller parties or large flocks it feeds on flowering eucalypts and visits gardens and orchards in search of pollen, nectar, fruit, insects and their larvae. Nomadic, sometimes ranging far inland. Breeds September-December. Nests in hollow trees near water. Endemic.
Sexes: *alike.*
Immatures: *sometimes no purple on crown.*
Voice: *loud shrill buzzing.*
                                                                  H&JB

22   RAINBOW LORIKEET *Trichoglossus haematodus*   32cm
Large flamboyant mobs of the Rainbow Lorikeet congregate noisily in flowering gums to take nectar and pollen. They also come readily as tame visitors to gardens and tourist parks such as that at Currumbin on the Queensland Gold coast where thousands of birds descend daily on the honey trays provided. They occur in all types of timbered country. Introduced in WA. Breeds August-January, or variably in the north. Nests in tree hollows.
Sexes: *alike.*
Immatures: *duller.*
Voice: *metallic screeching.*
                                                                  D&MT

23   RED-COLLARED LORIKEET *Trichoglossus rubritorquis*   31cm
Its plumage is similar to that of the Rainbow Lorikeet except for the nape and belly colour. The two
are sometimes regarded as races of the same species and their habits are similar. The Red-collared is
more abundantly found in the wetter more northerly parts of its tropical habitat. Mostly sedentary.
Nests in tree hole near water. Endemic.
Sexes: *alike.*
Immatures: *duller, bill and eye brown.*
Voice: *like the Rainbow Lorikeet.*   D&MT

24   SCALY-BREASTED LORIKEET *Trichoglossus chlorolepidotus*   24cm
This predominantly green parrot is usually seen in flocks, often in company with Rainbow Lorikeets.
Its favourite haunts are open forests, where it feeds on the nectar and pollen of eucalypts and melaleu-
cas. Fruits, seeds and cultivated grains also form part of its diet. In its swift flight, the orange under-
wings are distinctive. Nomadic to follow flowering trees. Breeds May-January. Nests in tree hollows.
Endemic.
Sexes: *alike.*
Immatures: *shorter tail; eye and bill brownish.*
Voice: *more shrill than the Rainbow Lorikeet.*   CC

25, 26   RED-WINGED PARROT *Aprosmictus erythropterus*   33cm
The Red-winged Parrot is one of the most spectacularly handsome of Australia's parrots. In varied
habitats from the tropics to the south-eastern inland, rarely far from water, it may be seen in all types
of timbered scrub country, open sandy plains, or in the mangroves of the north. It spends its day in the
treetops, foraging acrobatically for nectar, blossoms, berries and insects. It comes to ground only to
drink, or occasionally to investigate fallen fruit or nuts. Generally common, it appears in pairs, family parties or small flocks. The young male takes at least two years to acquire adult plumage and to
begin breeding, remaining with the family group until that time. Breeds from May (north), August-
February (south). Nests deep in a hollow tree with a high entrance.
Immatures: *like adult females.*
Voice: *flight call 'crillik-crillik', soft feeding chatter, alarm screeching.*   D&MT

27   AUSTRALIAN KING PARROT *Alisterus scapularis*   44cm
This parrot mainly frequents mountain forests, but often visits gardens and parks. It feeds on native
fruits and seeds in flowering trees, and also raids orchards and cereal crops. During winter it migrates
from the highlands to coastal plains, then returns to breed October-January. Nests deep in hollow tree
with entrance sometimes over 10m high. Endemic.
Female: *mostly green, lower breast and belly red.*
Immatures: *like adult females, eye brown.*
Voice: *three or four penetrating pure musical notes.*   D&MT

28, 29   SUPERB PARROT *Polytelis swainsonii*   42cm
The Superb Parrot has one of the most restricted ranges of any Australian parrot and is found usually
between the Namoi-Castlereagh River system of New South Wales and the Murray-Lachlan system of
southern New South Wales and northern Victoria. Intensive clearing of its principal habitat for agricultural development and illegal trapping for the cage-bird market have reduced its numbers, and some
fear that the species is endangered. It is usually seen in well-bonded pairs or small flocks and is seldom found far from water. It spends most of its time on the ground foraging for seeds, sometimes
along roadsides. Partial to cultivated grain crops and spilt grain, it will also take nectar from flowering eucalypts. It is gracefully streamlined both in repose and in effortless flight. Nomadic throughout
its range, and many birds migrate to southern New South Wales to breed in September-December.
During the breeding season, flocks seem to be composed entirely of males. Nests very high in tree
holes. Endemic.
Immatures: *face blue-green, eye brown.*
Voice: *deep warble, twittering.*   D&MT

276

30   PRINCESS PARROT *Polytelis alexandrae*   46cm
John Gould named this elegant and uncommon parrot in honour of Princess Alexandra. It is found in
the dry interior in pairs or small flocks and feeds on or near the ground searching for seeds, especial-
ly those of spinifex. It is also partial to acacia blossoms and mistletoe berries. Highly nomadic. Breeds
September-January. Usually nests in a hollow in a eucalypt near water, often in colonies. Endemic.
Female: *duller, shorter, tail shorter.*
Immatures: *like adult females.*
Voice: *mainly silent; rolling unmusical note often in flight, softer notes and twittering.*   D&MT

31   REGENT PARROT *Polytelis anthopeplus*   41cm
Uncommon in the east, abundant in the south-west where the birds are greener and duller and may
appear in large flocks. Near water, in woodland, scrub or mallee it forages mainly on the ground for
seeds, also in flowering gums. Seasonally migratory in WA. Breeds August-January. Nests in tree hol-
lows. Endemic.
Female: *duller, pink markings on undertail.*
Immatures: *like adult females.*
Voice: *rolling warble rather like the carol of the Australian Magpie.*   D&MT

32   CRIMSON (Yellow) ROSELLA *Platycercus elegans*   34cm
This 'blue-cheeked' rosella is usually seen in pairs and parties along inland rivers, mainly the Murray
and Murrumbidgee, amongst red river gums or in mallee, grassland or orchards associated with the
river systems. It has a diet of seeds, berries, blossoms, insects and their larvae. Relatively timid.
Sedentary. Breeds September-January. Nests in tree hollows at varying heights. Endemic.
Sexes: *alike.*
Immatures: *back and wings olive-green, underparts yellow-green.*
Voice: *shrill calls, piping and whistling, soft feeding chatter.*   D&MT

33   CRIMSON (Adelaide) ROSELLA *Platycercus elegans*   36cm
Inhabiting the Mount Lofty Ranges and adjacent areas including suburban Adelaide, it appears in pairs
and parties amongst eucalypts and is also at home in cultivated environments and is similar in its
behaviour to the other 'blue-cheeked' rosellas. It often feeds on spilt grain around farms and drinks
from stock troughs. Plumage colour may vary: breast and back markings are usually red, but orange-
yellow may predominate in some birds. Sedentary. Breeds September-February. Nests high in tree hollows. Endemic.
Sexes: *alike.*
Immatures: *dark green with red markings.*
Voice: *shrill calls, piping and whistling, soft feeding chatter.*   D&MT

34, 35   CRIMSON ROSELLA *Platycercus elegans*   37cm
Often called the Mountain Lory, the Crimson Rosella is the most widely distributed of the 'blue-
cheeked' rosellas. It is represented by two populations, birds in the north being smaller and darker. Its
natural habitat is rainforest and eucalypt woodland, both heavily timbered and more open, but it commonly frequents suburban gardens and parks. Often seen on the ground, it feeds on seeds, nectar, fruit
and scale insects, and is usually in pairs or family parties, with flocks of largely immature birds being
formed at times. It is a confident and confiding bird, allowing a close approach especially when feeding. Mostly sedentary. Breeds September-February. nests 8-30m high. Endemic.
Sexes: *alike.*
Immatures: *may be green up to 18 months.*
Voice: *shrill calls, piping and whistling, soft feeding chatter.*   D&MT

36   GREEN ROSELLA *Platycercus caledonicus*   36cm
This 'blue-cheeked' rosella is confined to Tasmania and the larger islands of Bass Strait. It is abundant in Tasmania in all wooded habitats and is a familiar sight on the fringes of urban areas. Usually in pairs or parties, flocks may gather in winter. it feeds on the ground or in the trees and is partial to hawthorn berries. It also raids orchards and grain crops. Sedentary. Breeds September-January. Nests high in tree hollows. Endemic.
Sexes: *alike.*
Immatures: *head and underparts yellow-green.*
Voice: *very loud, piercing 'cussick, cussick' flight call; double bell-like whistle, fluting and piping.*   TW

37   EASTERN ROSELLA *Platycercus eximius*   34cm
Prolific and familiar, this vibrant parrot is one of the 'white-cheeked' group of rosellas. Usually in pairs or family parties, though larger flocks may congregate during winter. It frequents woodlands and grasslands and is often seen in the suburbs and around farms. It forages quietly on the ground or in trees for seeds, nectar, fruit and insects. Sedentary. Breeds August-January. Nests in hollow. Endemic.
Female: *duller on head and breast.*
Immatures: *crown and nape patchy green.*
Voice: *pleasant whistling, metallic, 'kwink-kwink-kwink'.*   D&MT

38   PALE-HEADED ROSELLA *Platycercus adscitus*   32cm
Another of the 'white-cheeked' rosellas, its plumage varies considerably. North of Cairns, birds have a patch of violet on the lower face instead of white. There are hybrids between the Pale-headed and Eastern Rosellas where their ranges overlap. The preferred habitat is open forest, clearings, or edges of grassland; it also visits orchards, grainfields and patches of weed such as thistle and burr. Sedentary. Breeds September-December (south), February-June (north). Endemic.
Sexes: *alike.*
Immatures: *duller, may show grey or red head markings.*
Voice: *similar to Eastern Rosella, perhaps sharper.*   D&MT

39   NORTHERN ROSELLA *Platycercus venustus*   30cm
The remote distribution of this rosella of the 'white-cheeked' group separates it from the other rosellas. It is a quiet bird, not easy to locate, approachable and only takes refuge in nearby trees when disturbed. It prefers open forest near water, or mangroves, but visits cropfields and gardens in search of seeds. It is usually seen in pairs or family groups and is not given to flocking. Mainly sedentary. Breeds June-August. Nests in tree or post hollows. Endemic.
Sexes: *alike.*
Immatures: *duller.*
Voice: *short succession of two-syllable metallic notes.*   D&MT

40   WESTERN ROSELLA *Platycercus icterotis*   26cm
This, the smallest and quietest of the rosellas, has yellow cheeks and is confined to the south-west corner of Western Australia. It frequents open country and sparse woodland and is usually seen on the ground feeding on grass seeds, often at roadsides. Mostly sedentary. Breeds August-December. Nests in hollow tree limbs. Endemic.
Female: *less brilliantly coloured.*
Immatures: *lack yellow cheeks, less red on underparts.*
Voice: *soft musical repeated whistles.*   D&MT

41   AUSTRALIAN RINGNECK *Barnardius zonarius*   37cm
(A) Race *zonarius* Port Lincoln (illustrated) (B) Race *semitorquatus* Twenty-eight. The species occurs in two forms: the yellow-breasted Port Lincoln Parrot, found mainly in the inland areas, and the green-breasted Twenty-eight Parrot, found only in the wetter heavily-timbered south-west corner of Western Australia. The two populations interbreed where they meet. Breeds August-February. Endemic.
Sexes: *similar.*
Immatures: *duller.*
Voices: (A) - *high-pitched whistles resembling 'kwink';* (B) - *double-noted 'twenty-eight' call from which it is named.*
                                                                                              D&MT

42   AUSTRALIAN RINGNECK *Barnardius zonarius*   35cm
(A) Race *barnardi* (Mallee Ringneck) Southern birds favour mallee scrub; northern birds eucalypt watercourse. Pairs and family parties forage for seed, blossoms, insects and their larvae. Sedentary. Breeds August-January. Nests in tree holes. Endemic.
(A) **Male:** back and mantle deep blue-black; (B) **Sexes:** *similar.*
Immatures: *like adult females.*
Voice: *ringing 'twink-wink-wink'*   LR

(B) Race *macgillivrayi* (Cloncurry Parrot). This species includes the smaller isolated Cloncurry Parrot of north-west Queensland, which has pale yellow underparts and lacks a red frontal band.

43   RED-CAPPED PARROT *Purpureicephalus spurius*   37cm
Called the King Parrot in Western Australia, it occurs only in a relatively small area in the south-west corner. In pairs and small groups, it feeds quietly in the treetops, favouring one particular eucalypt, the marri, both for its seeds and for nesting. It also feeds on grass seed and cultivated fruit. Sedentary. Breeds August-December. Nests high. Endemic.
Female: *duller.*
Immatures: *duller, with crown green.*
Voice: *grating metallic call, whistling in flight, alarm shrieks.*   D&MT

44   RED-RUMPED PARROT *Psephotus haematonotus*   28cm
In pairs or small parties, it mostly frequents lightly-timbered grasslands, cultivated paddocks and trees bordering watercourses. It congregates in flocks in winter. It spends most of its time on the ground foraging for grass seeds or spilt grain and is partial to the leaves and blossom of certain thistles. Mainly sedentary. Breeds August-December. Nests in hollow stumps and limbs. Endemic.
Female: *much duller and more grey-green.*
Immatures: *paler.*
Voice: *shrill two-syllable whistle and pleasant warbling.*   D&MT

45   MULGA PARROT *Psephotus varius*   30cm
Widespread, but nowhere abundant, this bird of the interior lives quietly and inconspicuously in lightly timbered country and scrub. Solitary, in pairs or small parties, it is often seen on the ground feeding on grasses, herbaceous plants and shrubs. Sedentary or nomadic during drought. Breeds July-December or after rains. Nests in tree holes. Endemic.
Female: *head, neck and upper breast green-brown, dull red on nape and shoulder, rump green.*
Immatures: *duller.*
Voice: *repeated whistling 'jeep'.*   LR

46 PARADISE PARROT *Psephotus pulcherrimus* 30cm
Once acclaimed as Australia's most beautiful parrot, it is now feared to be extinct. It used to frequent the sparsely timbered grasslands of south-east Queensland and northern NSW in pairs and small flocks and appeared to be wholly seed-eating. It bred August-December, sometimes later, and nested in cavities excavated in termite mounds, river banks and occasionally low in a tree stump. It laid from three to five eggs.
Female: *duller.*
Voice: *'sweet, plaintive piping, not unlike that of a young bird' (Chisholm). The mounted specimen of a male bird photographed was donated to the National Photographic Index of Australian Wildlife in 1970 by the late Sir Edward Hallstrom.* D&MT

47, 48 GOLDEN-SHOULDERED PARROT *Psephotous chrysopterygius* 27cm
The survival of this rare parrot, found only in a relatively small area of Cape York, is threatened by the depredation of illegal bird trappers. The species is noted for its skill in excavating nesting chambers in the slab-sided termite mounds which abound in the area. Remarkably, all of these point north/south so that a minimum area is exposed to the heat of the mid-day tropical sun. A tunnel about 40cm long is enlarged at the end into a chamber in which the eggs are laid, then incubated by the female. When the young hatch they remain with the family group, the males not attaining the full plumage glory until their second year. Seen in pairs and flocks, it feeds on grass seeds and herbaceous plants. Sedentary. Breeds April-September. Endemic.
Immatures: *like adult females; young males have brighter colour.*
Voice: *soft whistled 'fweep'.* H&JB

49 HOODED PARROT *Psephotus dissimilis* 27cm
The sooty black forehead of this Northern Territory bird gives it its name and distinguishes it from its close relative, the Golden-shouldered Parrot of Cape York. The Hooded Parrot is perhaps more often seen in flocks, otherwise their feeding and nesting habits are identical and the two birds are sometimes regarded as races of a single species. Sedentary, local movement. Breeds April-July. Nests in termite mound. Endemic.
Female: *lacks black crown, in general light olive-green.*
Immatures: *duller.*
Voice: *similar to Golden-shouldered Parrot.* B&BW

50 BLUE BONNET *Northiella haematogaster* 35cm
    (A) Race *haematogaster* (Yellow-vented)
    (B) Race *haematorrhous* (Red-vented) illustrated
    (C) Race *pallescens* (Lake Eyre)
    (D) Race *narethae* (Nullarbor)
Races (A) and (B) intergrade where they meet; (C) is pallid; (D) is isolated and distinctive. A species of semi-arid open country where trees provide nesting hollows and is a ground feeder. Breeds August-December. Nests below 10m. Endemic.
Female: *less blue on face, duller red or yellow on belly.*
Immatures: *duller.*
Voice: *whistling, harsh 'chuck'.* D&MT

51 BOURKE'S PARROT *Neophema bourkii* 22cm
Crepuscular - moving after dusk and before dawn - and semi-nocturnal, it is sometimes active even in total darkness. It frequents mulga and inland scrub and spends much time on the ground feeding, merely fluttering off to cover if disturbed. Usually in pairs or small family parties, but flocks may throng at water during drought. Sedentary or nomadic. Breeds August-December or after rains. Nests in tree 1-3m from ground. Endemic.
Male: *similar but forehead sky blue.*
Immatures: *like adult females, less pink on breast.*
Voice: *soft 'chu-wee' in flight, also warbling and whistling.* K&BR

7

52   BLUE-WINGED PARROT *Neophema chrysostoma*   23cm
The Blue-winged Parrot is a gregarious bird that has adapted to a variety of habitats from forested valleys to coastal dunes, mallee and inland saltbush plains. It feeds mainly on the ground and is approachable. If disturbed the whole flock will rise as one and fly to cover, then cautiously return in small groups. Seasonally migratory throughout its range, including to and from Tasmania. Breeds October-January. Nests in tree hollow, sometimes very high. Endemic.
Female: *duller and more olive-green.*
Immatures: *duller, less blue.*
Voice: *soft twittering, melodious tinkling notes.*   LR

53   TURQUOISE PARROT *Neophema pulchella*   21cm
Once common around Sydney, the Turquoise Parrot was portrayed by the convict artist Watling in the earliest days of colonial settlement. It is found in open forest, timbered rocky slopes and ridges, or along watercourses and has responded well to the little-disturbed country of the Warrambungle National Park. It feeds on the ground in pairs or small flocks. Nomadic. Breeds August-December. Nests in a dead tree-spout, hollow limb or fence post. Endemic.
Female: *paler, no red on wing.*
Immatures: *duller; young males have faint red wing patch.*
Voice: *two-syllable whistle usually in flight.*   LR

54   ELEGANT PARROT *Neophema elegans*   24cm
While closely resembling the Blue-winged Parrot, its yellow markings are brighter and it lacks the extensive blue on the wing. Although its distribution is interrupted by the Nullarbor Plain, the two populations appear to be identical. In the east, it is sometimes seen in the company of Blue-winged Parrots where their ranges overlap; in the west, it is extending its range and numbers. A ground feeder, it is not easily flushed but when disturbed will rise high and fly off. Partly nomadic. Breeds August-November. Nests in tree holes. Endemic.
Sexes and immatures: *similar.*
Voice: *sharp 'zit-zit' in flight.*   D&MT

55   SCARLET-CHESTED PARROT *Neophema splendida*   21cm
Very rare in some of its former haunts, this bird is now generally found only in the inland areas where it frequents mallee, mulga scrub, spinifex, eucalypt and casuarina woodland. Unobtrusively in pairs or small parties, it feeds on seeds on the ground. It seldom goes to water and probably gets its moisture from dew or plants. Breeds August-January or after rains. Nests in a tree hollow. It has been seen carrying aromatic leaves into the nest presumably for deodorising or humidifying purposes. Endemic.
Immatures: *duller.*
Voice: *feeble twittering.*   D&MT

56   ORANGE-BELLIED PARROT *Neophema chrysogaster*   21cm
This very rare species, found only in Tasmania and in small parts of Victoria and South Australia, is the subject of on-going intensive surveys in an effort to save it from extinction. Mainland birds migrate to Tasmania to breed during the summer. Nests in tree hollows. Endemic.
Female: *duller.*
Immatures: *duller than adult females.*
Voice: *distinctive continuous buzzing.*   TP

57   ROCK PARROT *Neophema petrophila*   23cm
The Rock Parrot frequents often bleak and exposed coastal areas and rocky offshore islands. In pairs and small flocks it feeds inconspicuously on the ground on seeds and fruits of littoral plants. Relatively tame but, when alarmed, it flits off to nearby rocks and bushes. Between coast and islands the flight is swift and high and it circles overhead before landing. Mostly sedentary. Breeds August-October on islands. Nests in rock crevices or under overhanging ledges. Endemic.
Sexes: *alike.*
Immatures: *lack blue band on forehead.*
Voice: *'tsit-tseet', twittering.*   D&MT

7

58   SWIFT PARROT *Lathamus discolor*   25cm

Often seen together with lorikeets, this swift-flying parrot is characterised by a thin pointed red-brown tail. It has a brush tongue, like the lorikeets, though it is unrelated and its activities are similar. It clambers with agility amidst top-most foliage in search of nectar, berries, fruit and insects such as lerpscale. When feeding it chatters busily. It breeds in Tasmania September-January and most migrate to the mainland to overwinter. Nests in tree holes 6-18m high. Endemic.

Sexes: *alike.*
Immatures: *duller.*
Voice: *torrent of notes 'clink-clink', chattering, fluting rather than screeching.*   GC

59, 60   BUDGERIGAR *Melopsittacus undulatus*   20cm

The Budgerigar occurs throughout the vast inland areas of the continent and is thought to be the most numerous of all Australian parrots. It is highly nomadic and ranges over great distances in quest of water and seeding grasses. It is a great survivor. During periods of high temperature it will remain totally inert in the shade of trees and bushes to conserve body moisture. It has a prolific capacity to breed when conditions are favourable and it can make up losses suffered through drought and heatwave at an astonishing rate.

Sexes: *alike but female has brown cere when breeding.*
Immatures: *duller, may lack black throat spots.*
Voice: *animated conversational chatter, pretty warbling.*   59 D&MT; 60 LR

61   GROUND PARROT *Pezoporus wallicus*   32cm

This ground-frequenting species makes its home in damp coastal heath and grasslands. Timid and elusive, its long legs enable it to retreat swiftly through the undergrowth when threatened. When flushed, it rises with a rush of wingbeats and flies away on a zigzag course at great speed, alternatively beating and gliding before diving back to cover. It is particularly active and vocal towards nightfall and again at sunrise. Breeds September-December and nests on the ground. Endemic.

Sexes: *alike.*
Immatures: *heavier black breast markings.*
Voice: *thin high-pitched ascending notes.*   GC

62   NIGHT PARROT *Pezoporus occidentalis*   24cm

The elusive and rarely seen Night Parrot ranges widely over the vast arid inland areas, and is probably highly nomadic. It frequents spinifex when in seed, and salt-lake and flood-plain vegetation at other times. It remains silently concealed by day and, if flushed, flies a short distance and runs off at a tangent to cover on landing. It apparently feeds, drinks and calls only after dark. Breedings - recorded in July and August. Nests found tunnelled into clumps of spinifex and 'samphire bush'. Endemic.

Sexes: *alike.*
Immatures: *duller.*
Voice: *sweet, low, two-tone whistle uttered frequently.*
Frog-like croaks when alarmed.   Painting by TRL

1   FOREST KINGFISHER *Todiramphus macleayii*   23cm
The two Australian populations are separated by the Gulf of Carpentaria. Singly or in family parties, it frequents forest, swamps, mangroves and woodland, but may be found far from water. Frogs, worms and insects are its diet. Breeds August-December, sometimes twice. Nests in termite mounds and in river banks. Eastern birds migrate to New Guinea. **Recognition:** *violet-blue crown and white under-parts. Western birds - back bluer and white wing patch, seen in flight, larger.*
Males: *back of neck white.*
Immatures: *duller.*
Voice: *trills and whistles.*   EZ

2   RED-BACKED KINGFISHER *Todiramphus pyrrhopygia*   24cm
Widespread, and adapted to live in the arid and semi-arid areas, often far from water - presumably obtaining enough moisture from its food of insects, frogs, reptiles and even young birds. Singly, in breeding pairs or in very small parties, it frequents a variety of habitat, often in timber along dry rivers and creeks. Highly nomadic. Southern birds migrate northwards to winter. Breeds August-February. Nests in a burrow in a creek bank or in a tree hollow. Endemic.
Recognition: *orange-tan rump, streaked crown.*
Sexes: *similar but female duller.*
Immatures: *white-flecked wings.*
Voice: *mournful descending whistle.*   GC

3   SACRED KINGFISHER *Todiramphus sanctus*   23cm
The familiar Sacred Kingfisher is seen throughout all but the arid centre of the Australian continent. It perches high, and is often solitary. Its food includes lizards, insects and occasionally aquatic life. Many birds migrate northwards to winter. Breeds September-March and nests in a creek bank, termite mound or tree hollow. **Recognition:** *after breeding the deep buff of the breast is often worn and discoloured to dull ivory.*
Sexes: *similar but female duller.*
Immatures: *like females.*
Voice: *repeated 'kee-kee-kee' and a series of churring scolding notes.*   T&PG

4   COLLARED KINGFISHER *Todiramphus chloris*   29cm
Also known as the Mangrove Kingfisher. In Australia, this large kingfisher is predominantly a mangrove dweller; and can often be seen perching on bare branch tops. It feeds on insects, small animals and nestlings. Southern birds migrate northwards to winter. Breeds September-March and nests in tree hollows, termite mounds or earth banks. **Recognition:** *like the Sacred Kingfisher but larger and has whiter underparts.*
Female: *duller.*
Immatures: *flecked white.*
Voice: *some notes like Sacred Kingfisher, some like Kookaburra.*   JP

5, 6   YELLOW-BILLED KINGFISHER *Syma torotoro*   21cm
In Australia the small and inconspicuous Yellow-billed Kingfisher occurs in the remote tropical rainforests of Cape York Peninsula. Usually solitary, it lives in relative obscurity, but during and after breeding it is seen in pairs and sometimes small family parties. It perches on a branch to scout with concentrated intensity for insects, lizards and worms. Some may migrate to overwinter in New Guinea. Breeds November-January and nests in termite mounds or hollow tree limbs.
Sexes: *similar but male has black neck patch, female has black head patch.*
Immatures: *flecked with black.*
Voice: *mournful ascending trilling call.*   D&MT

7   BUFF-BREASTED PARADISE-KINGFISHER *Tanysiptera sylvia*   36cm
Unlike any other of Australia's kingfishers, this species of the rainforests of Cape York Peninsula has two long (18cm) stiff white tail feathers. In November, the birds arrive from New Guinea in a burst to breed, but once the bustle of territory-claiming and nest-building is over, they become quieter and retiring. Nesting takes place in a low termite mound and three or four weeks are spent tunnelling into it and excavating the nesting chamber (about 15cm in diameter). By the time the young have been reared in the confines of such a small space, the parents' plumage is stained and worn. The adults begin returning to New Guinea in March and most have left by the end of April.
Sexes: *alike.*
Immatures: *lack long tail streamers and have fine scallopings of light grey on breast.*
Voice: *series of 'chop-chop' notes, loud scream, persistent trilling.*   LR

8

8   AZURE KINGFISHER *Alcedo azurea*   19cm
A true fishing kingfisher which dives to seize fish and other aquatic life in either salt or fresh water. It perches for long periods on a low branch overhanging water, quiet, solitary and intent, waiting to dart for its prey. Sedentary. The northern birds are smaller and bluer on the flanks. Breeds September-January (south), October-April (north). Nests in a channel dug in a stream bank, with a terminal chamber lined with fishbones and shells.
Sexes: *alike.*
Immatures: *less glossy, paler underparts.*
Voice: *shrill whistling in flight.*   CW

9   LITTLE KINGFISHER *Alcedo pusilla*   13cm
This fishing kingfisher, the smallest of the kingfishers in Australia is confined to two separate populations - in Cape York Peninsula and the Northern Territory. Birds west of Normanton have bluer backs and larger wing patches. The species frequents mangroves, estuaries and rainforest creeks where it dives for small fish. It has been known to catch as many as eight a day. It is solitary and seldom seen. Breeds October-March. Nests in creek banks or in termite mounds.
Sexes: *alike.*
Immatures: *areas of turquoise-grey.*
Voice: *very high shrill whistle, usually in flight.*   TH

10   RAINBOW BEE-EATER *Merops ornatus*   28cm
The Rainbow Bee-eater is aptly named for it displays every hue of the rainbow when pirouetting on the wing, and does eat bees which, with other insects, form a substantial part of its diet. The sting is rendered harmless and the bee killed before it is swallowed. It occurs in mallee and all types of open country, especially where there are sandy river banks. Breeds November-January and nests at end of a tunnel in a bank or on the ground. Migrates northwards to overwinter.
Sexes: *similar but central tail feathers shorter in female.*
Immatures: *lack black throat bar.*
Voice: *soft musical trilling.*   T&PG

11   DOLLARBIRD *Eurystomus orientalis*   30cm
The Australian Dollarbird is so named from the pale blue coin-spot seen under each wing during flight. It perches strategically to dart out and seize large flying insects, returning to its perch to batter the prey before swallowing it. Usually seen singly or in pairs. It frequents woodlands and timbered environs of settled areas. Seasonally migratory. Breeds October-February. Nests in cavities of high trees on the edges of forests or in open woodland.
Adults: *similar with bluish-purple throat and crimson feet.*
Voice: *harsh squawks followed by calls of 'kak-kak-kak'.*   JB/NPI

12, 13, 14   LAUGHING KOOKABURRA *Dacelo novaeguineae*   40-46cm
Few native species have adapted to city and suburban life as successfully as the endemic Laughing Kookaburra, and it is as familiar in gardens as it is in its natural state in large-timbered country and woodlands. It sits patiently for long periods scanning for prey. It eats snakes, lizards, rodents, small birds and insects, and bashes its victim to pulp before swallowing it. The northern birds are smaller, and those in Western Australia, Tasmania and Kangaroo Island are descended from releases from eastern Australia. Breeding is from September-January, nesting mostly in tree holes.
Sexes: *alike. Male distinguished by blue rump.*
Immatures: *shorter tail, bill all-black.*
Voice: *the famous call is usually joined by several birds in chorus which can rise in a riotous and deafening crescendo, particularly at dawn and dusk.*   12 & 14 D&MT, 13 JohnC/APL

15   BLUE-WINGED KOOKABURRA *Dacelo leachii*   44cm
The range of this smaller blue-winged relative of the Laughing Kookaburra extends right across the tropical and sub-tropical top end of the continent and northwards into New Guinea. There is some variation throughout its range, the western population generally being paler and the Cape York population smaller. In Queensland where the territories of the Blue-winged and Laughing Kookaburra overlap, the former will be found more often in the wetter tropical coastal fringes. It rests quietly during the heat of the day, and is more retiring that its relative. Otherwise, the habits and diet of the two species are similar. Sedentary. Breeds September-January. Nests in a termite mound or tree hollow.
Female: *rufous tail barred blue-black.*
Immatures: *brown on underparts, head paler.*
Voice: *does not laugh but utters very loud fiendish howls especially at dawn, usually with several birds joining in.*   CS

THE PASSERINES
Sections 9–16 with Sections 4 (part) and 5

The order Passeriformes represents about half of the world's living birds, and are known variously as Passerines, Songbirds or Perching birds. They occupy the top of the evolutionary tree, and are characterised by a number of distinctive anatomical features, especially by their four-toed feet in which the longer and stronger hind toe curls forward to meet the front toes to secure a grip when perching. (Non-passerines have a variety of very different feet). Passerines also have unique muscular arrangements of the voice box, or syrinx, which have endowed the majority of them with the gift of song. Australia's 33 passerine families of 326 species are represented in the eight Sections which follow, also in the first part of Section 4 and in Section 5. (The non-passerine Swifts are included in Section 9 for convenience of reference).

9 Cuckoo-shrikes and Allies

1   BLACK-FACED CUCKOO-SHRIKE *Coracina novaehollandiae*   33cm
Also known as the 'Blue Jay' or the 'Shufflewing', the latter because it folds and refolds its wings on alighting. It inhabits open timber, sometimes in small flocks, and comes to parks and gardens. It eats insects, berries and fruit, sometimes hovering, then diving to the ground. Partly nomadic. Breeds August-February. Nests 5-15m high.
Sexes: *alike.*
Immatures: *less black on face.*
Voice: *2 or more drawn out, husky 'cheeeer' sounds.*   CW

2   WHITE-BELLIED CUCKOO-SHRIKE *Coracina papuensis*   28cm
Also known as the Little Cuckoo-shrike. Only the northern race *hypoleuca* (illustrated), which spans the top end of the continent, has a white belly. The larger race *robusta,* which occupies eastern Australia, has a grey breast and belly and sometimes a black face and throat. It is usually seen in pairs and small flocks in forest and woodland, where it feeds mainly in the tree canopies. Some seasonal or nomadic movement. Breeds August-March.
Sexes: *alike.*
Immatures: *brown mottling.*
Voice: *rather reedy 'kiseek, kiseek', other calls like the Black-faced Cuckoo-shrike.*   D&MT

3   BARRED CUCKOO-SHRIKE *Coracina lineata*   28cm
Also called the Yellow-eyed Cuckoo-shrike. Singly and in pairs when breeding, and in flocks at other times, this bird frequents the coastal rainforests. It is constantly on the move foraging for its diet of fruit, berries and insects, often in the company of fruit pigeons and figbirds. Non-breeding birds roost communally at night. Breeds October-January. Nests in trees up to 20m from the ground.
Recognition: *barred underparts and yellow eye.*
Sexes: *alike.*
Immatures: *barring on breast is less distinct.*
Voice: *series of soft notes and pleasant chatter.*   EW

4   GROUND CUCKOO-SHRIKE *Coracina maxima*   36cm
A communal breeder, the species is seen mainly in groups of three or four, all of whom help to feed the young. Very wary, it is hard to approach in open country. At a distance it appears black and white, like a long-tailed magpie. It feeds on the ground in sparsely timbered areas, mainly inland. It nods the head pigeon-like when walking, and on alighting flicks the wings, more so when alarmed or calling. Nomadic. Breeds August-December. Nests 3-15m high. Endemic.
Sexes: *alike.*
Immatures: *faint barring.*
Voice: *peculiar rippling call note, and a series of piercing cries.*   JP

5, 6   VARIED TRILLER *Lalage leucomela*   18cm
This species lives mainly in coastal tropical and sub-tropical monsoon rainforests as well as mangroves, river margins and gardens. It eats both insects and fruit, scrutinising the foliage, and is sometimes seen in mixed feeding flocks. Sedentary, moving inland during the wet season. Breeds August-April. Nests 1-2m high. Recognition: could be confused with the much larger female Cicadabird, which also has a barred abdomen..
Immatures: *like adult females.*
Voice: *trilling, drawn-out 'k-a-r-r-'.*   NC

7, 8, 9   WHITE-WINGED TRILLER *Lalage sueurii*   18cm
When breeding, the male endlessly pours out beautiful musical notes, even when sitting on the nest and in flight. The female is noticeably quieter. Seen singly, in pairs or groups, it frequents lightly-timbered areas including suburban parks and gardens, foraging in foliage, amongst blossoms, or on the ground. Breeds September-February. The nest, a shallow cup, is often built with other species in the same tree, from 1-10m high. After breeding, males moult into an eclipse plumage of dull brown but this is rarely seen in the south. Migratory.
Sexes: *similar in non-breeding season.*
Immatures: *like females.*
Voice: *persistent melodious trilling and warbling.*   7GC; 8D&MT, 9KI

10   CICADABIRD *Coracina tenuirostris*   27cm **9**
The male of this small cuckoo-shrike utters a high-pitched buzzing during the breeding season resem-
bling the stridulations of the cicada. Arboreal and inconspicuous in the high foliage searching for
insects, singly or in pairs. West of the Gulf of Carpentaria, the birds are smaller. Seasonally migrato-
ry. Breeds October-March and nests in trees 3-48m above ground.
Male: *dark grey overall, face and wings blackish.*
Immatures: *like adult females.*
Voice: *male (as above); female a sharp whistling 'cheep'.*   JP

Woodswallows, Swallow-like Birds

11   WHITE-BROWED WOODSWALLOW *Artamus superciliousus*   19cm
Highly nomadic and wanders in search of food in large flocks, often with the Masked Woodswallow
to which it is closely related. Frequents open forest, woodland, orchards and gardens. Its brush tongue
enables it to take nectar and it also eats insects. Breeds August-January (usually when conditions are
suitable). Migratory after breeding. Endemic.
Female: *noticeably duller.*
Immatures: *mottled.*
Voice: *sparrow-like chirps in flight.*   D&MT

12   MASKED WOODSWALLOW *Artamus personatus*   19cm
The black face and throat of this species are prominent distinguishing marks. It chatters and hawks on
the wing for insects. In spring huge flocks join with the White-browed Woodswallow over southern Australia
prior to dispersing to start breeding. It breeds August-December and nests in bushes, fence posts etc. usual-
ly 1-2m above ground. Migratory after breeding. Endemic.
Female: *much duller, throat grey, no white collar (can be confused with the female Black-faced
Woodswallow).*
Immatures: *upper marts mottled.*
Voice: *soft chattering.*   T&PG

13   WHITE-BREASTED WOODSWALLOW *Artamus leucorhynchus*   17cm
Perches in groups of ten or more and together set up a constant animated chattering and chirping. It is
found in well-timbered country near water and feeds on insects taken in the air. Sedentary in the north.
Nomadic and seasonally migratory further south. Breeds August-January. Nests in a variety of situa-
tions, sometimes using a Magpie-lark's old nest. Recognition: a white rump and an all-black tail.
Sexes: *alike.* **Immatures:** *mottled.*
Voice: *harsh 'cheek', continuous chattering.*   GC

14   BLACK-FACED WOODSWALLOW *Artamus cinereus*   18cm
One of the commonest birds of inland Australia where it is mainly sedentary, preferring sparsely vegetated open savannah. It lives in pairs or family groups which roost in clusters at night. Occasional
large winter flocks occur in arid areas. It hawks for insects on the wing and takes passing prey while
perched, but also feeds on the ground. Breeds August-January. In arid regions breeding is quickly
responsive to rains. Nests 1-5m above ground in a bush or on a stump.
Sexes: *alike.*
Immatures: *grey-brown mottling.*
Voice: *a short subdued rolling chatter.*   D&MT

15   DUSKY WOODSWALLOW *Artamus cyanopterus*   18cm
In pairs and family groups, it frequents open forests and partly-cleared lands. The western population
- separated from the eastern by some 2 500kms - is partial to open tracts within the jarrah and karri
forests. Like both the Black-faced and Little Woodswallows, it hawks for insects on the wing and
roosts in close clusters. Breeds August-January. Nests within 11m of the ground in a wide variety of
situations. Eastern population nomadic after breeding. Endemic. Recognition: the white wing edge distinguishes this species from the other woodswallows.
Sexes: *alike.*
Immatures: *mottled.*
Voice: *constant chattering.*   TW

16   LITTLE WOODSWALLOW *Artamus minor*   12cm
The smallest of the woodswallows, it is seen in pairs and family groups. The inland birds frequent
rocky outcrops; the birds on the WA coast haunt the cliffs and those in Queensland inhabit the wood-
land fringes. The species takes insects while floating high in graceful flight and low over water,
sometimes with other woodswallows. Occasionally sips nectar. They roost in clusters at night.
Breeds October-January. Nests in cliffs and rock crannies in WA and in trees elsewhere. Endemic.
Recognition: *lacks white wing edge.*
Sexes: *alike.*
Immatures: *mottled.*
Voice: *softer than other woodswallows.*   KI

17   GLOSSY SWIFTLET *Collocalia esculenta*   11cm
This non-breeding summer visitor has been seen only on a few occasions in Australia - in
Cape York Peninsula and near Mackay. The smallest of the swiftlets, it is seen in small par-
ties or flocks and is reported to fly more slowly and lower than other small swifts.
Recognition: *distinguishable by its white belly and contrasting glossy black upper parts.*
Sexes: *alike.*   PK

18   WHITE-RUMPED SWIFTLET *Collocalia spodiopygus*   11cm
Flocks of this small swiftlet circling high betray the proximity of breeding sites located in caves and
gorges. These have been found at Cairns, near Mackay, Tully River, Chillago Caves, Dunk and
Bedarra Islands. It breeds September-February, and nests in dense colonies. The nest is a tiny cup of
grasses cemented to the rock face with saliva, and the bird guides itself in dim cave interiors with
echoes from its radar system. Caves are abandoned after nesting.
Sexes: *alike.*   T&PG

19   FORK-TAILED SWIFT *Apus pacificus*   19cm
A regular non-breeding migrant, arriving from northern Asia in early October and leaving in mid-
April. Sometimes in huge flocks. It will go anywhere where insects are plentiful and favours low pres-
sure zones where the humidity is high. Like all swifts, it takes insects in the air, and skims over water
to drink. It apparently sleeps on the wing, soaring at considerable heights. It has excellent twilight
vision.
Sexes: *alike.*   CF

20   WHITE-THROATED NEEDLETAIL *Hirundapus caudacutus*   20cm
Also known as the Spine-tailed Swift, it arrives mid-October in eastern and south-eastern Australia
from Asia, and departing mid-April. It is one of the world's fastest and most powerful flyers, achiev-
ing cruising speeds of 50-130kph, and is seen soaring high in parties to very large flocks. It hawks for
insects on the wing, and skims lakes and other stretches of water to drink. It has excellent twilight
vision. Occasionally clings to trees or rock ledges with its sharp claws using its tail spines as a prop.
Sexes: *alike.*   RD

21   WHITE-BACKED SWALLOW *Cheramoeca leucosternus*   15cm
In small flocks and colonies, it frequents open country including the drier inland areas. It has a graceful, fluttering flight and takes insects on the wing. It breeds August-December and nests in burrows
drilled into a sandy creek bank or road cutting and is the only Australian swallow to do so. It is highly sociable and up to twenty birds may roost at night in a nesting burrow. Clusters of birds have also
been found hibernating in a burrow in a torpid state during cold and inclement weather. Endemic.
Sexes: *alike.*
Immatures: *duller.*
Voice: *an attractive twittering song, with a 'check check' call in flight.*   GW

22   BARN SWALLOW *Hirundo rustica*   17cm
A non-breeding summer migrant from Asia, which is common almost throughout the northern hemisphere. It regularly occurs in the Kimberley area, but elsewhere sightings are sporadic. Most are in
northern Australia but it could turn up anywhere. Like the Welcome Swallow, its flight is swift and
graceful and it hawks for insects on the wing, sometimes close to water, over which it also skims to
drink. Recognition: thin blue-black band below throat.
Sexes: *alike.*
Immatures: *duller.*
Voice: *high-pitched 'tswit' or 'tswee' and rapid chatter.*   E&DH

23   WELCOME SWALLOW Hirundo neoxena   13cm
Familiar and endearing, this endemic swallow is indeed welcome when, in eastern Australia, it returns with
the spring from overwintering in the north to breed. Many use the same beautifully-made and softly-lined
mud nest year after year with the same partner. In autumn, lines of birds twittering on telegraph wires gath-
ering to take off for their winter migration make a pretty sight. The birds in the west are mainly sedentary.
Recognition: *the deeply forked tail and absence of a white rump distinguish this bird and the Barn
Swallow from the martins.*
Sexes: *alike.*
Immatures: *duller.*
Voice: *sweet twittering 'seet'.*   D&MT

24   TREE MARTIN Hirundo nigricans   13cm
Probably the most common and widespread of the swallow-like birds in Australia. It is partial to the
bigger trees which offer plenty of nesting sites, in open eucalypt woodland and likes to be near water.
It feeds on the wing on insects over tree canopies or water. Breeds July-January and nests in loose
colonies in small holes in trees, interstices in buildings, or cliff holes. Migrates northwards to over-
winter, including to New Guinea. In southern Australia, large flocks gather for the autumn migration.
Sexes: *alike.*
Immatures: *browner.*
Voice: *high-pitched twitter.*   R&DK

25   FAIRY MARTIN Hirundo ariel   12cm
Gregarious and favours open country near water. Takes insects in the air or over water. Breed August-
January in the south and May-March in the far north. The distinctive bottle-shaped nest of mud pellets,
has a down-sloping spout as an entrance, and is often built in large clusters on a variety of surfaces,
including under bridges and caves. Several birds may combine to build a single nest, and new birds often
take over old nests or build new ones over them. Southern birds are seasonally migratory. Endemic.
Recognition: *rusty-brown head, darker in WA.*
Sexes and immatures: *alike.*
Voice: *noisy twittering especially at dawn.*   MS

Sittellas and Treecreepers

There are five quite distinctive forms of Sittellas in Australia. These keep to particular
areas of the continent, except for fairly narrow zones of overlap where they interbreed and
produce intermediate forms. They inhabit woodland and dry forest and wander widely
within their areas, usually travelling in small flocks. Their days are spent busily scurry-
ing about among the branches of trees probing the crevices and prising up bark in search
of insects. They are extremely acrobatic and, unlike the treecreepers, they usually work
along branches from the tip and spiral down the trunk. They are communal breeders, living in family groups with several birds of a group helping to build the nest, usually in a
deep fork, and feeding the young. Number 27 is the nominate race.

26   (A) VARIED SITTELLA (White-winged) *Daphoenositta chrysoptera leucoptera*   10cm
       (B) VARIED SITTELLA (Striated) *Daphoenositta chrysotera striata*   10cm
These two races have white wing patches instead of orange. (A) (illustrated) frequents woodlands and
light timber. (B) (not illustrated) has the darkest head and is the most streaked of the sittellas. It fre-
quents forest and scrub. The two races breed July-October.
Sexes and immatures: *some differences.*
Voice: *see 27.*   GC

27 **VARIED SITTELLA** (Orange-winged) *Daphoenositta chrysoptera chyrsoptera* 12cm
An orange wing-patch and a dark grey-brown head characterise this the least distinctively marked
nominate race. It lives in most types of forest, except rainforest, and lightly wooded country.
Sexes: *similar, but throat of female is dusky white and speckled.*
Immatures: *paler, underparts speckled.*
Voice: *varied thin high-pitched incessant 'psees', 'dear-dip', 'wits' and 'chips', often in flight.* JG

28, 29 **VARIED SITTELLA** (Black-capped) *Daphoenositta chrysoptera pileata* 12cm
The most widespread of the orange-winged sittellas of southern Australia. It is distinguished by its
bold and striking markings and by its white (not mottled) underparts. It frequents forest and woodland
of the coastal areas and timber near water of the arid inland. Breeds usually September-January.
Sexes: *the black cap of the female extends over the forehead. The faces may be white or black in either
sex* (Boles 1980).
Immatures: *crown is greyish-black.*
Voice: *see 27.* H&JB

30 **VARIED SITTELLA** (White-headed) *Daphoenositta chrysoptera leucocephala* 12cm
The head and neck of this orange-winged sittella are wholly white. It lives in forest and woodland from
the high country of the Great Dividing Range to the more open coastal plains. Breeds July-October
and February-March.
Sexes: *similar, but the throat of the female is dusky instead of white.*
Immatures: *some may have grey heads.*
Voice: *see 27.* EZ

31 **WHITE-THROATED TREECREEPER** *Cormobates leucophaeus* 17cm
The species includes the smaller Queensland race *minor* 'Little Treecreeper', found only on the
Atherton Tablelands. An agile bird, which can hop along the underside of a branch, it zig-zags briskly
up a tree probing under bark with its long beak for insects, spiders, and especially ants. It frequents a
variety of wooded habitats. Breeds August-January, and nests in tree cavities from 5m above ground.
Endemic.
Male: *lacks orange neck spot.*
Immatures: *chestnut rump.*
Voice: *bursts of loud piping notes in a variety of songs briskly repeated.* K&BR

32 **RED-BROWED TREECREEPER** *Climacteris erythrops* 15cm
Less conspicuous than the White-throated Treecreeper, with which it shares its range. It frequents rain-
forest or dense eucalypt forest and, where the populations overlap, the Red-browed Treecreeper takes
to the higher trees. It breeds August-January and nests in trees 6-30m above ground. Endemic.
Females: *upper breast streaked.*
Immatures: *no eyebrow marking.*
Voice: *very high-pitched staccato chatter descending the scale.* JP

33 **WHITE-BROWED TREECREEPER** *Climacteris affinis* 14cm
Closely resembles the Red-browed Treecreeper in plumage. It is partial to a habitat of mulga, casuar-
ina, and other sparse vegetation and often forages on the ground among fallen timber for food. It will
however behave like other Treecreepers where taller timber borders its preferred habitat. Breeds
September-November and nests low, perhaps in a tree hollow or log. Endemic.
Male: *upper breast grey.*
Immatures: *no marked streaking of underparts.*
Voice: *loud strident call and weak song.* B

34   **RUFOUS TREECREEPER** *Climacteris rufa*   17cm
The most colourful of the treecreepers. It is often seen in family groups of three to five and is a com-
munal breeder. It frequents the open woodland, moist jarrah forest, and mallee of the south western
parts of Australia. Breeds September-December and nests in a tree up to 8m above the ground and
occasionally in a hollow log. All members of the family may help to feed nestlings. Endemic.
Sexes: *similar but female has breast feathers edged with red.*
Immatures: *plainer with rufous rump.*
Voice: *shrill repeated whistling like the Brown Treecreeper, but higher in pitch.*   GC

35   **BROWN TREECREEPER** *Climacteris picumnus*   17cm
The northern race *melanota* 'Black Treecreeper' holds a special place in the annals of ornithology as
it was first collected for John Gould by John Gilbert on the day in 1845 he was speared by aborig-
ines on Leichhardt's first expedition. The species lives in groups of up to five birds in a variety of
habitat and is common in eucalypt woodland. Breeds June-January (but earlier inland and later in
the east) and nests in trees 1-15m above ground, sometimes in a fence post. Endemic.
Female: *faint rufous breast markings.*
Immatures: *underparts faintly streaked.*
Voice: *repeated strident notes.*   K&BR

36   **BLACK-TAILED TREECREEPER** *Climacteris melanura*   20cm
(A) race *melanura;* (B) race *wellsi* (Allied Treecreeper). The latter race is paler and smaller and apparent-
ly lives quite separately from its northern relative. The species is the largest and darkest of the treecreep-
ers. Like the Brown Treecreeper, it usually keeps together in small groups and frequents open woodland
and savannah. Breeds August-January and nests in tree hollows 4-10m above ground. Endemic.
Female: *smaller, white throat and upper breast streaked rufous.*
Immatures: *faint white streaks on throat.*
Voice: *strident sharp calls.*   JP

10 Robins, Flycatchers, Whistlers and Thrush-like Birds

1, 2   FLAME ROBIN *Petroica phoenicea*   14cm
This spectacularly marked robin is remarkable for its complex seasonal movements. During the summer period, many breed and raise their young in the Australian Alps and the high Tasmanian mountains, where they live in eucalypt forest, woodland and heath. With the onset of winter, they disperse widely to lower latitudes, where they can often be seen in open country and pastures. Normally in pairs, the Flame Robin also congregates in flocks and is the only red-breast to do so. It will sit patiently on a post waiting to dive to the ground to snatch an insect or a worm. Sometimes it flicks its wings and tail while perched. The male may breed still in immature brown plumage. Breeds September-January. Nests low in tree cavities and rock fissures. Endemic.
Immatures: *like adult females but with buff markings.*
Voice: *soft musical 'you-may-come, if-you-will, to the sea'.*   1JP, 2RL

3   DUSKY ROBIN *Melanodryas vittata*   16cm
This robin is confined to Tasmania and Bass Strait islands, where it is moderately common. It prefers sparse forest and woodland with fallen timber and debris. It perches low and motionless waiting to dart to the ground or in the air to catch its prey. Feeds on insects, spiders and snails, and seeds in winter. Sedentary. Breeds July-December. Nests below 6m. Endemic.
Sexes: *alike.*
Immatures: *less pronounced white markings.*
Voice: *low 'choo-wee-choo-wee-er' monotonously repeated.*   TW

4, 7   SCARLET ROBIN *Petroica multicolor*   14cm
Both of the widely-separated populations of the Scarlet Robin breed in high forest country, then move to lower open areas, sometimes to cultivated farmland or suburbia. Like other robins, the Scarlet is an insect-eater, feeding on the ground. The tiny nest is favoured by cuckoos.
Immatures: *like females, but duller, no red at first.*
Voice: *a succession of sweet trilling notes.*   4T&PG, 7FD

5, 8   ROSE ROBIN *Petroica rosea*   12cm
The Rose Robin is Australia's smallest robin and perhaps the most captivating. Singly and in pairs, it frequents the rainforests, dense gullies and creeks of the south-east during the summer, some dispersing to the north of its range to overwinter, where it is seen more often in drier country. It feeds mainly on insects taken from foliage, sometimes on the ground or on the wing - where it displays much of the agility of a flycatcher. It flicks its tail when perched and flits quietly about with tail fanned. Inquisitive and trusting, it will sometimes approach to inspect a person within a few metres. Breeds September-January. Nests 1-20m high, often fosters cuckoo eggs. Endemic.
Immatures: *like adult females.*
Voice: *sweet trilling song and 'tick-tick-tick' calls.*   JP

6, 9   PINK ROBIN *Petroica rodinogaster*   14cm
The Pink Robin is more often seen in Tasmania and its offshore islands than anywhere else in its somewhat restricted southerly range. In quiet pairs or family groups, this trusting bird mostly lives and breeds in the fern gullies of dense wet forest. Males tend to remain in their breeding areas for most of the year, but wandering birds are sometimes seen in dry forest country and woody suburbia during the non-breeding season. The species is heard calling from cover more often than it is seen. It feeds on flying and ground insects. Breeds September-December. Nests in a leafy tree up to 20m high. Endemic.
Recognition: *the only 'red' robin with no white in tail. Its coloration is also variable.*
Immatures: *like adult female.*
Voice: *slight 'tick', simple but pleasant warble.*   JN

10, 11　RED-CAPPED ROBIN *Petroica goodenovii*　　　　　　　　12cm
Mainly a bird of the drier inland, this robin is seen in open forest and scrub. It is absent from most of
the tropic north and areas of high rainfall in the south, including Tasmania. It flicks its wings and tail
when perched, and takes insects on the ground, in foliage, and sometimes on the wing. Sedentary, but
nomadic in drought conditions. Some seasonal movement to the coast in winter. Adept at a feigned
injury display when its nest is threatened. Breeds July-December. Nests in a tree up to 10m above
ground. Endemic.
Immatures: *like adult females, but have pale red wash.*
Voice: *call note somewhat like the ticking of a clock, also feeble insect-like song.*　　　　10LR, 11JF

12　MANGROVE ROBIN *Eopsaltria pulverulenta*　　　　　　　　16cm
As its name suggests, this is a bird of the mangroves. Its range is limited to the northern coasts. Quiet
and seldom breaking cover, it is difficult to spot though it is not shy. It sits on a perch, darting to seize
insects and small crustaceans in foliage or mud, and is seen singly, in pairs and family parties, depending on the season. Sedentary. Breeds mainly in the winter dry period, April-September. Nests in shallow cup to 5m over mud.
Sexes: *alike.*
Immatures: *paler.*
Voice: *two drawn-out plaintive notes.*　　　　　　　　　　　　　　　　　　GC

13, 14　HOODED ROBIN *Melanodryas cucullata*　　　　　　　　17cm
This pied robin is wary and unobtrusive. Usually in pairs, it is seen in open drier forest or mulga scrub,
particularly where there is fallen timber on which it perches. It may be nomadic to follow food sup-
plies, mainly insects either gathered on the ground or taken on the wing. Its feigned injury display
when its nest is threatened is remarkable and includes tumbling over and over. Breeds July-December
(south), March-April (north). Nests in a tree fork or hollow 5-6m from ground. Endemic.
Immatures: *like adult females.*
Voice: *yapping notes by night and day, especially prominent in the dawn chorus.*　　13ES, 14D&MT

15　WHITE-BREASTED ROBIN *Eopsaltria georgiana*　　　　　　　　14cm
Where the plumage of the Eastern and Western Yellow Robin is yellow, that of the White-breasted
Robin is white. Otherwise, the birds are much alike. It lives in dense moist vegetation along creeks, in
gullies, or the understorey of karri, occasionally visiting country gardens and orchards. Like the
Yellow Robins, it will cling sideways to a tree trunk, low down, to watch for insects and their larvae.
Some seasonal movement. Breeds July-January. Nests in tree or shrub near water to 6m high.
Endemic.
Sexes: *alike.*
Immatures: *like adults but may be mottled brown.*
Voice: *somewhat harsh 'chit-chit'.*　　　　　　　　　　　　　　　　　　GC

16　WESTERN YELLOW ROBIN *Eopsaltria griseogularis*　　　　　　　　16cm
Like the Eastern Yellow Robin, except for a grey chest and upper breast instead of yellow, and simi-
lar in habits. It is partial to the drier habitats of the south-west and is found in open forest, woodland,
scrub and mallee. Some winter movement from highland to lowland. Breeds July-December. Builds
its nest in a tree fork or branch, up to 8m high, and decorates it with strips of bark or lichen. Endemic.
Sexes: *alike.*
Immatures: *duller.*
Voice: *repeated piping, harsh 'chit-chit'.*　　　　　　　　　　　　　　　GC

17   EASTERN YELLOW ROBIN *Eopsaltria australis*   17cm
One of the first birds to call at dawn and amongst the last to fall quiet at nightfall. It favours dry forest and woodland and frequently appears in picnic grounds and suburban gardens. Friendly and inquisitive, it feeds on the ground on insects, and characteristically clings sideways on a tree trunk to watch for prey. Some migration to the coast in winter. Breeds July-December. Nests usually below 7m but occasionally up to 25m. Endemic.
Sexes: *alike.*
Immatures: *duller.*
Voice: *'tchew-tchew'; soft piping.*   D&MT

18   PALE-YELLOW ROBIN *Tregellasia capito*   13cm
The two widely-separated populations of the Pale-yellow Robin live in coastal and upland rainforest. It is the most common of the birds on the Atherton Tablelands. It perches in middle level foliage or clings to a tree trunk ready to dart out to catch flies and other insects. It moves singly, in pairs or family parties, but seldom leaves dense cover. It is unafraid and inquiring. Sedentary. Breeds July-January. Nests in neat cup, mostly amongst lawyer vine creepers or low in a tree. Endemic.
Sexes: *alike.*
Immatures: *like adults but more brown and rufous.*
Voice: *series of penetrating whistles and squeaks.*   T&PG

19   WHITE-FACED ROBIN *Tregellasia leucops*   12cm
The range of this tame small bird is restricted to a small area of tropical rainforest of Cape York Peninsula. Its pattern of behaviour is similar to that of the Pale Yellow Robin. It frequents middle levels of foliage, and is found in pairs and sometimes largish feeding parties foraging for insects and small crustaceans. Sedentary. Breeds July-January. Nests in lawyer vine, or at a junction of tree fork and vine, low down.
Sexes: *alike.*
Immatures: *like adults but duller.*
Voice: *occasional short harsh 'chee-chee'.*   D&MT

20, 21   WHITE-BROWED ROBIN *Poecilodryas superciliosa*   17cm
(A) race *superciliosa* (White-sided); (B) race *cerviniventris* (Buff-sided)
This endemic robin divides into two races at the Gulf of Carpentaria. In the east it lives in rainforest bordering streams and in woodland near the coast; in the west waterside thickets and occasionally mangroves. Usually in pairs. It is largely a ground feeder, and flits and hops from foliage to ground and back again, dropping its wings and flicking its tail as it forages for caterpillars, green ants, beetles and other insects, or crabs, molluscs and other small invertebrates in mangroves. It also clings to tree trunks probing crevices for prey. Although shy, it can be observed at close range if approached quietly. Sedentary. Breeds July-March. Nests in tree fork up to 9m high.
Recognition: *race (B) has orange-buff flanks and under tail coverts, and sooty-black crown and face patch.*
Sexes: *alike.*
Immatures: *like adults.*
Voice: *loud repeated piping whistle.*   20 Race (B) GC, 21 race (A) T&PG

22   GREY-HEADED ROBIN *Heteromyias albispecularis*   17cm
The Grey-headed Robin is commonly seen and heard in the rainforests of the Atherton Tablelands and the coastal highlands of northern Queensland. It often appears on the edges of clearings and tracks and clinging to tree trunks. Solitary or in pairs, it spends much time on the ground foraging. Sedentary. Breeds August-January. Nests in a tangle of vine, shrub or tree 1-10m high. Endemic.
Recognition: *characteristic upright posture.*
Sexes: *alike.*
Immatures: *patchy brown and white underparts.*
Voice: *gentle whistling.*   LR

23 **SOUTHERN SCRUB-ROBIN** *Drymodes brunneopygia* 23cm
This scrub-robin lives in mulga and mallee scrublands, especially where there is broom-bush. Usually seen only singly or in pairs, it hops along the ground or flits to low branches, flicking wings and tail. Feeds on insects. Sedentary. Breeds July-January. Nests in shallow lined ground depression, only one egg to a clutch. Endemic.
Sexes: *alike.*
Immatures: *light brown and white.*
Voice: *animated and far-carrying calls of 'chip-pip-er-ee'; will answer imitations.* GC

24 **NORTHERN SCRUB-ROBIN** *Drymodes superciliaris* 23cm
The remote habitat on Cape York Peninsula of this ground-frequenting bird makes it one of Australia's least-known species. It was recorded in the Roper River area of the Northern Territory in 1910, but there have been no recent sightings there. Solitary or in pairs, it frequents rainforest floor or the edges of clearings, hopping from place to place and turning over litter for insects. Sedentary. Breeds October-January. Nests in depression in ground.
Sexes: *alike.*
Immatures: *lighter brown head and neck.*
Voice: *a loud shrill whistle.* D&MT

25 **YELLOW-LEGGED FLYCATCHER** *Microeca griseoceps* 12cm
An unobtrusive bird with distinctive yellow legs, sometimes mistaken for a Lemon-bellied Flycatcher or a Pale-yellow Robin. It lives mostly in New Guinea and was discovered in Australia only in 1913. Here it is confined to a small area of tropical rainforest and bordering woodland in Cape York Peninsula. An Australian nest was not found until 1977. Singly or in pairs, it is active amongst foliage, stirring up insects and often rising to catch them on the wing. Breeds November-January. Small cup-shaped nest.
Sexes: *alike.*
Immatures: *duller.*
Voice: *zzt-zzt.* D&MT

26, 27 **LEMON-BELLIED FLYCATCHER** *Microeca flavigaster* 14cm
The depth and hue of yellow on the underparts of the Lemon-bellied Flycatcher varies from east to west - from bright yellow south of Cape York to white in the Kimberley. Singly and in pairs, it lives in eucalypt forest, woodland and rainforest clearings in Queensland; in dense vegetation on the Gulf of Carpentaria; in rainforest and sometimes mangroves in the Northern Territory; and in dense mangroves in the Kimberley. The eastern birds feed on a variety of insects, including ants, and caterpillars; the Kimberley birds on flies and invertebrates of the mangroves, including crabs. Eastern and northern populations breed August-January. Tiny cup-shaped nests are built in a tree 10-12m high.
Recognition: *the Kimberley birds, which resemble the Jacky Winter, lack the white-edged tail.*
Sexes: *alike.*
Immatures: *paler.*
Voice: *varied sweet and musical phrases.* 26 Kimberley form , 27 Cape York form GC

28 **JACKY WINTER** *Microeca fascinans* 14cm
Well known for its clear sweet song, this brown flycatcher is found over most of the continent in well wooded areas. Unusually amongst perching birds, it is able to hover in the air for some seconds, with the white-sided tail often fanned in flight. It is an assiduous feeder, even after dusk has fallen, taking all kinds of spiders, moths, flies and butterflies. Sedentary. Breeds July-February. Nests in tiny frail saucer to 20m high. May be parasitised by cuckoos.
Sexes: *alike.*
Immatures: *mottled.*
Voice: *varied and profuse phrases: 'jacky, jacky' or 'peter, peter'.* . GC

29   SPECTACLED MONARCH *Monarcha trivirgatus*   16cm

The Spectacled Monarch's fussy activity of jerking and tumbling seems designed to flush out prey of flies, moths, spiders and snails from the foliage of middle and upper layers of forest or woodland canopy. It seldom takes its food on the ground or on the wing. Some southern birds migrate northwards in winter. Breeds October-February. Nests in tree fork or vine tangle 1-7m high.

Sexes: *alike.*

Immatures: *less black on the head.*

Voice: *repeated whirring 'pree-pree-pree'; whistling.*   T&PG

30   BLACK-FACED MONARCH *Monarcha melanopsis*   19cm

In tropical or temperate rainforest or moist gullies, this bird forages for insects amongst middle level foliage, more rarely taking them in flight, hovering briefly. It may be seen in small groups during migration. The migratory pattern is complex: southern birds move northwards in winter, northern ones may be sedentary or move to bolster resident populations in New Guinea. Breeds October-January. Nests in tree fork 1-12m high.

Sexes: *alike.*

Immatures: *grey where adults are black.*

Voice: *clear whistling 'why-yew-which-you'; chattering.*   D&MT

31   BLACK-WINGED MONARCH *Monarcha frater*   15cm

A breeding migrant from New Guinea, it arrives in Australia in October and leaves in March, although some may remain over the winter. It was considered a race of the Black-faced Monarch, but is now retained as a separate species because of the differences in plumage, notably pearl-grey upperparts which give it the alternate common name of Pearly Flycatcher. It sits quietly on a branch with tail quivering, on the watch for insects. Nest is goblet-shaped, in a tree fork to 10m high.

Sexes: *alike.*

Immatures: *grey and buff instead of black markings.*

Voice: *like the Black-faced Monarch.*   TRL/RM

32   YELLOW-BREASTED BOATBILL *Machaerirhynchus flaviventer*   12cm

This is a lively bird which works its way at great speed through the foliage of rainforest, creek vegetation or eucalypts, snapping up insects; or it may rise into the air from its perch to take flying insects on the wing. Sometimes it cocks its tail like a wren. It is solitary and sedentary. Breeds September-March. Nests in forked branch 2-25m high. **Female:** *paler.*

Immatures: *like adult females.*

Voice: *pretty trilling song and twittering.*   R&DK

33   WHITE-EARED MONARCH *Monarcha leucotis*   14cm

Hovering and fluttering around the treetops in wet eucalypts or rainforest to snap up insects flushed from foliage or bark crevices, this flycatcher may appear in small groups. Possibly some seasonal migration southwards to breed, the breeding season being September-January. In the northern part of its range it nests so high in the tree crown that they were undescribed for 70 years; in the south, nests are lower. Endemic.

Sexes: *alike.*

Immatures: *brown-and-cream where adults are black-and-white.*

Voice: *three-syllable song phrase with last one descending; whistling.*   T&PG

34   FRILLED MONARCH *Arses telescophthalmus*   16cm

Named from its habit of frequently raising a frilly white collar, especially in courting displays. In rainforest and adjacent eucalypts it flits from branch to branch to pick insects from the foliage; occasionally it spirals up the trunk like a treecreeper. A vivid blue eye ring and the absence of a black chest band separates it from the Pied Monarch. Sedentary. Breeds September-January. Nests in a cup slung between two vines 1-10m high.

Male: *lacks grey lores.*

Immatures: *black areas tinged brown.*

Voice: *soft churring, whistles and creaks.*   D&MT

35   PIED MONARCH *Arses kaupi*   16cm
The Pied is a more southerly relative of the Frilled Monarch. Like the latter, it raises a frilly white collar, often as it briskly and boldly flits and hops in spirals up a tree trunk in the rainforest. It grips the
bark with sharp claws and long toes as it flushes out beetles, moths and flies from crevices, then darts
out after them. The tail is fanned in flight. Sedentary. Breeds October-January. Nests between two
vines 1-10m high. Endemic. **Female:** *black breaks the white collar on sides of neck.*
Immatures: *grey-brown mantle and breastband.*
Voice: *like Frilled Monarch.*   H&JB

36, 39   SATIN FLYCATCHER *Myiagra cyanoleuca*   17cm
Glossy plumage separates the Satin from the Leaden Flycatcher. Another distinguishing feature where
their ranges overlap is that the Satin Flycatcher prefers the treetops of wetter forests and mountain
ranges. It is constantly active and vocal, and darts out to take insects, including grasshoppers and
wasps on the wing. Breeds September-February. There is migratory movement from south to north
after breeding. Nests are placed openly on a tree branch, and perhaps because of this are much
favoured by Bronze and Pallid Cuckoos. Nests may be at heights of 3-25m.
Immatures: *like adult females, but are difficult to separate from immatures of Leaden Flycatcher.*
Voice: *deep 'chee-chee', grating note, nasal buzzing.*   GC

37, 38   SHINING FLYCATCHER *Myiagra alecto*   19cm
The male is the only all black flycatcher. Active body movements such as quivering of the tail, crest-
raising, and darting sallies to seize prey, are characteristic. Its habitat is mangrove and other dense vegetation associated with water. Here it takes insects from foliage, but more often it creeps along the mud
in search of ants and tiny shellfish. Probably sedentary. Breeds August-March. Shining Flycatchers
nest low or to 3m high on a branch or fork over water. The nest is parasitised by cuckoos.
Immatures: *like adult females.*
Voice: *extended whistling 'cheee'; melodious trilling by both sexes.*   37T&PG; 38JP

40   BROAD-BILLED FLYCATCHER *Myiagra ruficollis*   16cm
In mangroves, monsoon forest or scrub, it perches for long periods on a branch, characteristically quiv-
ering its white-shafted tail. It will fly out to take insects on the wing, or from leaves. Out of breeding sea-
son, it is solitary. Sedentary. Breeds October-February. Nests in a mangrove tree close to water, or in a
paperbark up to 7m high. **Recognition:** *can be confused with the female Leaden and Satin Flycatchers.*
Sexes: *similar but female paler and duller.*
Immatures: *like females.*
Voice: *loud buzzing, croaking, whistling.*   GC

41, 42   LEADEN FLYCATCHER *Myiagra rubecula*   16cm
Sometimes called Frogbird from its croaking call. In dry scrub and woodland in the south, mangroves
and wooded vegetation near water in the north, it is robustly active. It darts out to take its prey of a
wide selection of insects including bees, termites and cicadas; on the perch it is equally busy, with
rapid quivering of the tail, raising of the neck feathers and vivacious calling. Rare in Tasmania and the
southern part of its range, southern birds migrate northwards in winter. Both sexes call from the nest.
Breeds August-February. The nest is placed on a tree fork 3-25m high.
Immatures: *like adult females.*
Voice: *clear high whistled 'too-whee' or 'too-whit'; nasal buzzing.*   JG

43   RESTLESS FLYCATCHER *Myiagra inquieta*   21cm
A notable feature is the peculiar grating call from which derives its common name of Scissors Grinder.
It is often confused with the Willie Wagtail which it resembles, but can be distinguished by its white
throat and the absence of a white eyebrow. Frequenting scrub or woodland in the search for insects, it
often hovers close to the ground like the Jacky Winter, with crest raised. Nomadic or seasonal move-
ments. Breeds July-March. Nests near water 1-22m high.
Sexes: *similar.*
Immatures: *brown above.*
Voice: *beautiful penetrating musical 'tu-whee tu-whee'; grinding notes.*   GC

44   WILLIE WAGTAIL *Rhipidura leucophrys*   21cm
Willie Wagtail is one of Australia's best known and loved birds. It is familiar and tame in parks and gardens, endearingly switching its tail from side to side while running about snapping up insects, and expanding its white eyebrows conspicuously when agitated. It is strongly territorial and drives off much larger birds. Some nomadic or seasonal movements. Breeds June-February. Fibrous nest on horizontal branch.
Sexes: *alike.*
Immatures: *buff feather tips.*
Voice: *'sweet-pretty-creature'; match-box rattling alarm call, often at night.*   GC

45   RED-WHISKERED BULBUL *Pycnonotus jocosus*   23cm
Introductions of this bird to Sydney a century or more ago became established slowly, but it has now spread into country areas. It has also been sighted occasionally in Melbourne. At one time dealers sold it as a 'Persian Nightingale'. It lives in thick bush, parkland and gardens, taking insects and feasting on fruit. It calls from high vantage points. Breeds August-March. Nests in vegetation 2-3m from ground.
Sexes: *similar.*
Immatures: *duller.*
Voice: *tuneful animated chattering; call of 'kink-a-jou' and other notes.*   D&MT

46   GREY FANTAIL *Rhipidura fuliginosa*   16cm
Inquisitive and unafraid, the Grey Fantail conspicuously flits restlessly among foliage often with spread tail and darts after insects on the wing. Breeds August-January.
Sexes: *alike.*
Immatures: *browner.*
Voice: *sweet musical trilling and 'cranky' chattering.*   PG

MANGROVE GREY FANTAIL *Rhipidura phasiana*   15cm
Recently classified as a separate species, the Mangrove Grey Fantail is restricted to the coastal mangroves of north-western Australia. It is smaller, with longer bill, shorter tail, and fainter throat bar than its widespread relative. Breeds July-December.

47   NORTHERN FANTAIL *Rhipidura rufiventris*   18cm
Similar to the Grey Fantail, but with a grey-brown bib and less white in the plumage, the Northern Fantail is more subdued in its behaviour, indulging less in tail-fanning and restless flitting from perch to perch. Generally solitary, it is sometimes found in small companies of mixed birds feeding at the edges of rainforest, or in mangrove or open forest. Breeds August-January. Nests 2-20m high.
Sexes: *alike.*
Immatures: *duller.*
Voice: *musical silvery-toned 'just-keep-away-you'; notes of 'chunk-chunk' or 'chip-chip', continued after dark.*   D&MT

48   RUFOUS FANTAIL *Rhipidura rufifrons*   16cm
Taking its name from its lovely fanned flame-like tail, this tame bird darts in quick jerky runs or flights in pursuit of insects. It lives in the lower levels of the dense foliage of rainforest gullies, and migrates northwards beyond the shores of the continent in winter; some straying into drier country or cultivated areas. Breeds October-February. Nests 1-10m high.
Sexes: *alike.*
Immatures: *like adults.*
Voice: *high-pitched tinny but sweet song; call of 'chip'.*   NC

49, 50   CRESTED BELLBIRD *Oreoica gutturalis*   23cm
The Crested Bellbird lives mostly in lightly wooded country of Australia's arid areas. It is seen singly, in pairs, sometimes in loose flocks, and spends much of the time foraging on or near the ground - hopping rapidly as it goes. Its food consists of a variety of seeds, insects including beetles, and especially hairy caterpillars. It has the strange habit of maintaining a larder of these in a live but incapacitated state around the rim of its large nest. As many as 12 caterpillars have been counted, with their hairs often shed. The male chooses a bare vantage point to deliver his song, with crest raised - all the while turning his head from side to side to give a ventriloquial effect. Breeds August-January or in response to rainfall. Nests 1-3m high. Endemic.
Immatures: *like adult female.*
Voice: *the Aboriginal name for the bird Pan-pan-panella reflects its chief song of far carrying melodious notes; also distinctive liquid 'plonks'.*   49GC, 50JG

51   CRESTED SHRIKE-TIT *Falcunculus frontatus* Race *whitei* Northern form   16cm
This uncommon, even rare race, is found only in restricted areas of the Northern Territory and in the Kimberley. There have been few sightings and Graeme Chapman's photograph is therefore of special interest. Compared with its nearest relative, the Eastern Shrike-tit, it is smaller, its upperparts are yellower and its black throat and foreneck have some white barrings. Endemic.
Voice: *like nominate race.*

52, 54   CRESTED SHRIKE-TIT *Falcunculus frontatus* Nominate race Eastern form   19cm
The crested head, robust body and strong bill are features common to all three races of this species. The bill is used to open seed pods or to prise bark off trees to get at larvae. The sound of chunks of bark being ripped away can often be distinctly heard. Solitary or in family parties, it keeps mostly to the highest branches. Sedentary or nomadic. Breeds August-January. Nests in tree fork up to 30m high. Endemic.
Immatures: *browner wings.*
Voice: *several low chattering phrases resembling 'knock-at-the-door'; plaintive piping.*   52EZ, 54JP

53   CRESTED SHRIKE-TIT *Falcunculus frontatus* Race *leucogaster* Western form   17cm
The extreme south-western corner of the continent is the home of this form of the Crested Shrike-tit. A white belly separates it from the northern and eastern forms. Like them, this bird is often located by its calls and by the noise of shredding bark when it is searching for insects and spiders. Endemic.
Male: *similar, except for black throat and more prominent crest.*
Immatures: *like adult females.*
Voice: *like nominate race.*   GC

55, 56   RUFOUS WHISTLER *Pachycephala rufiventris*   17cm
Widely distributed throughout almost the whole of the continent except in heavy forest, the Rufous Whistler's outstandingly beautiful song is amongst the most joyously exuberant of all Australian birds. It will burst into song in response to a clap of thunder, hence its popular name of Thunderbird. It feeds arboreally mainly on insects, occasionally berries, in the south-west it is locally nomadic, and in the south it is migratory, arriving in August and departing around April. Breeds September-February. The female Rufous Whistler is as accomplished a vocalist as the male. Seen in pairs or small migrating groups. Nests low to 10m high.
Immatures: *like adult females but with rufous wing edges.*
Voice: *repeated ringing 'ee-chong' with whipcrack ending; rippling musical 'pee-pee-pee' or 'joey-joey-joey'.*   55D&MT, 56PG

57, 60   WHITE-BREASTED WHISTLER *Pachycephala lanioides*   21cm
Pairs of this striking whistler are to be seen searching for small crustaceans on the muddy floors of northern mangroves, or foraging among foliage for insects. It is an inquisitive and approachable bird, readily responding to imitations of its lively call. Sedentary in well-defined territories. Breeds March-November. Nests in dense mangrove fork 2-5m above the mud. Endemic. **Recognition:** *where their habitats overlap, the female White-breasted Whistler may be differentiated from the female Rufous Whistler by its larger size and bigger bill, and less rufous coloration below.*
Immatures: *male - brown washed olive, white throat; female - like adult female.*
Voice: *rich and musical penetrating whistles 'per-weet', scolding alarm note.*   GC

58, 61   GOLDEN WHISTLER *Pachycephala pectoralis*   18cm
Singly or in pairs, sometimes in small parties, it frequents the dense vegetation of brush, scrub or eucalypt forest, and moves purposely through foliage searching for insects and berries. It may move to open forest to winter. Both sexes are particularly fine and strong singers, especially during the breeding season. Immature birds may wander considerably. Sharp noises like thunderclaps evoke a quick vocal response. Breeds September-January. Nests in bush or tree to 6m high. **Recognition:** *because the male Golden Whistler goes through various plumage changes before he finally and permanently retains his golden colouring, and may often breed in brown plumage, it is not always easy to distinguish the sexes.*
Immatures: *like adult females with rufous margin on wing feathers.*
Voice: *lovely clear whistles with a whipcrack ending*
'chee-chee-chee-chee-tu-whit', and variations.   58BL; 61LR

59, 62   MANGROVE GOLDEN WHISTLER *Pachycephala melanura*   17cm
Very similar in appearance to its close relative the Golden Whistler, except for its black tail, longer bill and slightly smaller size. There are two races: *melanura* Black-tailed Whistler (illustrated) occurring along the north-west coast of WA to the Kimberley region; and *robusta* Robust Whistler occurring along the coasts of the Northern Territory and Queensland. Confined to mangroves and marginal vegetation, it feeds on grubs, ants and beetles, sometimes feeding on the ground.
Voice: *fluid resonant whistles, slower and richer than Golden Whistler.*   GC

63, 64   GILBERT'S WHISTLER *Pachycephala inornata*   20cm
In 1840, John Gould described a specimen collected in South Australia and named it *Pachycephala inornata* (meaning unadorned). In 1845, he also gave species rank to another specimen of the darker and more richly coloured Western Australian population, collected in the York district near Perth by John Gilbert, and named it *Pachycephala gilberti* as a tribute to his young and gifted assistant. Unfortunately, the two populations were later deemed to constitute a single species and the name *gilberti* lapsed under the international rule of priority - leaving Gilbert's name unrepresented among scientific bird names. The species lives in mallee and open forest. Usually in pairs, it quietly forages on or near the ground for insects, berries and seeds. Locally nomadic. Breeds September-December. Nests near the ground in a shrub or low tree. Endemic. **Recognition:** *black in front of eye; female greyish like small Grey Shrike-thrush.*
Immatures: *brown eye instead of red.*
Voice: *variety of rich notes, some ventriloquial; whistling, short 'chop-chop'.*   63B&BW, 64BL

65, 66   OLIVE WHISTLER *Pachycephala olivacea*   22cm
This species has Tasmanian and mainland races. In the north, it is uncommon in its haunts of beech forest at the tops of the highest mountains, where its call is wistful and elusive. In the south, it is more abundant in mountain and coastal thickets and in gardens. Here its lovely bursts of song are ringing, melodious and ventriloquial. Its calls are remarkably varied and it is probably the best songster of all the whistlers. It lives on insects and berries. Locally nomadic. Breeds September-January. Nests low. Endemic.
Immatures: *like adult female with reddish wing tips.*
Voice: *song of 'cheer-weet' or 'I'll-whit-choo' (south),*
'peee-pooo' (north).   65K&BR, 66TW

67   RED-LORED WHISTLER *Pachycephala rufogularis*   21cm
This shy and solitary bird shares a restricted range with that of Gilbert's Whistler, with which it is sometimes confused. It frequents mainly mallee scrubs with dense cover and spends much time on the ground feeding unobtrusively on insects, larvae, seeds and berries. It is very vulnerable to clearance of its habitat. Sedentary. **Recognition:** *cinnamon in front of eye, face and throat, and buff-bellied. Breeds September-December. Nests very low. Endemic.*
Male: *brighter.*
Immatures: *eye brown.*
Voice: *rich clear whistle followed by reedy sibilant notes 'see-ee-saw'.*   GC

68, 69   GREY WHISTLER *Pachycephala simplex*   15cm
This bird is common in the monsoon coastal rainforests and mangroves of the Northern Territory and
Cape York Peninsula. It is sedentary and lives mostly in the treetops, seldom descending to lower levels. It feeds quietly on a variety of insects. Usually solitary, but Cape York birds sometimes forage in
flocks with other birds. There are several races in New Guinea; two in Australia.

68 Race *simplex* (Northern Territory form) **Recognition:** *pale grey-brown above and dull white below.*
Breeds all months and nests sometimes near the ground in a vine tangle, or high in the tree canopy.
Sexes: *alike.*
Immatures: *rufous brown.*
Voice: *persistent melodious and varied song.*   GC

69 Race *peninsulae* (Cape York form) **Recognition:** *tinged greenish-olive above; pale lemon yellow
below.* Breeds September-February. Nests low in vines or high in trees.
Sexes: *alike.*
Immatures: *rufous brown.*
Voice: *persistent melodious and varied song.*   D&MT

70   LITTLE SHRIKE-THRUSH *Colluricincla megarhyncha*   19cm
(A) Race *rufigaster* (illustrated). (B) Race *parvula* (pale rufous below, whitish throat, black bill).
A bird of rainforest, mangroves, gullies, parks and gardens. It forages at all levels of foliage, but main-
ly on the ground in rainforest, for insects and their larvae. It may appear in small feeding parties or in
large mixed flocks. Sedentary. Breeds September-February. Nests 3-5m high.
Sexes: *alike.*
Immatures: *wing coverts edged brown.*
Voice: *rich melodious 'to-whee-wot-wot'. Race parvula: 'eeee, butch-butch-butcher'.*   JP

71, 72   GREY SHRIKE-THRUSH *Colluricincla harmonica*   23cm
The rich melodious voice of this familiar and graceful bird puts it high on the list of the world's best
songbirds. Its pure notes are far-carrying, and are often borrowed by lyrebirds and other mimics.
The species also occurs in New Guinea, and there are several races - three in Australia. These are:
harmonica (Grey Thrush) of the east and south-east; *brunnea* (Brown Thrush) of the far north; and
rufiventris (Western Thrush) of the centre and south-west. Plumages vary progressively (clinally)
from north to south and from east to west, without sharp divisions between the races. The natural
habitat of the species is forest and open woodlands. In the south-east it has adapted well to living
alongside humans, and it is often seen and heard in parks and gardens. In the south-west however,
it has yielded ground to encroaching cultivation. It is carnivorous, and eats a wide range of insects,
lizards, small mammals, nestlings and sometimes carrion. Sedentary. Breeds July-February. Nests
in a wide variety of sites including buildings.
Female: *grey lores.*
Immatures: *bright rufous eyebrow and wing coverts rufous.*
Voice: *a glorious repertoire of melodious notes.*   D&MT

73   BOWER'S SHRIKE-THRUSH *Colluricincla boweri*   21cm
Bower's Shrike-thrush is restricted to the highlands (above 400m) and frequents dense rainforest.
Sometimes visits nearby gardens. Perching quietly and inconspicuously, it watches for prey before tak-
ing insects and their larvae in foliage or on the ground. Sedentary. Breeds October-January. Nests in
tree or vine tangle 1-8m high. Endemic. **Recognition:** *compared with the Little Shrike-thrush, it is a
little larger, has a grey back and head, and is more streaked on the throat and breast.*
Sexes: *alike.*
Immatures: *browner and duller.*
Voice: *varied repertoire of musical calls; silent in winter.*   JP

74   SANDSTONE SHRIKE-THRUSH *Colluricincla woodwardi*   26cm
Named for its habitat in the sandstone gorges and cliffs of northern Australia, this is a terrestrial species, hopping with great agility over rocky outcrops, cliffs and caves in search of insects, especially grasshoppers and spiders. It often sings from a lofty crag, the song ringing and resounding through the natural rock amphitheatre. It is not rare, but rarely observed closely. Sedentary. Breeds November-January. Makes a nest of spinifex roots in rocky fissure. Endemic.
Sexes: *alike.*
Immatures: *darker wings and duller breast.*
Voice: *rich musical songs, clear whistling.*   GC

75   SONG THRUSH *Turdus philomelos*   23cm
This bird was introduced from Britain in 1863 to Melbourne where it has become fairly common in parks and gardens. Introductions elsewhere however all failed and the bird is not seen beyond Melbourne. A ground feeder, it pulls worms from lawns and is fond of snails using a rock as an 'anvil' to smash their shells. Breeds September-January and nests low in dense vegetation.
Sexes: *alike.*
Immatures: *like adults.*
Voice: *a glorious song of repeated phrases which it pours out for hours*
on end, especially at dawn and dusk.   BC/ANT

76   (A) BASSIAN THRUSH *Zoothera lunulata*   Tail 10.7-12.2cm 25-28cm
       (B) RUSSET-TAILED THRUSH *Zoothera heinei*   Tail 8.9-9.8cm 25.5-27.6cm
Previously treated as a subspecies of the Australian Ground Thrush, and with much in common, these two species exhibit distinct differences in voice, plumage, size, habitat and behaviour. The Bassian Thrush occurs widely in Eastern and Southern Australia from Atherton to near Adelaide - and is endemic. The Russet-tailed has a more restricted distribution from northern NSW to near Gympie in Queensland. Where the species overlap on either side of the NSW/Queensland border the Bassian Thrush appears to prefer higher latitudes, and there is no evidence of interbreeding. Both species live in rain forest and wet eucalypt forest, with the Bassian also frequenting heath and teatree. Both hop along among dense ground litter foraging for worms, insects and molluscs - pausing to watch and listen for prey. They often freeze if disturbed. Largely sedentary. Solitary, in pairs or small parties. Males sing particularly at dawn and dusk to proclaim territory in the breeding season. Breeds July-January. Nests in tree stump or fork to 13m high.
Recognition: *very difficult to separate; Russet-tailed a little rustier on rump and upper tail and shows white on outer tail in flight.*
Sexes: *alike.*
Immatures: *like adults.*
Voices: *Bassian - beautiful flute-like song like Blackbird. Russet-tailed - two note*
whistle 'pooo-peeee'. Both species have very sibilant 'seeeet' contact call.   JP

77, 78   COMMON BLACKBIRD *Turdus merula*   25cm
This all-black member of the thrush family was introduced by the Zoological Acclimatization Society of Victoria in Melbourne in 1862 and subsequently to the Hobart Zoo. On the mainland, it has spread slowly northwards, and is still doing so, but the birds remain more numerous in the south. In Tasmania, it is now abundant. It is a familiar sight in gardens, parks, orchards, as well as in natural habitats. It spends much time on the ground and is partial to lawns and short grass where it can probe for worms. In typical thrush fashion, it patters the ground with its feet (perhaps to emulate the sound of falling raindrops) then stops with head turned on one side to 'listen' for a worm. Insects, berries and fruit also form a part of its diet. Breeds September-January and nests in low bushes.
Immatures: *more rufous brow than adult females.*
Voice: *a true prima donna among bird songsters. From a high vantage point, it pours out its melodies in long recitals, especially early and late in the day, and its song carries over long distances. When disturbed, it rushes away protesting loudly with a torrent of*
scolding notes.   77 F&BP/ANT, 78LS

1, 2   SUPERB FAIRY-WREN *Malurus cyaneus* Mainland form   13cm
Popularly known simply as the Blue Wren, it lives in low dense bushy vegetation and will frequent
parks and gardens. It is strongly territorial and, when vocal warnings of the male to competing males
do not suffice, it may engage in aerial battles. It will also attack its image in windows. It often bathes
in a shallow pool, or skims over deeper water, and delights in showering in the rain or under a garden
sprinkler. Normally sedentary, but some individuals become nomadic in winter. Breeds July-March
and may raise several broods. Usually nests low in a bush or tangled thicket. Endemic.
Immatures and young males: *see following note.*
Voice: *light trilling like the tinkling of a small alarm clock.*   1GW, 2PG

Immatures and young males
An intriguing ornithological experience in Australia in the winter months is to encounter a family of
Superb Fairy-wrens on the move in which a single blue male leads a retinue of perhaps a dozen, or
even more, brown birds, which could easily be taken for females. Thanks to close observation, it is
now known that the brown birds comprise a majority of immatures from the nestings of the preceding
breeding season in association with surviving males in eclipse winter plumage from progeny of previous years. The new immature males can be picked out by their black bills and light underparts, and
the older males in eclipse plumage additionally by their blue tails. Shortly after nesting, the dominant
female can often be identified by her tatty and frayed tail. As spring approaches, she drives her daugh-
ters away to find mates of their own, but one or two young males may stay. The female nests several
times during a season, and she is able to do this by the relief afforded from parental duties in feeding
and rearing the young by members of the family who assume the role of 'helpers'. These may be the
older males who stayed or birds from earlier broods who, on reaching maturity, assist with the siblings
of later broods. It may take four years or more before a male ceases to moult into eclipse winter
plumage and wear full adult plumage throughout the year.

3   SUPERB FAIRY-WREN *Malurus cyaneus* Tasmanian form   14cm
The Tasmanian bird is larger than its mainland cousin, has a longer tail, and is a deeper
blue. Its bib is also blue instead of black.   TW

4, 5   SPLENDID FAIRY-WREN *Malurus splendens* Nominate race   13cm
This brilliant blue wren, the south-western counterpart of the Superb Blue Wren, was thought by John
Gould to be more gorgeous than any other of its race. It inhabits dense bushy woodland. Maturing
young stay with the family for one or more seasons, and territories are jealously guarded. Sedentary.
Breeds September-January. Nests within 1m of the ground. Endemic. **Recognition:** *The male, and that
of its close relative the Black-backed Wren (6), are distinguished by their bright violet-blue underparts
crossed with a black band on the upper breast. In most respects its behaviour is similar to that of the
Superb Fairy-wren. It is however markedly shyer, especially the male*
Female: *note bluish tail.*
Immatures: *like females, but tail brown.*
Voice: *trilling, and a single sharp note.*   4AT, 5B&BW

6   SPLENDID FAIRY-WREN *Malurus splendens* Race: *melanotus* Black-backed Wren   13cm
This bird resembles its close relative the nominate race in almost all respects except for a black lower
back and rump. It lives as a widely separate population in mallee, woodland and scrub. It is also shy
and relatively rarely seen. Nests low in a bush.
Female: *brown, tail dull blue, bill light brown.*
Immatures: *like adult female.*
Voice: *high-pitched trilling.*   H&JB

7   SPLENDID FAIRY-WREN *Malurus splendens* Race: *callainus* Turquoise Wren   14cm
The dun colours of mulga scrub, spinifex and saltbush of the arid centre habitat, are the antithesis of
the luminous blue-green colouring of this wren. Within the context of differing environments, its
habits are similar to the others of the species, but it is somewhat more nomadic. Breeds variably, main-
ly November-April. Nests on or close to the ground, well hidden. Endemic.
Female: *like non-breeding male, bill light brown, tail dull blue.*
Immatures: *like females.*
Voice: *trilling.*   AF

8, 9   VARIEGATED FAIRY-WREN *Malurus lamberti* Nominate race   14cm

Living to the east of the Great Dividing Range, the Variegated Fairy-wren is the best known of the chestnut-shouldered wrens. It is shyer than the Superb Fairy-wren, with which it shares territory, and so is less frequently seen. Families up to 10 frequent heathland and open forested country, occasionally parks and gardens. Sedentary. Breeds August-January. Nests on or near ground in dense cover.
Female: *distinguished by a chestnut bill, and a chestnut patch ringing the eye. The tail is dull grey-blue and longer than that of the female Superb Fairy-wren.*
Immatures: *like adult females.*
Voice: *brief high-pitched trills, softer than the Superb Fairy-wren, but more metallic.*   JP

10, 11   VARIEGATED FAIRY-WREN

Malurus lamberti Race: *assimilis* Purple-backed Wren   14cm

The most widely-distributed of the chestnut-shouldered wrens and common in the drier inland areas of all States. Its habitat includes mallee, lightly timbered grassland and a wide variety of low-growing vegetation. Usually in small family parties. Sedentary. Breeds variably, mainly September-January. Nests on or close to the ground. Endemic. **Recognition:** *the male has deeper violet-blue tonings than the males of the nominate race of the Variegated Fairy-wrens, but the differences are slight and difficult to detect in the field.*
Female: *like males in eclipse plumage, but bill chestnut.*
Immatures: *like adult females.*
Voice: *like nominate race.*   10GC, 11T&PG

12   VARIEGATED FAIRY-WREN

Malurus lamberti Race: *dulcis* Lavender-flanked Wren   14cm

This race of the Variegated Fairy-wren is distinguished by the lavender flanks of the male (although not always obvious) and the blue-grey upperparts of the female. It lives among the rugged sandstone ridges of the Kimberley and Arnhem Land, in low vegetation. It is continually on the move usually in small parties. Breeds October-December. Nests low. **Female:** *blue-grey upper parts and tail.*
Immatures: *like females.*
Voice: *short sharp notes and trills.*   GC

13, 16   LOVELY FAIRY-WREN *Malurus amabilis*   14cm

Restricted to the humid coastal parts of Cape York Peninsula south almost to Townsville, the Lovely Fairy-wren frequents the edges of mangroves, rainforest and streams. In pairs and family parties, it forages on or close to the ground, usually in dense cover. Sedentary. Breeds September-December. Nests low or on the ground in dense cover. Endemic. **Recognition:** *the female, unlike the females of the other blue wrens, is almost as brightly coloured as the male.*
Immatures: *like adult females; young males have black bills.*
Voice: *faint trilling, more feeble than the others of the species.*   H&JB

14, 17   BLUE BREASTED FAIRY-WREN *Malurus pulcherrimus*   14cm

The indigo-blue breast of the male, when caught in strong light, beautifully sets off the chestnut shoulders, and distinguishes him from the black-breasted male of the very similar Purple-backed Wren whose range partially overlaps. It lives in scrubby mallee, heathland or swampy areas of southern Western Australia and in South Australia. Its behaviour is similar to but quieter than the other fairy wrens. Typically the male is shyer and keeps in the background. Gregarious, it forages in small parties on or near the ground. Sedentary. Breeds August-September. Nests well hidden low in a small bush.
Immatures: *like female, but bill brown.*
Voice: *thin trilling.*   GC

15, 18   RED-BACKED FAIRY-WREN *Malurus melanocephalus*   13cm
The Red-backed Fairy-wren is one of the smallest of the fairy wrens and the name Elfin Wren is among its alternative names. It is also unique in the complete absence of blue in its plumage, but its flashing scarlet 'saddle' nevertheless makes it a spectacular little bird. The toning of this red is however variable and may fade in different seasons. Sometimes too, the male breeds in brownish plumage. It is seen in pairs or family parties and favours thick grassland associated with a wide variety of other vegetation. It is common within its range. Sedentary. Breeds August-January. Nests low.
Female: *pale-brown above, with no chestnut around eye.*
Immatures: *like adult females.*
Voice: *trilling.*   CW

19   WHITE-WINGED FAIRY-WREN
        Malurus leucopterus Nominate race: Black-and-white Wren   13cm
The black-and-white form of the species was the first to be discovered - by the French naturalists Quoy and Gaimard in 1818 on Dirk Hartog Island off the west coast of Australia. It is also to be found on Barrow Island some 500km to the north. It moves in pairs and family groups through the vegetation of the islands. Sedentary. Breeds July-September. Nests in dense bush close to the ground. Endemic.
Female: *light brown above, paler below.*
Immatures: *like females.*
Voice: *weak trilling.*   B&BW

20, 21   WHITE-WINGED FAIRY-WREN
        Malurus leucopterus Race: *leuconotus* Blue-and-white Wren   13cm
On the mainland, the plumage of the species is always blue-and-white. It has a very wide range over the drier parts of the continent, and frequents treeless plains with shrubs, spinifex and grass thickets and is often the dominant bird. Habits are similar to those of other fairy wrens. The male is especially wary in the family party, which may number 20 birds, and many observers have commented on the ability of a whole family group to melt into the vegetation with astonishing speed when alarmed. Sedentary or locally nomadic. Breeds mainly July-September. Nests low. Endemic.
Immatures: *like adult females, tail brown.*
Voice: *like the sound of a fishing reel being wound.*   20TL, 21D&MT

22   RED-WINGED FAIRY-WREN *Malurus elegans*   14cm
Also known as the Elegant Wren. It lives in dense wet thickets fringing freshwater swamps and creeks and the undergrowth of jarrah and karri forests and is difficult to observe. Its name describes the rufous wing area common to all the chestnut-shouldered group. Slightly larger than its relatives. Gregarious and sedentary. Breeds August-January. Nests close to ground near water.
Female: *grey-brown above, pale below; tail dull blue.*
Immatures: *like females, tail brown.*
Voice: *trilling.*   GC

23   PURPLE-CROWNED FAIRY-WREN *Malurus coronatus*   to 15cm
Found only in two isolated areas of the far north of Australia, it is the least known and most unusual of the fairy wrens, being larger than the others. Its lovely lilac coloration, so distinctive, is not only unique among the wrens, but very rare in all Australian bird species. It was named by Gould from specimens collected on A.C.Gregory's expedition across north Australia in the 1850s. Sedentary. Family parties search for insects and their larvae, moving swiftly through dense riverside vegetation, keeping mainly in the shadows, but sometimes catching insects on the wing. Females and immatures are inquisitive; as usual, the male is more retiring. Breeds most of the year. Nests in grass or Pandanus thicket near water, bulkier than other wren nests.
Immatures: *similar to adult females, but crown brown.*
Voice: *loud sustained 'chicka-chicka-chickaa-chicka' often as a duet.*   GC

24, 25 SOUTHERN EMU-WREN *Stipiturus malachurus*   20cm
The eastern population of the Southern Emu-wren inhabits dense undergrowth in swampy areas, coastal dunes and heath, whilst in south-western Australia it occurs in dry sandplain heath. Like the fairy-wrens, the species lives in pairs and family groups. It is unusually timid and, except when flushed, seldom exposes itself. It will then quickly drop to cover and scurry away mouse-like to disappear in the undergrowth. At the time of settlement, the Southern Emu-wren was common around Sydney, but it is now much rarer, and always difficult to spot. Sedentary. Breeds July-January. Nests near ground. Endemic. **Immatures:** *duller.*
Voice: *thin very high-pitched trilling.*   24B&BW, 25F&BP

26   (A) RUFOUS-CROWNED EMU-WREN *Stipiturus ruficeps*   13cm
          (B) MALLEE-EMU-WREN *Stipiturus mallee* (illustrated)   15cm
The smaller first-named bird is distinguished by a plain rufous crown. Both species live in and nest in spinifex clumps - the first in sandy stony country, the second in the under-storey of mallee eucalypt country on the SA/Victoria border. They are extremely shy and secretive and feed on insects. Breed September-January. Endemic.
Females: *blue bib absent.*
Immatures: *like females.*
Voice: *thin high trills.*   BL

27   THICK-BILLED GRASSWREN *Amytornis textilis*   18cm
The species inhabits thick saltbush on inland plains and around salt lakes. Populations have declined alarmingly. Timid and elusive, it hides within base of bush during heat of day and is difficult to flush. Bounces hastily from bush to bush. In pairs or small groups it feeds on ants, beetles, or berries. Sedentary or nomadic. Breeding related to rainfall. Nests low. Endemic.
Female: *rufous patch on flanks.*
Immatures: *duller, less distinct markings.*
Voice: *silvery melodious song; reeling or buzzing call, squeaky alarm.*   GC

28   WHITE-THROATED GRASSWREN *Amytornis woodwardi*   21.5cm
Inhabiting the rugged sandstone escarpments of west Arnhem Land, it scurries secretively over rocky outcrops with head and tail lowered. Sometimes it watches intruders curiously from cover in rock crevices, or sits on an open perch to sing with the head thrown back. In pairs or parties it feeds in damp gullies on insects and seeds. Sedentary. Breeds December-March. Nests in porcupine grass tussock. Endemic.
Female: *more rufous underneath.*
Immatures: *duller, with buff abdomen.*
Voice: *high-pitched notes.*   GC

29   CARPENTARIAN GRASSWREN *Amytornis dorotheae*   17cm
Discovered only in 1913, this grasswren was named dorotheae after the daughter of the distinguished ornithologist H.L.White. Its habit of keeping low in the spinifex of the remote sandstone ranges of the Gulf country and sheltering among the rocks makes it one of Australia's most elusive and least known birds. Sedentary. Breeds October-March. Nests low in grass or bush. Endemic.
Female: *chestnut underparts.*
Immatures: *duller.*
Voice: *musical song; 'ticking'.*   GC

30   STRIATED GRASSWREN *Amytornis striatus*   17.5cm
The Striated Grasswren has the widest range of the grasswrens but its distribution is patchy. It frequents dense spinifex of inland sandy plains and mallee and exhibits extraordinary agility in threading its way through prickly porcupine grass. Singly or in pairs or small groups it bounces along rapidly near cover when feeding on seeds, ants and beetles. Shy but inquisitive during breeding. Sedentary or nomadic. Breeds variably according to rainfall. Nests in grass tussock. Endemic.
Female: *rufous flanks.*
Immatures: *duller.*
Voice: *silvery trilling, cheeping.*   GC

31   EYREAN GRASSWREN *Amytornis goyderi*   14cm
The Eyrean Grasswren mainly lives and nests in the sandhill canegrass tussocks which grow along the tops of the long ridging dunes of the Simpson Desert, from which it is hard to flush. It eats insects and cane-grass seed, hulling it with its exceptionally strong finch-like bill. Probably highly nomadic, seeking areas where canegrass is in seed following a chance fall of rain. Rainfall may also trigger its breeding. It gets moisture from insects and seems to show no interest in water. It characteristically hops with one foot in front of the other.
Sexes: *similar.*
Immatures: *duller.*
Voice: *high-pitched notes.*   D&MT

32   GREY GRASSWREN *Amytornis barbatus*   20cm
Confined to a few relatively small remote areas on the Bulloo, Diamantina and Cooper River systems, it lives in tall dense clumps of lignum and swamp canegrass, and eats seeds, insects and some water snails. It hops briskly, tail cocked, when feeding, chirping constantly. When calling, it often perches prominently. Dashes to cover when alarmed, tail trailing. Often wanders in groups of up to 15 out of breeding season. Flies low and swiftly. Breeds July-August. Nests low. Endemic.
Female: *less distinct breast markings.*
Voice: *prolonged cricket-like twittering from thicket, especially when disturbed.*   LR

33   BLACK GRASSWREN *Amytornis housei*   23cm
Confined to the Kimberley region of rocky outcrops, gullies and tumbled rocks interspersed with dense spinifex. It forages in small parties for insects and seeds, and darts over the ground with head and tail lowered. It makes short low flights to a rock perch, flicking its tail on alighting. Climbs up and down rocks instead of flying, keeping mostly to the shadows. Sedentary, but small groups wander when not breeding. Breeds probably in the wet season, December-April. Nests in porcupine grass tussock. Endemic. **Female:** *chestnut below.*
Immatures: *duller.*
Voice: *trilling, with bell-like notes.*   GC

34   DUSKY GRASSWREN *Amytornis purnelli*   17cm
Very like the Thick-billed Grasswren except for its thinner bill; it differs chiefly in its preferred habitat of spinifex on rocky hillsides. While grasswren scampering is often described as mouselike, it is most unrodent-like when it perches, tail cocked, on a rock or bush to sing musically, sometimes in duet. Often appearing in parties, it is shy but inquisitive. Distraction displays draw attention away from the nest. Sedentary or locally nomadic. Breeding related to rainfall. Nests low. Endemic.
Female: *similar; female has chestnut flanks.*
Immatures: *duller streaking.*
Voice: *silvery song ending with a quick jangle of notes.*   H&JB

35   FERNWREN *Oreoscopus gutturalis*   14cm
Dusky brown-green plumage helps the Fernwren blend perfectly with its dense shady environment in remote highland rainforest. It dwells on the forest floor, searching amongst leaf litter for insects, spiders and snails, constantly on the move, hopping, bowing the head, and flicking the tail. It is calmly tolerant of observation. Usually alone or in pairs. Sedentary. Breeds August-February. Nests low. Endemic.
Recognition: *its white collar is distinctive.*
Female: *duller.*
Immatures: *brown face and throat.*
Voice: *single high repeated whistle, cheeping and chattering.*   H&JB

36, 37   WHITE-BROWED SCRUBWREN *Sericornis frontalis*   11cm
The bold White-browed Scrubwren is abundant throughout its range and is one of the most popular of the small birds. It lives in undergrowth in a wide variety of low vegetation and is constantly on the move in pairs and parties briskly foraging for insects such as beetles and moths. It advertises its presence with incessant 'zitting'. There are many geographical and taxonomic variations. Illustrated at 37 is the eastern and nominate race (A and B on the map), and at 36 the western subspecies *maculatus* known as the Spotted Scrubwren (D on the map). The Tasmanian subspecies *humilis* (C on the map and not illustrated) is larger, plainer and darker. Sedentary. Breeds July-January. Nests low. Endemic.
Female: *duller.*
Immatures: *duller and browner.*
Voice: *an incessant 'zit-zit' and some oft-repeated musical notes.*   36B&BW, 37JW

38   YELLOW-THROATED SCRUBWREN *Sericornis citreogularis*   14cm
An outstanding songster and an accomplished mimic, incorporating into its song imitations of dozens of other birds. It sings especially at daybreak, generally while moving over the forest floor. It lives deep in rainforest in dense moist gullies. Its long pendulous nest is nearly always slung over water in a dark, sunless spot, a habit which accounts for its being known as 'devil-bird' in Queensland. Sedentary. Breeds August-March. Endemic.
Female: *brown face patch.*
Immatures: *like females.*
Voice: *range of beautiful melodious notes including mimicry; also a sharp 'tchit'.*   JW

39   LARGE-BILLED SCRUBWREN *Sericornis magnirostris*   12-13cm
It is a resident of the same sort of damp forest as the Yellow-throated Scrubwren. However, it feeds in middle or upper foliage levels, not on the ground. It is active and agile, flushing out prey by much fluttering, twittering and chattering. It is seen in groups of up to ten but in the more northerly part of its range it may join mixed flocks of similarly-occupied birds. Sedentary. Breeds July-January. Nests to 10m high, or takes over nest of Yellow-throated Scrubwren, often in turn parasitised by cuckoos. Endemic.
Sexes: *alike.*
Immatures: *paler.*
Voice: *harsh 'chew', twittering; minor mimic.*   D&MT

40   ATHERTON SCRUBWREN *Sericornis keri*   13cm
Only in recent years has this resident of a very restricted range on the Atherton Tablelands been declared a separate species from the Large-billed Scrubwren, which it closely resembles, and the minimal differences make them difficult to identify in the field. Usually solitary, rarely in pairs. Sedentary. Breeds possibly July-February. The only nest so far reported was close to the ground. Endemic. **Recognition:** *(cf the Large-billed Scrubwren): slightly larger, longer legs and bill, forehead and face darker, feeds on the ground.*
Sexes: *alike.*
Immatures: *bright yellow-ish underparts.*
Voice: *chatter.*   T&PG

41   TROPICAL SCRUBWREN *Sericornis beccarii*   11cm
This small scrubwren occurs in Australia only in the northern rainforests of Cape York Peninsula. In pairs and parties, the species actively forages in middle levels of foliage for insects. Probably sedentary. Breeds October-December. Nests close to ground in dense cover.
Sexes: *similar.*
Immatures: *rufous wash on flanks.*
Voice: *musical warblings, grating calls.*   D&MT

42   **RUFOUS FIELDWREN** *Calamanthus campestris*   13cm
This shy bird is patchily spread through arid and semi-arid country and lives in a variety of low vegetation. It hops on the ground, tail erect, when searching for insects and seeds, and scurries mouse-like to cover when alarmed. Usually in pairs and small parties. The male may sing from the top of a shrub, particularly at dawn and dusk. There are many geographical colour variations, but birds in the south-west tend to be greyer. Sedentary. Breeds July-December. Nests on the ground. Endemic.
Sexes: *alike.*
Immatures: *duller and more finely streaked.*
Voice: *'whirr-whirr-chick-chick-whirr-ree-ree'.*
                                                                           GC

43   **STRIATED FIELDWREN** *Calamanthus fuliginosus*   13cm
Confined to the south-eastern corner and Tasmania, it lives in moist coastal swamp and heath. Seen singly, in pairs and small parties, it creeps mouse-like through the undergrowth. It feeds on insects and seeds - hopping on the ground with tail cocked. Males sing from a conspicuous perch sometimes wagging their cocked tails from side to side. Sedentary and strongly territorial. Breeds July-December. Nests on or near the ground in dense cover. Endemic.
Female: *buff-yellow throat tinge.*
Immatures: *like adult females.*
Voice: *similar to Rufous Fieldwren.*
                                                                           TW

44   **REDTHROAT** *Pyrrholaemus brunneus*   12cm
A small chestnut throat patch distinguishes this otherwise drab bird. It is widespread on inland plains and semi-arid areas, and is common in WA. It frequents thick scrub and saltbush, also mulga and mallee. Often calls from the top of a bush. In pairs and family groups it searches low vegetation for insects. Sometimes in flocks of up to 30. Sedentary. Breeds August-December. Nests in a bush clump close to the ground, sometimes used by cuckoos. Endemic.
Female: *lacks throat patch.*
Immatures: *paler than adult female.*
Voice: *twittering and chattering, a rambling melodious song, and a splendid mimic.*   B&BW

45   **SHY HEATHWREN** *Hylacola cauta*   14cm
The Shy Heathwren in the east lives in mallee, a habitat which separates it from the Chestnut-rumped Heathwren. It is in serious danger from mallee clearance. In the west, it lives in dry heathland. Despite its name, it does not appear to be any shyer than its relative - both are timid and elusive. Sedentary. Breeds August-November. Nests near the ground. Endemic.
Female: *duller.*
Immatures: *fawn wash on throat and breast.*
Voice: *'chee-chee-chick-a-dee', some mimicry.*
                                                                           BL

46   **CHESTNUT-RUMPED HEATHWREN** *Hylacola pyrrhopygia*   14cm
This bird with a cocked tail, is usually encountered singly in thick undergrowth of heath, woodland and forest. It is not only an accomplished songster in its own right but has exceptional skill in mimicking the calls of many other birds, one observer identified in a continuous song the voices of fifteen species, ranging from the small Yellow Robin to the large Yellow-tailed Black Cockatoo. Sedentary. Breeds June-November. Nests low. Endemic. Female: duller.
Immatures: *no streaking on underparts.*
Voice: *long variable melodic song with mimicry of other birds.*
                                                                           D&MT

47   **SCRUBTIT** *Acanthornis magnus*   12cm
Confined to Tasmania, the Scrubtit is found mostly in the quiet ferny gullies, forests and thickets of the west and south-west of the State. Retiring, but it can be 'chirped-up'. It is a most active little bird, scrutinising leaf foliage for insects and hopping up tree trunks in the manner of treecreepers. Sedentary. Breeds September-January. Nests low, often among ferns. Endemic.
Recognition: *(cf the White-browed Scrubwren): longer curved bill, underparts pale lemon-yellow.*
Sexes and immatures: *similar.*
Voice: *whistled 'to-wee-to'.*
                                                                           JP

12 Warblers

1 SPECKLED WARBLER *Chthonicola sagittatus* 12cm
This small ground-frequenting warbler lives mostly in open woodland. Usually in family parties, often in company with thornbills, it hops briskly over the ground foraging for insects and seeds among grass and leaf litter. It is often parasitised by the Black-eared Cuckoo with matching chocolate-red eggs coloured with a rub-off pigment. Breeds September-January. Domed nest on ground near cover. Endemic.
Male: *eyebrow black instead of red-brown.*
Immatures: *less streaking on underparts.*
Voice: *subdued warbling song, also short 'zzt' contact call; accomplished mimic.* GW

2 ROCKWARBLER *Origma solitaria* 14cm
The Rockwarbler is the only Australian bird restricted to New South Wales, where it lives in coastal sandstone between the Hunter River and the Clyde River. It is unique among Australian warblers in building its nest in a cave or deep rock crevice, sometimes even in the dark places of man-made structures. It feeds on insects and seeds. Breeds August-December. The spherical nest with side entrance is suspended from the rock undersurfaces with spider's web. Endemic.
Sexes: *similar.*
Immatures: *duller.*
Voice: *sad shrill 'goodbye' also a chattering note; minor mimic.*
Sings even when being handled by bird banders. GW

3 BROWN GERYGONE (Warbler) *Gerygone mouki* 10cm
Common in pairs and small parties usually feeding in middle storey of rain forest. The birds north of Mackay (race *mouki*) are greyer above and buffer below than those south of Queensland (race *richmondi*). An intermediate race *amalia* is named for Frau Amalie Dietrich, the German naturalist who spent the years 1864-72 in the Queensland bush collecting for a Hamburg museum. Breeds September-February. Intricate, beautiful hanging nest near water. Endemic.
Sexes: *alike.*
Immatures: *like adults.*
Voice: *(south) busy repetitive 'what-is-it', 'which-is-it'; (north) musical*
'having-a-good-time'; minor mimic. JDW

4 LARGE-BILLED GERYGONE (Warbler) *Gerygone magnirostris* 12cm
In Australia the Large-billed Gerygone is often called the Floodbird because of its habit of building a nest hanging over water skilfully camouflaged as flood debris. It frequents coastal moist vegetation and forages on middle and lower levels of foliage for insects. Usually seen singly or in pairs. Sedentary. Breeds September-April. Nest is a loose slender dome with ragged tail 50cm long, and often near a wasp nest.
Sexes: *similar.*
Immatures: *similar to adults, brown eye.*
Voice: *long cadence of repeated notes gradually slowing and descending*
like a spring unwinding. EZ

5 DUSKY GERYGONE (Warbler) *Gerygone tenebrosa* 12cm
This, the largest of the warblers, frequents the mangroves, swamps and scrubby creeks of the north-western coasts and is one of the least known. Its habits are apparently similar to those of other warblers, including working over foliage to snap up insects, sometimes in small loose feeding groups. Breeds October-March. Domed suspended short-tailed nest. Endemic.
Sexes: *alike.*
Immatures: *underparts washed pale yellow.*
Voice: *a hesitant four-note warble.* GC

6 MANGROVE GERYGONE (Warbler) *Gerygone levigaster* 12cm
The Mangrove Gerygone occurs in Australia as two races: race *levigaster* along the north coast, smaller and white below, and race *cantator* on the east coast, rustier above. The latter has slowly extended to south of Sydney in the past twenty years. Usually in pairs mostly in coastal mangroves and margins of rivers and creeks and forages for insects. Unafraid and extremely active. Breeds September-April, longer in the north. Domed suspended nest 1-8m above ground.
Sexes: *alike.*
Immatures: *underparts pale yellow wash.*
Voice: *sweet jaunty warble descending the scale.* EZ

7 WESTERN GERYGONE (Warbler) *Gerygone fusca* 10cm
Also known as the White-tailed Gerygone. This species occurs in several isolated populations across the continent. It differs from all the other warblers of the genus in its adoption of the drier inland areas where it lives in open forest and mallee scrub. Singly or in pairs, it forages mostly in the canopy for insects. Breeds September-January. Nest slender-tailed suspended from twig. Endemic.
Recognition: *broad band of white to base of tail.*
Sexes: *alike.*
Immatures: *underparts pale yellow wash.*
Voice: *similar but slower than White-throated Gerygone.* GC

8 GREEN-BACKED GERYGONE (Warbler) *Gerygone chloronotus* 10cm
This species occurs in Australia only in the northern monsoon rainforests and mangroves from the Kimberley region to Arnhem Land, where it is abundant. It is a common garden bird in Darwin and is fearless. In pairs and loose flocks it forages for insects in the outer foliage. Breeds mainly October-April. Nests in small trees up to 10m.
Sexes: *similar.*
Immatures: *duller.*
Voice: *delicate warbling song similar to the White-tailed Gerygone.* IM

9 WHITE-THROATED GERYGONE (Warbler) *Gerygone olivacea* 11cm
Popularly known as the Bush Canary for its distinctive song which is one of the first to be heard in spring. It is quiet and unobtrusive during the non-breeding period. Its habits are similar to those of other warblers, except for the northwards migration of the southern birds to overwinter. Breeds sporadically in the north and often nests in ant-infested trees up to 12m.
Sexes: *similar.*
Immatures: *yellow on throat.*
Voice: *repeated cascades of falling silvery notes.* KI

10, 11, 12 FAIRY GERYGONE (Warbler) *Gerygone palpebrosa* 11cm
The range of the Fairy Gerygone spreads from New Guinea into eastern Australia, where two races are recognised - (A) *personata* Black-throated Gerygone (illustrated) in Cape York to about Cooktown and (B) *flavida* to the south. The former is characterised by the black/brown throat of the male which progressively disappears where the two populations intergrade in the region of Cooktown. The females of the two races are indistinguishable and the markedly different male plumage of race *personata* is the only instance in Australia where a warbler is sexually dimorphic. The species frequents coastal rainforests and mangrove and forages in the outer foliage for insects. It is seen in pairs during the breeding season and is strongly territorial. It gathers in family parties in the non-breeding period sometimes with other species. Breeds sporadically throughout the year, especially October-March, and has the remarkable habit of siting its nest close to a wasp nest. It plays unwilling host to egg-laying by bronze-cuckoos.
Recognition: *the female of (A) is easily confused with the Green-backed Honeyeater (Section 13 no. 15). The eye of the gerygone has a distinctive red iris.*
Sexes: *race flavida similar.*
Immatures: *yellow wash on throat.*
Voice: *twitters constantly, tinkling undulating warble.* 10EZ, 11,12D&MT

13,14   WEEBILL *Smicrornis brevirostris*   8cm
The smallest bird in Australia, with an unusually short bill - hence Weebill and brevirostris which means
'short bill'. Widespread almost throughout the continent. Plumage grades regionally from brown in the southern populations to yellow in the interior, the north and the west of the continent with many intermediate variations. The brown and yellow birds were formerly recognised as two species *S.flavescens* (Yellow Weebill)
and *S. brevirostris* (Brown Weebill). In pairs or in loose parties, it frequents a wide range of habitats, with a
preference for the drier eucalyptus forests and woodlands. It behaves much like the thornbills in flitting and
hovering in and over foliage in search of insects. Breeds August-February, south; October-May, north. Neat
domed nest with narrow spout-like entrance suspended in tree 1-10m or more from ground. Endemic.
Sexes: *alike.*
Immatures: *duller.*
Voice: *short clear whistling coil 'wee-winnie-wield', sometimes sustained song.*   13K&BR, 14JE

15   MOUNTAIN THORNBILL *Acanthiza katherina*   10cm
This species is confined to rainforest and nearby stream vegetation above 400m between Townsville and
Cooktown. It feeds actively on insects in high foliage in pairs and small parties. Although its plumage is
normally yellow-green, this varies according to locality, becoming less yellow at increasing altitudes. Breeds
September-January. Domed nest with slightly hooded entrance of grass and stalks faced with moss. Endemic.
Recognition: *although closely resembling the Brown Thornbill, the most distinguishing characteristic is a
creamy-white eye.*
Sexes: *similar.*
Immatures: *duller.*
Voice: *sweet warbling similar to Brown Thornbill.*   H&JB

16.   BROWN THORNBILL *Acanthiza pusilla*   10 cm
Singly and in pairs, it frequents wet areas with dense undergrowth and sometimes seen in gardens. An
acrobatic feeder in the foliage while looking for insects and spiders. Five races are recognised, the northern
birds being brighter, the northernmost race *mcgilli* (from Eungella) is very yellow. In western Victoria it
intergrades with the Inland Thornbill. Breeds August-December. Rather an untidy nest of fibre and moss
close to the ground. Endemic.
Recognition: *large dark-red eye and streaked breast.*
Sexes: *alike.*
Immatures: *duller,*
Voice: *varied musical notes and 'tzit-tzit' calls. Accomplished mimic and, like the Rock Warbler, is reported
to sing even while being banded.* .

17   INLAND THORNBILL *Acanthiza apicalis*   11cm
Also called the Red-rumped and Broad-tailed Thornbill, replacing the Brown Thornbill in the drier country
over much of the continent. It also inhabits wet eucalypt forest in the west. Singly or in pairs it forages for
insects mainly in low shrub, but also in trees. There are variations in plumage and rump colour and three
races are recognised. Breeds July-December. Nests in low branches of tree or shrub. Endemic.
Recognition: *rump brighter red and forehead more scalloped than Brown Thornbill.*
Sexes: *alike.*
Immatures: *duller.*
Voice: *strong song with mimicry.*   GC

18   TASMANIAN THORNBILL *Acanthiza ewingii*   10cm
Confined to Tasmania and the Bass Strait Islands, it is difficult to distinguish from its close relative, the
Brown Thornbill, which also occurs in Tasmania. It, however, prefers the wet forest while the latter keeps to
dry forest. They co-exist where their ranges meet without inter-breeding. Breeds August-December. Nests in
outer branches of small tree or shrub. Endemic.
Recognition: *longer legs, smaller bill and paler underparts than the Brown Thornbill.*
Sexes: *alike.*
Immatures: *paler.*
Voice: *musical warbling.*   JP

19   CHESTNUT-RUMPED THORNBILL *Acanthiza uropygialis*   10cm
The Chestnut-rumped Thornbill, whose bright rufous rump is very apparent in flight, is seen in family parties and small nomadic flocks. Its range includes the drier inland areas. It frequents a variety of habitats including woodland, scrub and garden and is often seen near buildings. It feeds on the ground on insects and seeds. Breeds July-December. Nests in variety of places including hollow timber and buildings. Endemic.
Recognition: (cf Inland Thornbill) *pale eyes.*
Sexes: *alike.*
Immatures: *duller.*
Voice: *animated twitter and occasional mimic.*   ILM

20   SLATY-BACKED THORNBILL *Acanthiza robustirostris*   9cm
Dense scrub and mulga in isolated arid inland territory is the home of this small thornbill. Probably season-ally nomadic. It usually forages in pairs arboreally for insects and caterpillars, also on the ground. Breeding is rainfall-related. Nests in slender branches, usually about 2m high. Endemic.
Recognition: *iris dark red-brown; forehead streaked black (c/f Inland Thornbill) breast is not streaked.*
Sexes: *alike.*
Immatures: *like adults.*
Voice: *loud vigorous with call like 'wi-pu-chew'; also sibilant 'ssew' like Chestnut-rumped Thornbill.*   JD

21   WESTERN THORNBILL *Acanthiza inornata*   10cm
This plain bird is common in the woodland areas of south-west Western Australia, including Kings Park in Perth. It forages in pairs or small parties of 5-15 birds for tiny insects in the foliage or on the ground. Breeds July-December. Nests close to the ground in low shrub. Endemic.
Recognition: *plain plumage, short tail, pale eye.*
Sexes: *alike.*
Immatures: *paler*
Voice: *feeble tinkling twittering, with mimicry.*   BG

22   BUFF-RUMPED THORNBILL *Acanthiza reguloides*   11cm
The Buff-rumped Thornbill varies in appearance and habit throughout its range. The most distinctive variant is the race *squamata*, ranging from the Atherton Tablelands south to Mackay, which has much brighter yellow underparts and rump. The northern birds, also known as the Varied Thornbill, frequent the tree tops as often as the ground, while the southern birds are mainly terrestrial. The species is fairly common and usually seen in small flocks of up to 15 birds. Breeds August-December. Variety of nest sites less than 2m from ground. Endemic.
Sexes: *alike.*
Immatures: *duller*
Voice: *very similar to Yellow-rumped Thornbill, less melodious.*   T&PG

23   SLENDER-BILLED THORNBILL *Acanthiza iredalei*   9cm
Also known as the Samphire Thornbill. Sparsely distributed across its range, with some geographic plumage variations, it characteristically frequents samphire and saltbush on margins of inland salt lakes, saltbush or dense arid mallee heath and is usually seen in small parties searching for insects. It is shy and groups quickly scatter to cover. Breeds mainly July-November. Nests in low vegetation. Endemic.
Sexes: *alike.*
Immatures: *like adults.*
Voice: *quiet twitter, warbles especially in flight.*   GC

24   YELLOW-RUMPED THORNBILL *Acanthiza chrysorrhoa*   10cm
The best known and most widespread of the terrestrial thornbills. In pairs and small parties, often with other thornbills, it is seen in all foliaged areas including parks and gardens. It is relatively unafraid of humans. Breeds June-December, or after rain. Nests in drooping foliage 2-10m high, sometimes in nests of other birds. For reasons unknown, it builds an open cup false nest over the domed structure in which the eggs are laid. Endemic.
Recognition: *bright yellow rump and black spotted crown.*
Sexes: *alike.*
Immatures: *like adults.*
Voice: *described as a showering silvery cadence of animated notes.*   EZ

25   YELLOW THORNBILL *Acanthiza nana*   9cm
This, the yellowest and smallest of the thornbills, frequents a wide variety of habitats ranging from forest to parks and gardens where it readily accepts the proximity of people. It feeds on insects on outer foliage especially of acacia and casuarina and is rarely on the ground. Inland birds are paler. Breeds August-December. Nest suspended 3-12m up from outer branches of trees. Endemic.
Recognition: *(cf) Weebill) bill longer, pale eyebrow absent.*
Sexes: *alike.*
Immatures: *like adults.*
Voice: *constantly repeated sharp metallic 'ts-ts', 'ts-ts-ts' with a thin note through it.*   K&BR

26   STRIATED THORNBILL *Acanthiza lineata*   10cm
Forages mainly in the canopy of eucalypts for leaf-dwelling insects. It is sociable and is at home in suburban gardens. There is some geographic variation and four races are recognised. Small flocks of 15-20 birds may gather in the non-breeding season often with other species. A banded bird, retrapped after an interval of 11 years suggests that the species has a long life span. Breeds July-December. Nest is suspended from a branch from 3-10m up. Endemic.
Sexes: *alike.*
Immatures: *darker and duller.*
Voice: *extremely high-pitched continuous chatter, 'zit-zit-zit'.*   RG

27   SPINIFEXBIRD *Eremiornis carteri*   15cm
In reluctant feeble fluttering flight, the ground-frequenting Spinifexbird seems to be hindered by its heavy wedge-shaped tail (a diagnostic feature). It hops quickly across open ground with tail erect and moves through clumps of spinifex by clinging to the stems, with its tail used for balance. It feeds on insects and plant matter. Breeds August-April. Nests in a spinifex clump. Endemic.
Sexes: *alike.*
Immatures: *paler.*
Voice: *a rapid chirrup, with repeated variations 'chidlee-dt', 'chpee-it'; contact call a repeated 'tk'.* GC

28   SOUTHERN WHITEFACE *Aphelocephala leucopsis*   10cm
This bird is still as familiar around country homesteads as it once was in the outskirts of towns of the south before domestic and feral cats helped reduce its numbers. In family or mixed parties, it hops busily over the ground in search of grass seeds, often with thornbills. There is minor variation of flank colour progressively across Australia and three races are recognised. Breeds July-December. Nests in shrubs and low trees, and in any convenient repository around farm buildings. Endemic.
Sexes: *alike.*
Immatures: *like adults.*
Voice: *twitters and sweet silvery song.*   D&MT

29   BANDED WHITEFACE *Aphelocephala nigricincta*   11cm
Widespread in the arid inland, it lives in spinifex or on stony flats with scattered shrubs, and behaves very much like other whitefaces. In pairs and small parties, it hops over open ground foraging for seeds and moist-bodied insects. It moves seasonally as conditions dictate. Breeds February-August. Bulky domed nest in prickly bush, lined with flowers and feathers, and with narrow entrance tunnel also lined. Endemic.
Sexes: *alike.*
Immatures: *browner and paler.*
Voice: *twittering when feeding; musical trill sometimes in flight.*   D&MT

30   CHESTNUT-BREASTED WHITEFACE *Aphelocephala pectoralis*   10cm
In remote gibber plains and desert tablelands studded with low shrubs in South Australia, this bird lives out its life away from the eyes of all except those who set out to track it down. In pairs and small companies, often with other whitefaces, it hops over the ground in search of seeds and insects. It is nomadic, according to seasonal conditions, and is shy, flying to cover if disturbed. Breeds August-September, sometimes seasonally. Loose globular nest with side entrance. Endemic.
Sexes: *similar.*
Immatures: *paler chest band, with some dark spots.*
Voice: *softer, more plaintive than Banded Whiteface.*   GC

31   TAWNY GRASSBIRD *Megalurus timoriensis*   17-19cm
During the nesting season, the male performs an impressive display flight, soaring to hover in a crescendo of song to proclaim its territory. It frequents rank grassy vegetation or open forest with thick understorey. It is extremely secretive, and rarely shows itself except when climbing briefly to stem top to observe intruders. Sedentary or occasionally nomadic. Breeds August-April. Cup shaped nest in deep grass.
Sexes: *alike.*
Immatures: *darker brown.*
Voice: *(in cover) persistent 'tsi-lik'; (in flight) loud musical trill, ascending then descending the scale.*   JP

32   LITTLE GRASSBIRD *Megalurus gramineus*   15cm
This smaller grassbird of the wetlands keeps close to the cover of moist reedbeds near the edge of water.It is equally difficult to see, even when its song comes from a point close by. It can, however, be coaxed from cover by mimicry. Sometimes scurries over mud in search of insect prey. Calls from top of bush. Sedentary but may make long flights to temporary inland swamps. There are minor plumage variations over its widely spread distribution. Endemic.
Sexes: *alike.*
Immatures: *paler.*
Voice: *plaintive, drawn-out three-note 'pip-pooo-pooo'.*   GC

33   CLAMOROUS REED-WARBLER *Acrocephalus stentoreus*   17cm
The Reed Warbler is notable for its glorious song and in Australia lives in moist wetlands where reeds grow, but is scarce in Tasmania. Southern populations in eastern Australia migrate northwards after breeding. Breeds September-February. Nests in skilfully-woven cups 'laced' to reed stems or willow branches over water.
Sexes: *alike.*
Immatures: *darker brown.*
Voice: *its wonderfully melodious song is poured forth constantly in the breeding season, at night too, and is unsurpassed even by the European Nightingale.*   RMcL

34, 35   GOLDEN-HEADED CISTICOLA *Cisticola exilis*   10cm
It nests in vegetation where it can cobble living leaves into the structure, hence the previous name of Tailorbird. These are stitched together along their edges in combination with grasses using a thread of spider-web or fibre - and even cotton, rayon and wool where the birds live near inhabited areas. The female uses her beak as a needle and the male gathers the 'thread' for her. The number of leaves used varies with their size and counts have ranged from three to forty-five in a nest built in a verbena bush. Nests are entered from the side and are softly lined. The male has a golden crown only during the breeding season. At other times, his head becomes streaked like that of the female and he grows a longer tail. The species frequents reed beds and swampy vegetation in open areas and is often abundant. It feeds on insects. Breeds September-March. Nests in thick vegetation close to the ground.
Female: *lacks golden crown of breeding male.*
Immatures: *yellow underparts.*
Voice: *incessant buzzing and pretty ventriloquial song of liquid notes usually delivered briefly on popping up to a reed top or some other vantage point.*   34T&PG, 35CW

36   ZITTING CISTICOLA *Cisticola juncidis*   10cm
This species has only recently been reported in Australia from a few isolated coastal areas. Its habits are similar to those of its Golden-headed relative, from which it is difficult to distinguish, except for the head markings of the male Zitting which remain striped during the breeding season. Breeds December-April. Builds nest in grass clump near the ground with green leaves occasionally stitched in. The calls however differ.
Female: *crown more streaked.*
Immatures: *similar to female but duller.*
Voice: *male - 'zit-zit' or 'lik-lik'; female calls infrequently*   GC

13 Honeyeaters

1   WHITE-NAPED HONEYEATER *Melithreptus lunatus*   14cm
The birds in the south-west are larger with longer bills and some have a greyish-white eye skin. In the
east and south-east the eye skin is orange-red, and the white nape band fainter. In wet and dry forest
it forages in pairs and parties for insects, keeping mainly to high foliage, and amidst blossoms for nectar and pollen. In the south-east it is migratory, moving northwards in autumn in noisy flocks, returning in spring. Breeds July-January. Nests 5-16m from ground, sometimes host to cuckoos. Endemic.
Sexes: *alike.*
Immatures: *duller, nape crescent indistinct.*
Voice: *subdued, leisurely piping call also a hissing note.*   R&DK

2   WHITE-THROATED HONEYEATER *Melithreptus albogularis*   14cm
Replaces the White-naped Honeyeater in most of tropical Australia. Although the two species overlap
from northern NSW to the Atherton Tablelands, the White-throated differs in having bluish-white skin
above the eyes, and the white nape crescent reaches to the eyes. In the Kimberley they are smaller and
paler. Inhabits forest and woodland, parks and gardens. Breeds January-October. Nests 5-16m from the
ground.
Sexes: *alike.*
Immatures: *duller.*
Voice: *rapid hissing notes; loud clear whistling.*   R&DK

3   BROWN-HEADED HONEYEATER *Melithreptus brevirostris*   13cm
Living in mallee, open forest, arid scrub, parks and gardens, it overlaps much of the range of the White-
naped Honeyeater, whose immatures it resembles. Populations westward have increasingly dark head
plumage. Acrobatically active in foliage, it investigates bark crevices for insects; it also feeds on nectar.
Occurs in small stable flocks when not nesting. Sedentary or locally nomadic. Breeds August-December.
Nests 3-15m from the ground. Endemic.
Sexes: *alike.*
Immatures: *eye patch pale blue, nape crescent duller.*
Voice: *loud and noticeable; calls of 'chick-chick'.*   K&BR

4   BLACK-CHINNED HONEYEATER *Melithreptus gularis*   16cm
In the south-east this honeyeater has an olive-green back and bluish eye crescent. In savannah woodland and dry eucalypt forest it actively keeps to the upper foliage, feeding on insects and nectar. Like
the White-eared Honeyeater it collects hair for its nest. It usually occurs in largish parties, sometimes
in mixed feeding flocks. Sedentary or locally nomadic. Breeds July-December. Nests high in outer
foliage. Endemic.
Sexes: *alike.*
Immatures: *head brown, bill and legs orange.*
Voice: *various high-pitched calls including 'chirrup'; prolonged bursts of singing.*   K&BR

5   GOLDEN-BACKED HONEYEATER *Melithreptus gularis laetior*   16cm
This is the northern race of the Black-chinned Honeyeater, and distinguished from it by a striking gold-
en-yellow back and yellow-green eye crescent. It lives in a variety of habitat from open woodland to
desert scrub. Often in flocks, it feeds on nectar and insects. Sedentary, nomadic in drier regions.
Breeding probably related to rainfall. Very few nests have been found; one in a bauhinia tree was 3m
from ground. Endemic.
Sexes: *similar.*
Immature: *duller, head brown.*
Voice: *like Black-chinned Honeyeater; loud rollicking 'o-swallow-swallow' repeated.*   GC

6   BLACK-HEADED HONEYEATER *Melithreptus affinis*   14cm
Confined to Tasmania and the Bass Strait Islands where it is common. It is the only bird of the
Melithreptus group to lack a whitish nape. It lives in forest, woodland and heath, and forages in noisy
flocks in middle and outer foliage for a variety of insects. Occasionally takes nectar. Nomadic in win-
ter. Breeds October-January. Nests to 20m high in outer foliage; host to cuckoos. Endemic.
Female: *smaller.*
Immatures: *paler; throat whitish yellow.*
Voice: *sharp whistling; soft 'chip'.*   TW

7   STRONG-BILLED HONEYEATER *Melithreptus validirostris*   18cm
Confined to Tasmania and the Bass Strait Islands, where it is common in forest and scrub and is usu-
ally seen in pairs and flocks. It feeds mainly on insects, their larvae and spiders. These are often prised
from trunks of trees and flocks splitting and stripping bark in a patch of forest, calling as they go, set
up quite a noise. Falling debris also marks their presence. It is seldom seen in blossom seeking nectar.
Breeds July-December. Nests 5-25m from the ground, possibly in loose colonies. Endemic.
Female: *smaller.*
Immatures: *bill, legs and eye patch orange.*
Voice: *loud rattling noises; call of 'cheep'.*   TW

8   GREEN-BACKED HONEYEATER *Glycichaera fallax*   12cm
This predominantly New Guinea honeyeater is confined in Australia to a small area of rainforest at the
top of Cape York Peninsula. Usually in pairs, it moves non-stop from the tree-tops down almost to the
ground, actively foraging for insects in the foliage.
Sexes: *alike.*
Immatures: *unknown.*
Voice: *thin peeps and twitters.*   D&MT

9   DUSKY HONEYEATER *Myzomela obscura*   14cm
This plain long-billed honeyeater is common in humid tropical rainforest and coastal vegetation of the
north-east. Singly and in pairs, it feeds high in the blossoms for nectar, often with other honeyeaters.
It also takes flying insects on the wing. Locally nomadic. Breeds September-January. Nests in tree
tops.
Sexes: *alike.*
Immatures: *duller.*
Voice: *squeaky trilling chatter 'chrip-chrip-chrip', and harsher notes.*   D&MT

10   SCARLET HONEYEATER *Myzomela sanguinolenta*   11cm
The smallest of the honeyeaters it lives in tall flowering trees and briskly works over the canopy
among the blossoms in loose parties, often with other honeyeaters, probing for nectar and taking
insects with darting and hovering movements - singing as it goes. It is nomadic following the blossoms; the southern birds migrate northwards to winter. Breeds July-January. Nests in foliage to 10m
high.
Female: *upperparts olive-brown, underparts off-white.*
Immatures: *like females.*
Voice: *male's song is a clear and beautiful warble.*   KI

11   BROWN HONEYEATER *Lichmera indistincta*   15cm
Widespread in tropical rainforest, mangrove edges, heath and arid scrub, this honeyeater has one of
the most beautiful songs of all Australian birds. Singly, in pairs and sometimes large flocks in blossom
feeding on insects and nectar. It is much attracted by the red-flowering callistemons. Southern birds
migrate northwards to winter. Breeds June-January. Nests up to 7m.
Female: *smaller, crown olive-brown like back.*
Immatures: *lack yellow behind eye.*
Voice: *a glorious melodious song, very much like the Reed Warbler's.*   EZ

12   WHITE-STREAKED HONEYEATER *Trichodere cockerelli*   16cm
Distinguished by its unusual ruffled throat feathers and also known as the Brush-throated Honeyeater,
this species is found only north of Cooktown on Cape York Peninsula. It lives in eucalypt woodland,
rainforest and watercourse vegetation. Singly, in pairs and small groups, it forages energetically in the
upper foliage for nectar and insects. Locally nomadic, it sometimes gathers in large feeding flocks.
Breeds January-May. Nests low down in bush or small tree often over water. Endemic.
Sexes: *similar.*
Immatures: *duller brown upperparts and yellow on throat.*
Voice: *rarely quiet, with whistling and scolding.*   D&MT

13   RED-HEADED HONEYEATER *Myzomela erythrocephala*   13cm
The Red-headed Honeyeater lives in mangroves and coastal eucalypts of the tropical north. It flits and darts tirelessly among the blossoms in pairs or small flocks feeding on nectar, sometimes in mixed flocks. It also takes insects. Breeds March-September. Nests low in mangrove fork.
Female: *browner, red wash over forehead, cheeks and chin; upperparts grey-brown.* **Immatures:** *like females.*
Voice: *brisk hard 'chirrups'; jingling song.*   GC

14   RUFOUS-BANDED HONEYEATER *Conopophila albogularis*   13cm
A common garden bird in Darwin and recognised by its white throat and reddish breast. It forages actively and acrobatically in tropical blossom and foliage for a wide variety of insects and nectar. It is partly nomadic in search of blossoming trees. Seen in pairs or loose companies, or in mixed feeding parties. Breeds September-April. Nest low over water or to 6m above ground.
Sexes: *alike.*
Immatures: *breast band absent or indistinct.*
Voice: *pretty melodious song with a note of 'swee-wit' or 'swee-swee'.*   JE

15   RUFOUS-THROATED HONEYEATER *Conopophila rufogularis*   14cm
A noisy and conspicuous wanderer in small to large groups in tropical eucalypt forest and woodland following the blossoming trees and shrubs to feed on nectar. It also takes insects from the ground and on the wing. It is never far from water, and often bathes. It is aggressive, and there is much squabbling and fighting within groups, accompanied by display threats of fluffing up neck feathers and raising wings. Breeds mainly September-April. Nests to 7m above ground. Endemic.
Sexes: *alike.*
Immatures: *throat white, belly cream.*
Voice: *constant chattering notes and sharp 'zit-zit' calls.*   GC

16   GREY HONEYEATER *Conopophila whitei*   12cm
Not discovered until 1903, this honeyeater is found only in the remoteness of the inland areas, and has been observed infrequently. In pairs or small parties, it frequents acacia scrub, mulga and spinifex, sometimes in company with thornbills. It feeds on insects and mistletoe berries. Probably nomadic. Thought to breed August-November or in response to rainfall. Nests close to the ground. Endemic.
Sexes: *alike.*
Immatures: *cheeks and throat washed yellow; buff around eye.*
Voice: *succession of rapid high-pitched sibilant notes.*   B&BW

17, 18   PIED HONEYEATER *Certhionyx variegatus*   18cm
The habitat of the Pied Honeyeater ranges from spinifex and mallee scrub of the inland to eucalypt woodland nearer the coast. An unobtrusive and quiet bird except when breeding, it is seen in pairs and small parties, and feeds on blossom, native fruits and occasionally insects. The male performs a territorial flight, rising high while singing, then diving vertically to cover with tail fanned and wings closed. Nomadic in the southern part of the range in autumn. Breeding variable, mainly September-February. nests in a low bush. Endemic. **Recognition:** *(cf male Black Honeyeater): the Pied Honeyeater is much larger and the male lacks black on its belly.*
Immatures: *like females.*
Voice: *whistling 'te-tiee-tee-tee'.*   17GC, 18RayG

19, 20   BLACK HONEYEATER *Certhionyx niger*   12cm
The Black Honeyeater is highly nomadic wherever flowering shrubs are blossoming, with a special liking for red emu-bush (Eremophila). In pairs and flocks, sometimes large, it darts and hovers among the blossoms probing for nectar with its long bill. It also takes insects. Southern birds migrate northwards to winter. During the breeding season the males perform steep song flights. Breeds mainly October-November. Nests low in a bush. Endemic.
Immatures: *like females; greyer.*
Voice: *insect-like 'peeeee'; sparrow-like chirping.*   B&BW

21   **BANDED HONEYEATER** *Certhionyx pectoralis*   14cm
This black and white bird is highly nomadic and wanders in pairs and small parties through the wooded and shrubby country of the tropical north following the flowers and blossoms of such trees as eucalypts, paperbarks, melaleucas and grevilleas. Very large flocks can descend on areas where an exceptional effusion of blossom has occurred. Breeds October-April. Flimsy, almost see-through nest, to 3m high. Endemic.
Sexes: *similar.*
Immatures: *crown brown, underparts buff, breast band brown, mantle scalloped golden-brown.*
Voice: *brisk sharp calls and cheerful song.*   GC

22   **PAINTED HONEYEATER** *Grantiella picta*   16cm
This honeyeater, lives more on mistletoe berries than on the nectar of the flowers of that plant. It is nomadic in pursuit of its favourite food. It may also take insects on the wing. At times it is high and inconspicuous in a tree, but is easily located by its distinctive calling. Singly, in pairs or colonies. Breeds October-March. Nests so frail as to be net-like, 3-20m high. Endemic.
Female: *smaller, duller.*
Immatures: *like females, underparts more spotted.*
Voice: *double whistle with emphasis on second note and loud clear calls of 'georgie-georgie'.*   GW

23   **BROWN-BACKED HONEYEATER** *Ramsayornis modestus*   12cm
The Brown-backed Honeyeater lives in coastal paperbark swamp and mangrove, and feeds on nectar from flowering trees, sometimes in mixed flocks. Also takes insects on the wing. Southern birds migrate northwards to winter, some possibly to New Guinea, where there is also a resident population. They leave in April and return in August. Breeds August-March. Its nest is like the Bar-breasted Honeyeater's.
Sexes: *alike.*
Immatures: *breast more streaked.*
Voice: *typical call of 'mick-mick'; chattering.*   T&PG

24   **BAR-BREASTED HONEYEATER** *Ramsayornis fasciatus*   15cm
A honeyeater of tropical rainforest, woodland near water, and mangrove swamp. Usually in pairs, it works over flowering trees for nectar and insects. Large flocks sometimes gather when blossom is abundant. Breeds mainly October-March. Nest is usually built overhanging water, and its distinctive feature, shared alone with its close relative the Brown-backed Honeyeater, is a side entrance.
Female: *fainter markings.*
Immatures: *head brown not scalloped; bold brown streaking on breast.*
Voice: *rapidly repeated shrill piping note.*   B&BW

25   **STRIPED HONEYEATER** *Plectorhyncha lanceolata*   23cm
The name *lanceolata* (lance-shaped) relates to the bird's long spiky feathers on the throat and upper breast. Its habitat ranges from inland mallee scrub and native pines to dense stands of casuarinas and paperbarks towards the coast. It is active and fearless, and forages in pairs and small parties mainly for insects and fruit, sometimes raiding orchards, less often for nectar. Breeds August-January. Nests in deep cup hung by rim from twigs, 1-10m from ground, often close to the Grey Butcherbird's nest. Endemic.
Sexes: *alike.*
Immatures: *less distinct markings.*
Voice: *loud, rolling melodious song, more tuneful than most other honeyeaters.*   GA

26   **WESTERN SPINEBILL** *Acanthorhynchus superciliosus*   15cm
Restricted to the woodlands, heath and gardens of south-west WA, and frequents Kings Park, Perth. Usually in pairs, it works over a range of flowering shrubs for nectar, such as dryandras, banksias, myrtles, and particularly kangaroo paws. Pollen rubbed off from its hanging flowers onto the spinebill's back is thus carried to pollinate other kangaroo paws. It also takes insects. Breeds September-January. Nests in low bush or tree. Endemic.
Female: *upperparts olive-grey, throat buff-brown, paler orange collar.*
Immatures: *like females.*
Voice: *staccato piping 'kleet-kleet'.*   B&BW

27   EASTERN SPINEBILL *Acanthorhynchus tenuirostris*   16cm
The awl-shaped bill typical of honeyeaters attains its greatest length in the spinebill, and enables it to reach into long tubular flowers. Like hummingbirds, it hovers while feeding, with audible beating wings. Singly or in small groups, it frequents forest, woodland and suburban gardens wherever there are nectar-bearing blossoms. Also takes insects. Breeds October-January. Nests in bush or low tree. Endemic.
Female: *duller, crown grey.*
Immatures: *upperparts grey-olive, underparts fawn.*
Voice: *rapid succession of high piping notes and a soft 'chee-chee'.*   TW

28   LEWIN'S HONEYEATER *Meliphaga lewinii*   21cm
An inhabitant of rainforest, wet eucalypt forest, brigalow, heath, gardens and orchards, from the coast to the higher altitudes. Feeds on native fruits and nectar, hanging acrobatically from branches, also spirals up tree trunks and hovers over foliage for insects. It fearlessly drives off competitors, and is inquisitive. Breeds August-January. Nests are suspended 2-6m above ground. Endemic.
Sexes: *alike.*
Immatures: *not streaked, underparts greenish-yellow.*
Voice: *far-carrying rapid volleys of notes, sometimes likened to machine-gun fire.*   D&MT

29   YELLOW-SPOTTED HONEYEATER *Meliphaga notata*   18cm
The range of this species partly overlaps that of the similar looking Lewin's Honeyeater, but is identifiable by its smaller size, rounder yellow ear patch and different calls. It frequents coastal rainforest, mangroves and gardens, and flits around shrubs and middle level foliage foraging for insects, native fruits, berries and nectar. Breeds September-February. Nests smaller than Lewin's, 1-3m above ground. Endemic.
Sexes: *alike.*
Immatures: *paler, underparts washed ochre.*
Voice: *sharp repeated 'queak" and melodious 'chit'.*   LR

30   GRACEFUL HONEYEATER *Meliphaga gracilis*   16cm
The Graceful Honeyeater is the smallest of the Australian trio of look-alike honeyeaters with yellow facial spots. It lives inconspicuously in coastal forest, mangrove, lantana thickets and gardens, which it shares with the Yellow-spotted Honeyeater. It is slightly smaller, its bill is longer and thinner and it tends to forage higher in the tree canopy, and is particularly acrobatic. Breeds October-February. Pretty suspended cup nest above 2m from ground.
Sexes: *alike.*
Immatures: *alike.*
Voice: *utters sharp 'click' sounds continuously.*   LR

31   WHITE-LINED HONEYEATER *Meliphaga albilineata*   19cm
This infrequently seen bird of the Kimberley region and Arnhem Land lives in pockets of monsoon forest in rocky gorges and sandstone escarpments. Singly, in pairs and in loose flocks it eats native fruits, seeds and insects as well as nectar from flowering trees where it forages high in the canopy. When feeding will drive off smaller birds, and it is inquisitive. Breeds perhaps August-February. Nests 1-5m above ground. Endemic.
Sexes: *alike.*
Immatures: *alike.*
Voice: *up and down whistles: (Arnhem Land) drawn out; (Kimberley) rapidly repeated.*   K&BR

32   WHITE-EARED HONEYEATER *Lichenostomus leucotis*   21cm
This species becomes very tame during the breeding season and a female will fearlessly land on one's head to pluck a hair or onto a sweater to pull a strand for lining its nest (see illustration). In pairs and small parties, it frequents coastal and alpine wooded habitats. It feeds on manna, nectar and insects prised from bark. The western race *novaenorciae* (named after the famous Benedictine monastery just north of Perth) is smaller and darker. Breeds July-April. Nests below 3m. Endemic.
Sexes: *alike.*
Immatures: *duller, crown green, earpatch buff.*
Voice: *ringing notes and 'chop, chop'.*   JF

33   YELLOW-THROATED HONEYEATER *Lichenostomus flavicollis*   21cm
One of Tasmania's endemic honeyeaters. Its habits are similar to those of the White-eared Honeyeater,
including plucking human hair for its nest. It is widespread and abundant, and frequents a wide range
of habitat. Solitary and seen in family parties only during breeding season. Takes insects from foliage,
probes bark, and hawks for flying insects; also feeds on nectar and manna from foliage. Breeds July-
January. Nests in low bush or grass clump, sometimes in foliage to 10m. Endemic.
Sexes: *alike.*
Immatures: *paler.*
Voice: *various warbling notes, rapid 'tonk, tonk' uttered from top-most twig of low tree.*   TW

34   BRIDLED HONEYEATER *Lichenostomus frenatus*   20cm
Restricted to the Cooktown, Atherton and Mount Spec areas, this is a bird with a notable yellow and black bill,
and mainly lives in the highlands; some descend to lower altitudes in winter. Singly, in pairs or small flocks it
frequents high forest and swampy woodland foliage. It is active and aggressive and feeds on insects, nectar and
native fruits. Breeds September-January. nests in cup of stems, ferns and vine tendrils hung in vines or trees up
to 8m from ground. Endemic.
Sexes: *alike.*
Immatures: *more extensive yellow throat patches.*
Voice: *clear melodious whistling and harsh rattling notes.*   T&PG

35   EUNGELLA HONEYEATER *Lichenostomus hindwoodi*   19cm
This bird was known for twenty years before it was named as a new species in 1983. In rainforests it follows flowering trees and mistletoe. Movement to lower altitudes have been reported. In non-flowering
periods it occurs in singles and pairs only, but when flowers are prolific large numbers assemble. Usually
quiet, but noisy when in numbers at food source. Breeds possibly August-December. Nest cup-shaped in
a low bush. Endemic.
Sexes: *alike. Females slightly smaller.*
Immatures: *crown has rufous coloration.*
Voice: *very loud calls, or single note.*   TL

36   SINGING HONEYEATER *Lichenostomus virescens*   19cm
Loud duet singing by pairs from prominent perches may account for the name 'singing', as several other honeyeaters have more tuneful voices. This, the most widespread of honeyeaters, lives in pairs and small flocks in
open habitat ranging from arid scrub to coastal woodland. It feeds on nectar, native fruits and seeds. Northern
birds are smaller and paler and are less streaked on breast. Breeds July-February or depending on rainfall. Nests
low to 5m above ground. Endemic.
Female: *smaller.*
Immatures: *face band paler.*
Voice: *resonant trilling notes.*   GC

37   VARIED HONEYEATER *Lichenostomus versicolor*   20cm
Its bold varied notes are a familiar sound in mangroves and trees lining the streets and waterfronts of
Cairns and other coastal towns of north Queensland, and on the islands of the Barrier Reef.
Quarrelsome, inquisitive and active, in pairs and parties it flits among leaves and blossoms in search
of nectar and insects. Breeds April-December. Nests in mangroves or beachside trees 2-5m above
ground.
Sexes: *alike.*
Immatures: *back browner, not streaked.*
Voice: *varied resonant and melodious notes.*   D&MT

38   MANGROVE HONEYEATER *Lichenostomus fasciogularis*   20cm
Sometimes treated as a race of the Varied Honeyeater and commonly mistaken for it, this mangrove-dweller
has scalloping rather than streaking on the breast. They intergrade between Bowen and Cardwell. A flocking bird of coast and nearby islands, it also visits woodland and gardens near the mangroves to seek out
flowering trees. Breeds August-December, also April-May in the north. Usually nests in mangrove branches low over water. Endemic.
Sexes: *alike.*
Immatures: *upperparts brown, underparts paler.*
Voice: *varied resonant and melodious notes.*   KI

39   PURPLE-GAPED HONEYEATER *Lichenostomus cratitius*   16cm
Distinguished by a thin streak of purple or lilac skin (or wattle) extending from mouth to ear. The widely separate populations are similar, but Kangaroo Island birds have yellow facial streaks. It is shy and usually solitary. In mallee and heath, open woodland in WA, sometimes in gardens, it follows the blossom for nectar and may congregate around flowering trees in large numbers. It also eats insects from foliage, bark and by hawking. Aggressively territorial. Breeds August-December. Nests close to the ground. Endemic. **Sexes:** *alike.*
Immatures: *gape yellow.*
Voice: *harsh chattering notes.*   JP

40   GREY-HEADED HONEYEATER *Lichenostomus keartlandi*   16cm
This honeyeater lives in Australia's arid areas, and frequents low eucalypts, mulga scrub, wooded hillsides, stony gorges and desert dunes. In pairs and small flocks it is constantly on the move visiting florescent eucalypts and wattles for nectar, sometimes in competition with the White-plumed Honeyeater, which it resembles somewhat in behaviour and voice. It also eats insects and the honeydew and manna exuded from insect-damaged foliage. Breeds July-November. Nests in low shrub. Endemic.
Sexes: *alike.*
Immatures: *duller.*
Voice: *petulant 'chip-chip'; cheerful babbling 'chee-toyt'.*   D&MT

41   YELLOW HONEYEATER *Lichenostomus flavus*   19cm
The Yellow Honeyeater frequents open forest, riverside vegetation and mangroves. It is docile, friendly and inquisitive and is a regular visitor to gardens and orchards and is one of the most frequently seen honeyeaters in Townsville. It is jerkily active in search of nectar and insects, usually in pairs, sometimes in company with other honeyeaters. It is sedentary or locally nomadic. Breeds October-March. Nests in bark cup bound with cobweb, up to 19m above ground. Endemic.
Sexes: *alike.*
Immatures: *duller, bill paler.*
Voice: *agreeable and cheerful whistles and notes, with a brisk 't-weet'.*   LR

42   YELLOW-FACED HONEYEATER *Lichenostomus chrysops*   17cm
Common in east and south-eastern Australia and familiarly known as Chick-up from its cheerful call. Singly, in pairs and flocks, it frequents forest woodland and mangrove, and is familiar in suburban gardens. It feeds on nectar in spring and manna in summer and autumn, also insects and honeydew. In autumn huge flocks set of daily from the south to winter in the north, returning to their previous territories in spring. Breeds July-March, especially October-January. Endemic.
Sexes: *alike.*
Immatures: *duller, rump coloured rufous.*
Voice: *'chik-up' or 'quitch-up' amongst other whistles.*   D&MT

43, 44   YELLOW-TUFTED HONEYEATER *Lichenostomus melanops*   19-21cm
Lives in loose colonies of 10-100 birds in eucalypt woodland and open forest in south-east Australia, usually along creeks. There are two races: *melanops* the smaller and paler and shorter-tailed which straddles both slopes of the Great Dividing Range; and *cassidix* (the Helmeted Honeyeater) which is distinguished by the raised yellow helmet on its crown, and is restricted to a tiny area near Yellingbo in Victoria. The species eats nectar, insects, honeydew, and manna. Insects are also taken from leaves, from bark and on the wing. It raises the tufts at the sides of its head when disturbed. Birds of the high country tend to migrate northwards and to lower altitudes in winter. The population of the Helmeted Honeyeater, which is the faunal emblem of Victoria and one of Australia's rarest birds, was once found over a large area east of Melbourne. It has declined to only 100 to 150 birds within a few hectares in the Yellingbo State Wildlife Reserve. Sustained efforts are being made to save it from extinction. Breeds June-March. Nests below 4m. Endemic.
Sexes: *alike.*
Immatures: *the yellow patches are greener.*
Voice: *very varied repertoire ranging from sweet whistling to harsh nasal notes.*   43GW;44FJ

45   WHITE-PLUMED HONEYEATER *Lichenostomus penicillatus*   17cm
This is one of the most widespread of the honeyeaters. Plumage varies from greenish in the south-east
to pale yellow in Central Australia. It frequents large eucalypts along watercourses, close and open
woodland, and is familiar in parks and gardens. Singly, in pairs or flocks, it feeds in trees on insects,
nectar and particularly manna. Fearless and aggressive. Breeds June-January. Nests low to 15m, often
host to cuckoos. Endemic. **Sexes:** *alike.*
Immatures: *duller, brownish-yellow bill.*
Voice: *musical 'chick-o-wee' and constant 'chip' chattering.*   D&MT

46   GREY-FRONTED HONEYEATER *Lichenostomus plumulus*   16cm
Also called Yellow-fronted Honeyeater, it ranges extensively through all but the most arid desert areas
of the centre, and lives in dense mallee, mulga scrub, eucalypt woodland and spinifex in some areas.
Singly and in pairs it feeds among foliage and blossoms for nectar. Large flocks sometimes gather to
feed when eucalypt blossoms are profuse. Breeds August-January. Nests in small trees within a metre
of the ground. Endemic.
Sexes: *alike.*
Immatures: *duller.*
Voice: *clear penetrating 'it-wirt, wirt, wirt', and single sharp notes;*
sometimes canary-like notes.   GC

47   YELLOW-TINTED HONEYEATER *Lichenostomus flavescens*   17cm
It is common in open forest and scrublands along watercourses. It feeds in foliage and blossom on insects
and nectar and gathers in quite large flocks at sources of food, water and bathing places. Breeds July-
November. Nests suspended 2-12m high, with normally one egg.
Sexes: *alike.*
Immatures: *bill brownish-yellow.*
Voice: *in part rather like White-plumed Honeyeater but slower and high pitch;*
also 'chy-uck-oo-wee' variable in pitch.   ES

48   YELLOW-PLUMED HONEYEATER *Lichenostomus ornatus*   16cm
A honeyeater of the wetter mallee in southern Australia and tall eucalypt in the west of its range. It is similar in habits to the Grey-fronted Honeyeater and feeds on insects and nectar in pairs and small groups. It
is aggressive and quarrelsome when feeding in blossoming trees, with loud warning cries. The male rises
in steep display and song flights during the breeding season. Breeds August-December. Nests suspended
from low drooping branch. Endemic.
Sexes: *alike.*
Immatures: *duller.*
Voice: *calls well before sunrise. Loud animated 'chick-o-wee'; harsh sharp*
flight and alarm calls.   K&BR

49   FUSCOUS HONEYEATER *Lichenostomus fuscus*   15cm
Common in open forests, this noisy and gregarious honeyeater, usually in flocks of 6-12, feeds on nectar and
insects in the foliage, and is frequently quarrelsome. It will visit feeding tables and gardens and can become
tame. Sedentary in the north, nomadic in the south. Breeds July-March. Nests to 20m high. Endemic. Breeding
pairs have black eye-ring and black bills; out of breeding season eye-ring and base of bill is yellow. Plumage is
yellower in the north. Endemic.
Sexes: *alike.*
Immatures: *bill brown, yellowish at base.*
Voice: *a bright 'kitty-lin-tofftoff-toff' and calls like Yellow-tinted Honeyeater.*   EZ

50   WHITE-GAPED HONEYEATER *Lichenostomus unicolor*   20cm
Common across tropical Australia in riverine thickets, mangroves, swampy woodland, parks and gardens. It is noisy and aggressive, and hops along branches briskly, often with tail partly cocked (which is unique among honeyeaters), under the canopy or low in shrubs foraging for insects and spiders, sometimes even seeking them in houses. It also eats nectar, fruit and seeds. Breeds September-May. Nests in tree fork over water. Endemic.
Sexes: *alike.*
Immatures: *yellow wash on breast, gape yellow.*
Voice: *a great variety of pipings, sparrow-like chirping, and notes of 'whit-whit' or 'whit-o-wee'.* GC

51   MACLEAY'S HONEYEATER *Xanthotis macleayana*   20cm
Restricted to a small area of rainforest, woodland and mangroves, this honeyeater often frequents orchards and gardens, where its distinctive calls are familiar. It is deliberate in its movements and, usually alone or in pairs, it forages mostly in the foliage in the middle to upper layers beneath the canopy. It eats mainly insects and spiders, with some nectar and occasionally native and cultivated fruits, and is attracted to the blossom of Umbrella trees. Breeds October-December. Nests above 2m from ground. Endemic. **Sexes:** *alike.*
Immatures: *duller.*
Voice: *some calls like Yellow-faced Honeyeater, and a five-note 'to-wit-too-weee-twit'.*   H&JB

52   TAWNY-BREASTED HONEYEATER *Xanthotis chrysotis*   20cm
A bird of tropical rainforest and riverside galleries of vine scrub. Singly and in pairs, it forages deliberately and unobtrusively in the middle to upper strata of foliage. It eats insects - often extracted from dead clumps of leaves and from crevices of trunks - and to a lesser extent fruit and nectar. Breeds November-February. Nests in a bark cup-shaped nest from 4m above ground.
Sexes: *alike.*
Immatures: *duller above, paler below.*
Voice: *rich whistling, and a call of 'you-go-bang' with emphasis on either first or*
  last syllable.   D&MT

53   TAWNY-CROWNED HONEYEATER *Phylidonyris melanops*   16cm
The Tawny-crowned Honeyeater lives in coastal heath, mallee scrub and sometimes in open forest country on the coast. It sips nectar from low flowering shrubs, often foraging from the ground. It also takes flying insects, both by hawking over the vegetation and by sallying forth from a vantage point. It performs a spectacular high song flight during the breeding season. Breeds July-March. Nests on the ground or to 3m. Endemic.
Sexes: *alike.*
Immatures: *no tawny crown; yellow throat patch.*
Voice: *gentle airy, flute-like song with a ventriloquial quality.*   D&MT

54   WHITE-FRONTED HONEYEATER *Phylidonyris albifrons*   18cm
Highly nomadic, with its movements largely governed by the flowering of eucalypts, mistletoe, grevilleas, hakeas and eremophilas. It is usually in pairs and small parties, but in large flocks during effusions of blossom. It darts briskly among the foliage and flies in swift undulations from one bush to another. Breeds August-February, or in response to favourable conditions. Nests low on a branch or in the fold of bark against the trunk. Endemic.
Female: *browner.*
Immatures: *upperparts brown, throat whitish.*
Voice: *spirited melodious song including 'quak-peter-peet' phrases and various*
  metallic calls.   B&BW

55   CRESCENT HONEYEATER *Phylidonyris pyrrhoptera*   16cm
Most abundant in Tasmania where it is known as the Tasmanian Honeyeater. It frequents moist forest, dense heath and visits suburban gardens and is seen alone, in pairs or in loose companies. It feeds on nectar, honeydew and insects taken on the ground or from tree bark. In winter it migrates from highlands to low and coastal country. Breeds July-January or March-April. Nests to 2m from ground in bush or fern. Endemic.
Female: *duller.*
Immatures: *no crescent.*
Voice: *calls of 'egypt-egypt' amongst other notes.*   TW

56   NEW HOLLAND HONEYEATER *Phylidonyris novaehollandiae*   18cm
Also known as the White-eyed Honeyeater. The white beard, black cheek or white eye instantly differentiates it from the similar looking but dark-eyed White-cheeked Honeyeater. It is common on coastal heath, closely shrubbed woodland and gardens. In pairs and small flocks, it feeds principally on nectar from some 100 species of shrubs, but especially banksias in NSW. Breeds March-May and August-October. Nests to 3m from ground. Endemic.
Female: *smaller.*
Immatures: *streaking brown and grey rather than black and white.*
Voice: *chattering and single high notes.*   GC

57   WHITE-CHEEKED HONEYEATER *Phylidonyris nigra*   18cm
The large white cheek patch, black eye, and different voice distinguish this honeyeater from the look-alike New Holland. It inhabits heath lands and open timber and forages in pairs, loose colonies and flocks on flowering shrubs for nectar and insects. Breeds March-May, or August-October. Nests in low vegetation. Endemic.
Female: *smaller.*
Immatures: *browner and greyer, lores yellowish.*
Voice: *brisk 'chippity-chip', often in concert.*   MMcN

58   BLUE-FACED HONEYEATER *Entomyzon cyanotis*   32cm
A conspicuous facial patch, shading from vivid blue to pale turquoise characterises this large honeyeater. It lives in a variety of habitat throughout its exclusive range including fringes of rainforest and open woodland. Insects are its main diet, also nectar from blossoms, and native fruits. It also raids orchards and takes syrup from burnt sugar canes. Breeds June-January. Often uses discarded nests of other species such as babblers.
Sexes: *alike.*
Immatures: *eye skin green-yellow.*
Voice: *loud monotonous call of 'queet', alarm notes like the Noisy Miner.*   GC

59   REGENT HONEYEATER *Zanthomiza phrygia*   22cm
This strikingly-plumaged honeyeater is a nomad and may suddenly turn up anywhere in its habitat of woodland and open forest when there are flushes of blossom of flowering trees such as eucalypts and banksias, often in large feeding flocks. It feeds aggressively and quickly in the outer foliage and it also takes insects and native fruits. It may not return to a locality for many years. Its range and numbers are declining. Breeds August-January. Nests in tree-fork, up to 10m. Endemic.
Sexes: *similar.*
Immatures: *black parts grey or brownish.*
Voice: *a rich bell-like note and clicking sounds.*   GC

60   SPINY-CHEEKED HONEYEATER *Acanthagenys rufogularis*   26cm
An large endemic honeyeater characterised by its distinctive malar feathers. It is common in most areas of coastal woodland and across the open scrubby country of the arid and semi-arid inland. It feeds variously on insects both gleaned from foliage and flying, nectar from flowering trees, manna, native and grapes from vineyards. It is locally nomadic and flocks up to 100 can gather when there are flushes of blossom. Breeds variably, mainly June-January. Deep pendant nest up to 9m above ground.
Sexes: *alike.*
Immatures: *duller; yellow cheek spines.*
Voice: *liquid bubbling trills.*   GC

61   BELL MINER *Manorina melanophrys*   18cm
Popularly known as the Bellbird, this pugnacious species monopolises pockets of woodland from which it drives out other small birds, and often stays for many years. Its famous sharp 'pings' ring out all day and can sometimes be heard alongside a bush road. It eats mainly sap-sucking scale insects and their sugary lerps (scales). Breeds July-February and nests in trees normally 4-5m up. Endemic.
Female: *smaller.*
Immatures: *eye patch greenish-yellow.*
Voice: *'....sweeter than singing the notes of the bellbirds are running and ringing'. (Henry Kendall).*   PG

62   NOISY MINER *Manorina melanocephala*   28cm
The conspicuous and noisy bird is among the best known of the honeyeaters. It lives in open woodland in loose colonies of perhaps several hundred birds which erupt into an uproar of alarm calls when danger threatens, such as from a hawk overhead or the approach of a goanna, and mass mobbing follows. It feeds on insects, their honeydew and nectar. Breeds mainly June-December. Colonies of cup nests up to 20m from the ground. Endemic.
Sexes: *alike.*
Immatures: *washed brown on back and wings.*
Voice: *raucous alarm calls and rich musical notes.*   JF

63   BLACK-EARED MINER *Manorina melanotis*   26cm
In a very restricted habitat of mallee and riverine woodland where three southern state boundaries meet, this race - which is distinguished by a large black ear patch and greyish rump - is being hybridised out of existence through interbreeding with the nominate Yellow-throated Miner and extensive clearance of its habitat. It is shy and little known. Breeds August-January. Nests in communities of several breeding groups with females outnumbering males. Endemic.
Sexes: *alike.*
Immatures: *alike.*
Voice: *petulant and grating, rather like the Noisy Miner.*   JP

64   YELLOW-THROATED MINER *Manorina flavigula*   28cm
Common in patches in woodland, mallee and arid scrublands. A dark race obscura, once known as the Dusky Miner is confined to south-west Australia. Highly nomadic, but in other respects its habits including feeding are similar to the Noisy Miner. The yellow throat is faint but the white rump is prominent, and it is sometimes known as the White-rumped Miner. Breeds July-December. Nests in colonies. Endemic.
Female: *smaller.*
Immatures: *upperparts browner, wing coverts edged buff.*
Voice: *variety of strident calls, rather similar to the Noisy Miner.*   D&MT

65   LITTLE WATTLEBIRD *Anthochaera chrysoptera lunulata (Western race)*   32cm
Compared with the Little Wattlebird in eastern Australia, the crown is plain, the whitish feathers at the sides of the throat are more prominent, the bill is more slender and the eye is red. Often in loose companies, it wanders in search of blossoming trees and shrubs in woodland scrub and heath. In summer, it is partly migratory from inland to coast. Breeds July-October. Nest is often in a banksia. Only one egg is laid (the eastern relative lays two). Endemic.
Sexes: *similar, females sometimes smaller.*
Immatures: *browner.*
Voice: *cackles and chuckles, often by pairs in duet.*   GC

66   LITTLE (Brush) WATTLEBIRD
       Anthochaera chrysoptera chrysoptera (Eastern race)   31cm
The smallest of the wattlebirds, and without visible wattles. Birds in Tasmania are darker and larger. Solitary or in parties, it frequents woodland, heath, parks and gardens and feeds mostly on the nectar of flowering banksias, grevilleas and eucalypts. It also eats insects, manna and honeydew. It is active, continuously vocal, and aggressively drives off other honeyeaters. Breeds mainly July-December. Nests in trees up to 15m above ground. Endemic.
Sexes: *similar, females sometimes smaller.*
Immatures: *browner.*
Voice: *includes repeated braying phrases 'ke-kay-o', and one-syllable squawks such as 'yoiks'.*   D&MT

67   RED WATTLEBIRD *Anthochaera carunculata*   35cm
It is the largest of the mainland honeyeaters and is as well known in southern city gardens as in forest
and woodland. It is nomadic, sometimes in loose flocks up to 100, following the blossoms for their nec-
tar; also eats fruit , berries, insects, manna and honeydew. Its red wattles lengthen and deepen in colour
with age. Breeds mainly July-December. Some migration from highlands towards the coast in winter.
Nests 2-20m above ground. Endemic.
Sexes: *alike.*
Immatures: *no wattles.*
Voice: *loud harsh notes including characteristic 'tchock', sometimes in duet.*   GC

68   YELLOW WATTLEBIRD *Anthochaera paradox*   45cm
Confined to Tasmania and King Island, it is the world's largest honeyeater and is characterised by dangling
yellow-orange wattles. It lives in all but the rainforests of the west. It is strongly nomadic following the sea-
sonal flowering flushes of blossom for its nectar. Also feeds on spiders and insects, particularly those attack-
ing eucalypts foliage, and on cidergum sap. It migrates from highland to coast in winter. Breeds July-January.
Nests to 30m above ground. Endemic.
Sexes: *alike.*
Immatures: *no wattles.*
Voice: *extraordinary discordant gurgling and regurgitation noises.*   TW

69   LITTLE FRIARBIRD *Philemon citreogularis*   29cm
The smallest of the Australian friarbirds and the only one without a bill knob. The yellow throat to which
the specific name citreogularis refers applies only to immature birds. In pairs and small flocks and in
mixed parties, it frequents open woodland, orchards and vineyeards to feed on nectar, insects and fruit. It
also feeds on burnt-off sugarcane. Southern birds migrate northwards to winter. Breeds August-February.
Nests 2-11m above ground.
Sexes: *alike.*
Immatures: *yellow throat, back scalloped with white.*
Voice: *loud monotonous 'ar-coo'.*   E&DH

70   SILVER-CROWNED FRIARBIRD *Philemon argenticeps*   31cm
Like the Helmeted Friarbird, but its bill-knob is more prominent and the plumage on head and neck is
silvery white. It lives in tropical forest and woodland near water, and shares the nomadic habits of
other friarbirds, often in mixed flocks, following the blossoms of eucalypts and paperbarks, to feed on
nectar and the insects it attracts. Breeds September-March. Solitary bowl nest suspended 2-11m above
ground, often host to Koel. Endemic. **Sexes:** *alike.*
Immatures: *no bill-knob; white markings on back.*
Voice: *a variety of cacophonous calls, especially prominent in the dawn chorus.*   D&MT

71   HELMETED FRIARBIRD *Philemon buceroides*   36cm
The largest of the friarbirds. It often congregates in feeding parties of 10 to 30 with exceptionally noisy
squawking and flapping in woodland, mangrove or gardens, around flowering trees and shrubs - prob-
ing blossom for nectar. It also hawks for insects and eats more fruit than other friarbirds. Breeds
September-April. Nests up to 14m from ground. **Sexes:** *similar.*
Immatures: *some lack knob in bill; wings washed greenish-yellow.*
Voice: *constantly repeated call of 'poor devil', 'poor devil' and a medley of*
cacophonous clankings.   D&MT

72   NOISY FRIARBIRD *Philemon corniculatus*   36cm
This raucous and pugnacious bird is the barest headed of all the friarbirds. Singly, in pairs or flocks,
it frequents eucalypt forest and open woodlands, and feeds on nectar, insects, native and cultivated
fruits. Southern birds migrate northwards in winter, and to lower altitudes from the high country. It
breeds August-January and nests in trees up to 15m above ground. The northern birds are smaller.
Sexes: *alike.*
Immatures: *no bill-knob; white scallops on back and yellow on throat.*
Voice: *main call of 'four-o-clock' amidst an extraordinary jumble of sounds.*   EZ

14 Finches and Sparrows

1, 2   DOUBLE-BARRED FINCH *Taeniopygia bichenovii*   11cm
Double-barred Finches are black-rumped in the west and white-rumped in the east, and intergrade in a broad area south of the Gulf of Carpentaria. This owl-faced finch lives in sizeable parties, and frequents woodland with grassy understorey, low scrub, and is often seen on the margins of canefields, near homesteads, and in parks and gardens where it is relatively tame. It is a frequent visitor to cleared areas and is believed to have benefited from human settlement. Its habitat is always near water, where it gathers in large numbers. It drinks by sucking. It spends much time on the ground picking up seeds or jumping up to reach them from seeding grasses. Highly sociable in habits, it indulges in mutual preening and roosts communally. Northern birds breed from June-November, southern birds from January-March. Nests in bush or low tree, often thorny bushes like *Bursaria*. Endemic.
Females: *may have narrower black barring on back.*
Immatures: *duller; barring indistinct; upperparts greyish-olive.*
Voice: *soft kitten-like mews and 'tiaat-tiaat' calls.*   1D&MT, 2JP

3   PLUM-HEADED FINCH *Neochmia modesta*   11cm
In pairs or small to very large flocks, this finch is highly nomadic, and appears to be migratory in the southern parts of its range. In the north it has become rare. It frequents rank grass and reed vegetation and feeds on seeds on or near the ground. It often settles in gardens and is remarkably tame. Breeds August-March (north, September-January (south). Nests within 1m of ground. Endemic.
Female: *less claret-red on forehead; chin and throat whitish, less barring on underparts.*
Immatures: *no red patches, generally olive brown.*
Voice: *noisy when in flocks; calls of 'tlip' almost inaudible song of chirps and trills.*   D&MT

4   BEAUTIFUL FIRETAIL *Stagonopleura bella*   12cm
Tasmania's only native finch, it is now rare on the mainland and confined to the coastal strip there. It lives in scrub-covered country and thickly wooded gullies. Seldom seen in cleared areas. In sedentary pairs or small flocks. It has a strong arrow-like flight, and forages on the ground for seeds, hopping swiftly like a mouse. It is difficult to flush, but when it is it rises with a loud whirr of wings. It also picks small insects from foliage. Breeds September-January. Nests in low bush or tree to 6m above ground. Endemic.
Female: *no black on belly.*
Immatures: *duller, less distinct markings, blackish bill.*
Voice: *penetrating sorrowful 'weee'.*   TW

5   RED-EARED FIRETAIL *Stagonopleura oculata*   12cm
Restricted to south-west Western Australia, its range having contracted from former days. It frequents dense scrub, heavy forest and coastal paperbark swamp. It is solitary, never in flocks, and sedentary. With exceptional dexterity it weaves through low foliage foraging for seeds and insects. Breeds September-January. Builds large bottle-shaped nest with entrance tunnel up to 40cm long very high in tree up to 15m. Also builds an untunnelled roosting nest. Endemic.
Sexes: *similar, but breeding female paler ear patch.*
Immatures: *duller, no ear patch, bill black.*
Voice: *floating 'oowee' call, repeated faint 'quirk', harsh alarm notes.*   GC

6   DIAMOND FIRETAIL *Stagonopleura guttata*   11cm
Sometimes called the Diamond Sparrow. It prefers to be near watercourses in forest, mallee or sparse woodland, but will range further. It has been considerably displaced by land development. Feeds almost entirely on the ground, hopping rapidly, sometimes jumping up to reach grass seeds. Sedentary, often nesting in the same tree year after year. Usually seen in groups or flocks. Breeds August-January. Nests in bush, mistletoe or trees to 25m, occasionally under the roof of a building. Endemic.
Female: *smaller, narrow breast band.*
Immatures: *browner, breast band indistinct or absent.*
Voice: *call of 'twoo-hee', low rasping song.*   CG

7   PAINTED FINCH *Emblema picta*   10cm
A finch of the arid centre and north-west with a patchy distribution. It lives among spinifex and low scrub in rocky gullies and hills near water, and sometimes appears in station gardens. It is seen in pairs and small groups, rarely in large flocks and forages on the ground for fallen seeds. Breeding is related to rainfall. Nests in dense clump of grass, in ground depression, or on platform of earth and stones. Endemic.
Immatures: *much duller, no red on rump.*
Voice: *loud harsh call 'trut'; song 'che-che-che-weree-ooee'.*   D&MT

8   RED-BROWED FINCH *Neochmia temporalis*   12cm
This finch has a red rump like the firetails. On Cape York, birds have a brighter olive-yellow back, and white throat and abdomen; in South Australia it is browner. The Western Australian population is descended from aviary escapees. Common in wooded habitats and near habitation, it is trusting and confiding. Sedentary or nomadic; large flocks form out of breeding season. Breeds September-November (south), January-April (north). Nests in thorny bushes or shrubs. Endemic.
Sexes: *similar.*
Immatures: *browner, bill blackish, no red eyebrow.*
Voice: *incessantly-repeated call on the move of 'ssitt-ssitt' or 'ssee-ssee-ssee'.*   JP

9   STAR FINCH *Neochmia ruficauda*   12cm
The Star Finch lives in tall rank grass around water interspersed with bushes or low trees usually in small flocks, but these can sometimes be quite large. Plumage colour varies considerably, the northern populations are brighter and the intensity of red and the size of the white spots changes with age. It eats grass seeds, including spinifex, often taken from the plant head; also insects. Breeds December-August. Nests to 3m in a bush or tree. Endemic.
Immatures: *dull olive-brown above; grey crown, cheeks and breast.*
Voice: *high-pitched contact call 'tlit' or 'psilt' in flock; single contact call of 'sseet'.*   D&MT

10, 11   CRIMSON FINCH *Neochmia phaeton*   14cm
There are three isolated Australian populations and two forms: black-bellied in the northern and eastern populations, and white-bellied on Cape York Peninsula. In pairs and small family parties, it lives in the long grasses of eucalypt woodland, sometimes in pineapple groves and the margins of canefields - always near water. It feeds on the seeds of pandanus, grasses and insects. It flits somewhat like a butterfly between grass clumps and constantly flicks its long tail upwards. It has adapted to human settlement, appearing at homesteads or wherever water is available in wells and troughs. It is quarrelsome and will sometimes drive away bigger birds from its nest. Breeds September-May. Nests in a low bush, buildings or even rooms.
Immatures: *(black-bellied form) dull brown upper-parts, paler below, bills black.*
Voice: *call - loud penetrating 'chee-chee'; song - rasping sounds ending with three melodious notes.*   10D&MT, 11 painting by TL

12   ZEBRA FINCH *Taeniopygia guttata*   10cm
Popular with bird fanciers all over the world, it is the most widely-distributed and common finch in Australia and lives in a wide variety of open country habitats, always near water. Sedentary, sometimes in very large flocks. It eats grass seeds and insects. Breeds variably in colonies. Nests in bush, ground hollow or building. The most popular cage and aviary bird of all Australian finches, and many colour mutations have been bred.
Immatures: *like females; bill black.*
Voice: *calls of 'tiah' like a toy trumpet; aggressive 'wsst', elusive song with low ventriloquial trills.*   D&MT

14

13, 14 MASKED FINCH *Poephila personata* 12cm
The Masked Finch occurs in two isolated populations: race *personata* in northern Australia, and race *leucotis* (the White-eared Finch) on Cape York Peninsula. Masked Finches are amongst the most sociable of Australian grass-finches. They form strong pair bonds which persist even in the non-breeding season when they flock. Members of breeding colonies hold daily social gatherings at places outside the nesting area and indulge in a ritual of greeting with much chattering and mutual preening. The species frequents lightly timbered grasslands, and feeds on seeding grasses, termites, flies and foliage insects. It spends much time on the ground, and is never far from water. Unlike other grass-finches, it drinks only morning and evening, which enables it to forage for food far afield during the day. Flocks of hundreds may gather at water, sometimes in much greater numbers in dry conditions. It is particularly adept at drinking by sucking and can do so while hanging downwards from a branch to reach water or from the edge of a water trough. Breeds March-June. Nests in bush, tree or grass clump.
Sexes: *alike, but female smaller.*
Immatures: *duller, no black mask, bill blackish.*
Voice: *calls of 'twaat-twaat'; hissing aggressive call; loud song.* 13D&MT, 14H&JB

15 LONG-TAILED FINCH *Poephila acuticauda* 15cm
In pairs and flocks of 30 or more, often with Masked Finches, this finch frequents savannah usually near watercourses. Flocks may be of 1 000 or more during drought. It eats seeds on ground and catches flying insects. Bobs its head on landing. The bill changes colour from orange in the west to reddish in the east. Pair bonding is very strong. Breeds January-May. Nests in loose colonies in grass or low in trees. Endemic.
Female: *throat patch much smaller.*
Immatures: *duller; bill and legs black.*
Voice: *low 'tet', far-carrying floating 'weet' or 'tee-wheet'; plaintive flute-like song.* GC

16, 17 BLACK-THROATED FINCH *Peophila cincta* 10cm
The highly social Black-throated Finch is black-rumped in the north of its range (A) and white-rumped to the south (B). The northern population is common but the southern has declined greatly and is possibly extinct in southern-most parts including NSW. There is a broad band of integration where the two forms meet. Between Cairns and Normanton, the birds are rich fawn on the back and breast and paler grey on the head, and are known as Diggles Finches. The Black-throated Finch is the eastern counterpart of the closely-related Long-tailed Finch. The habits are similar including head bobbing and drinking by sucking, and the latter's long tail is the main difference between them. It frequents open timber with grassy understorey and pandanus clumps near the coast, especially in the vicinity of water. It is shy of settled areas. It eats seeds, often pulling the seed head to the ground. Breeds (north) after the monsoon from January to May, (south) August-January. Nests high in eucalypts or in pandanus palms near the coast. Endemic.
Females: *smaller throat patch.*
Immatures: *paler and duller.*
Voice: *similar to Long-tailed Finch, but hoarser calls and more flute-like song.* D&MT

18 BLUE-FACED PARROT-FINCH *Erythrura trichroa* 12cm
This bird, one of the so-called parrot-finches, is believed to be a relatively recent arrival in Australia, it is confined to coastal rainforest to 1 000m in far NE Queensland where the first breeding record was obtained only in 1944. Singly or in small groups, it forages in thick vegetation for seeds and insects. Breeding recorded in March and November. **Female:** *blue face patch duller and smaller.*
Immatures: *no blue face patch, dull green plumage.*
Voice *high-pitched call note; trilling followed by a whistle.* D&MT

19 YELLOW-RUMPED MANNIKIN *Lonchura flaviprymna* 10cm
The Yellow-rumped Mannikin is similar in many respects to the Chestnut-breasted Mannikin and the two feed and roost together, and nest in the same colonies, sometimes interbreeding. It is a ground feeder on seeds in grassland with scattered trees and shrubs near water. It seems to move southwards and away from the coast during the wet season. Breeds January-March. Nests in bush, sugar cane, bamboo, maize stalks, or green grass. Endemic.
Sexes: *similar.*
Immatures: *back and throat dark brown, breast pale grey, underparts grey-buff.*
Voice: *like Chestnut-breasted Mannikin.* D&MT

20, 21   GOULDIAN FINCH *Erythrura gouldiae*   14cm
This bird is named after John Gould's wife Elizabeth. About three-quarters of Gouldian Finches in a given population have black heads, a quarter red heads and, on rare occasions, yellow-ochre heads. The Gouldian Finch lives in open timbered grassland always near water, and in watercourse vegetation. Gregarious and highly social in habits, it is seen in small parties or flocks, which become quite large during the non-breeding season. It has only one partner, probably for life. It climbs grasses and reeds to reach the seed heads, and rarely feeds on the ground, except after fires. It also eats insects especially during the breeding season. Once widespread across the north of the continent, it has totally disappeared from some areas, particularly on Cape York Peninsula and country south of the Gulf of Carpentaria. Its numbers have also fallen alarmingly elsewhere; where flocks of a thousand or more used to be common at waterholes, fewer than thirty are now seen. Excessive trapping and over burning of grasslands are blamed for much of the decline. Breeds December-April. Nests uniquely in tree hollows or termite mounds. Endemic.
Female: *almost as colourful in some birds, duller in others.*
Immatures: *ash-grey; underparts ashy-brown.*
Voice: *generally rather silent; calls of 'ssitt'. Song has high-pitched,*
almost inaudible whistling, hissing and 'cluck'.   D&MT

22   CHESTNUT-BREASTED MANNIKIN *Lonchura castaneothorax*   10cm
In Australia this mannikin lives in two populations. Birds of the north-west are nomadic; those of the east coast are sedentary. Usually seen in tightly-knit parties and breeding colonies, or very large flocks, together with Yellow-rumped Mannikins. It frequents swamps, rice fields, crops etc., and climbs seeding heads to feed. Also catches flying termites. Breeds most months of the year. Nests in grass and crop stalks or bushes within 1m of ground.
Female: *similar.*
Immatures: *dark olive above, underparts whitish-buff.*
Voice: *tinkling, bell-like 'teet'.*   D&MT

23   PICTORELLA MANNIKIN *Heteromunia pectoralis*   11cm
Often seen in flocks flying over grassland. It is very vocal when gathering at water, drinking by taking rapid sips, then flying off. In the breeding season it is seen in groups of a dozen or less. A bird of open grassy plains with bushes, it is a mostly terrestrial insect and seed eater. Nomadic in dry conditions and moves away from the coast in the Wet. Breeds January-April (west), April-May (east). Nests low in bush or tussock. Endemic.
Immatures: *underparts brownish-grey, paler below.*
Voice: *call of sparrow-like 'chip', long drawn-out 'teet', almost non-existent song.*   D&MT

24   NUTMEG MANNIKIN *Lonchura punctulata*   11cm
This native of south-eastern Asia, also known in Australia as the Spice Finch, has colonised successfully as a result of introductions and escaped caged birds. It has become the 'house sparrow' of the north, and displaces the less vigorous finches in the bush. It eats seeds and scavenges on rubbish tips and on roads for carrion. Often seen flying in very large wheeling flocks. Breeds spring and summer (south), all months (north). Nests 1-6m high.
Sexes: *alike.*
Immatures: *upperparts light brown, underparts yellowish brown, unscalloped.*
Voice: *high-pitched 'chip' 'kit-teeee'. Almost inaudible song with whistling*
and bill- rattling.   D&MT

25   EUROPEAN GREENFINCH *Carduelis chloris*   15cm
Introduced from the northern hemisphere in the 1860's, it has spread patchily in south-eastern Australia and Tasmania. Out of the breeding season, it flocks with the Goldfinch. In the winter, small flocks move from city parks and gardens into farmland and woodland. It is a seed eater mainly in vegetation associated with introduced pines. Breeds October-January. Open cup nest 2-12m high in tree.
Female: *duller and less yellow.*
Immatures: *brown, streaked darker.*
Voice: *call is a hard dry 'ti-ti-ti-ti'; nasal 'dzhwee' by male during season; song*
is mixture of these two calls with musical warblings and twitterings.   TW

14

26   EUROPEAN GOLDFINCH *Carduelis carduelis*   13cm
A bird of the northern hemisphere, introduced to the three south-eastern states of Australia between 1860-1880. Escapees have become established around Brisbane, Perth and Albany. It lives in grassy settled areas often associated with weed infestations especially thistle, feeding mainly on seed. Seen in pairs and groups; out of season it forms large nomadic flocks. Breeds September-March. Open cup nest 2-12m high.
Sexes: *alike.*
Immatures: *duller head and face, body finely striped.*
Voice: *liquid 'tswitt-witt-witt' with pretty tinkling quality; song with harsh notes and canary-like twitterings.*   TW

27   RED BISHOP *Euplectes orix*   11cm
Native to Africa, this member of the large family of weaver finches was introduced into Australia some fifty years ago as caged birds. A colony established itself from escaped or released birds on the Murray River, south of Adelaide, but has apparently died out. The breeding male is one of the brightest-coloured of all the weavers and has one of the most interesting courtship displays before his harem of 2 or more females. (The bird illustrated was photographed in the aviaries of Taronga Park Zoo, Sydney and illustrates the neat construction of a weaver bird's nest).   D&MT

Other Small Brightly-coloured Birds

28, 29   HOUSE SPARROW *Passer domesticus*   15cm
The House Sparrow is the most successful, and familiar, of city and town dwelling birds. It is more closely attached to man than any other bird and has followed European settlement all over the world, including to North America and New Zealand, as well as to Australia. Introduced from Britain progressively from 1863, it is now very common in most parts of its Australian range. It has not succeeded in crossing the Nullarbor Plain, and the authorities in Western Australia and the Northern Territory maintain constant vigilance to prevent it spreading into their States. Arrivals, sometimes by ship, are shot on sight. It is bold and noisy and lives in flocks in trees and on the ground. It feeds on seeds, scraps dropped by humans, also insects especially when feeding young. It competes with native birds for nesting sites. Breeds spring and summer and variably when conditions are favourable. Nests are untidy and are built in a variety of situations, including trees, eaves and holes in buildings.
Immatures: *like females.*
Voice: *a variety of unmusical chirruping, cheeping and twittering notes.*   D&MT

30   EURASIAN TREE SPARROW *Passer montanus*   15cm
Introduced from Britain around 1860, the Tree Sparrow has spread little beyond Victoria. It lives in urban and cultivated areas, parks and gardens. It feeds on seeds and insects on the ground or in foliage, in small groups. Sedentary. Breeds September-January. Nests in bush or hollow, less frequently in buildings.
Recognition: *chestnut crown and nape; black ear patch. Slimmer than the House Sparrow and different calls.*
Sexes: *alike.*
Immatures: *paler.*
Voice: *flight call of 'tek'; shrill twittering.*   E&DH

31, 32, 33 SILVEREYE *Zosterops lateralis*   12cm

The Silvereye, widespread and familiar in Australia, also occurs on islands of the south-western Pacific and New Zealand. There are many plumage variations, but they can be grouped in six fairly distinct Australian races: the western race, the Tasmanian race, and four eastern races. Their distribution is continuous and they hybridise where the races meet. Silvereyes frequent low trees, bushes and gardens and feed on nectar, insects and fruit, sometimes making damaging raids on orchards. Usually they are seen in small numbers, but large flocks may gather in the non-breeding season. The Tasmanian birds migrate to the mainland to over-winter in huge flocks, often at night, and can be heard calling as they fly overhead. They disperse widely, some birds even reaching southern Queensland some 1 500km away. During the winter period, Tasmanian and mainland birds are often seen in the same areas. Silvereyes live to remarkable ages - one bird was recaptured ten years after banding. Breeds August-February, sometimes three broods. Nests in a bush 1-4m up.

Sexes: *female usually paler*
Immatures: *like adults.*
Voice: *joyous trills, some mimicry.*

31 Western form (race *gouldi*): perhaps the commonest small bird over much of south-west WA. Olive green upperparts, yellow throat.   GC

32 Tasmanian form (race *lateralis*): chestnut flanks, grey throat. (The area stippled on the map repre sents the winter range).   LP

33 Eastern forms (A) North of Mackay (race r*amsayi*): bright yellow throat and dark yellow under tail (illus-trated). (B) Barrier Reef form on the Capricorn-Bunker group of islands (race *chlorocephala*): much larger; throat yellow, white under tail. (C) South of Rockhampton to central Victoria (race *familiaris*): throat yellow. (D) Western Victoria to South Australia (race *halmaturina*): throat grey; flanks buff.   D&MT

34   YELLOW WHITE-EYE *Zosterops luteus*   10cm

In small parties to large flocks, Yellow White-eyes frequent mangroves and coastal scrub. The plumage of populations east of Wyndham in Western Australia is brighter. Nomadic. Breeds September-March. Nest is a deep neat cup of bark or grass bound with spiderweb suspended from a horizontal twig. Endemic.

Sexes: *alike.*
Immatures: *like adults.*
Voice: *similar to other white-eyes, but is reported to sing more loudly once described as a 'marvellous volume of song'.*   GC

35   PALE WHITE-EYE *Zosterpos citrinellus*   12cm

The Pale White-eye occurs only on the Lesser Sunda Islands of Indonesia (from Bali to Timor), on the islands of Torres Strait and the small offshore islands of northern Queensland. In pairs or parties, it frequents scrub-by thickets and feeds on insects, native fruits and berries. Reported to breed in June and December. Its nest is much larger and bulkier than its mainland relatives, and is suspended from a horizontal branch or fork.

Recognition: *a conspicuous yellow forehead.*
Sexes: *alike.*   AD

36, 37   YELLOW-BELLIED SUNBIRD *Nectarinia jugularis*   12cm

The Yellow-bellied Sunbird is common in the coastal rainforests, mangroves, parks and gardens of tropical Queensland, and is usually seen in pairs among the blossoms of flowering trees and shrubs. Its long narrow downcurved bill, often with side serrations, enables it to probe deeply into most flower heads to sip nectar, or pierce them at their base when they are too deep. Sucking is aided by its tubular tongue. It also catches insects on the wing, and sometimes plucks spiders from their webs. The sunbird darts swiftly from flower to flower and is sometimes compared with the hummingbirds of the Americas, but it more often clings to a petal or a leaf when feeding rather than hover like a hummingbird. It is unafraid of human beings and will enter houses. It builds a long spindle-shaped nest with a hooded side entrance suspended from a twig or a piece of rope or wire hanging from an eave or a verandah, and is oblivious to the comings and goings of people. Breeds most months but mainly August-March sometimes more than once during the year.

Immatures: *like adult females.*
Voice: *squeaky staccato notes.*   R&DK

38   RED-BROWED PARDALOTE *Pardalotus rubricatus*   10cm
A bird of arid country which is similar in behaviour to the Spotted Pardalote. Singly and in small parties, it is fairly readily seen in outer foliage of less leafy trees. Insects make up its diet. Breeds February-November. Nests at the end of a tunnel bored into an earth bank. Endemic.
Recognition: cf Striated Pardalote *P.s. melanocephalus: speckled head and small but distinctive orange-red eyebrow spot.*
Sexes: *alike.*
Immatures: *upperparts yellow-green; underparts yellow.*
Voice: *repetitive distinct five-note phrase.*   GC

39   STRIATED PARDALOTE *Pardalotus striatus melanocephalus*   11cm
A black non-striated head, and a red spot and a broad white stripe on the wings distinguish this race (often called the Black-headed Pardalote). The rump of northern birds is bright yellow; southern birds cinnamon brown. There is interbreeding with *substriatus* in the zones where the two races meet or overlap. Their habitats and habits are similar. Breeds May-December. Endemic.
Adults and immatures: *see nominate race.*
Voice: *loud sharp 'chip-chip' repeated monotonously.*   T&PG

40, 43   MISTLETOEBIRD *Dicaeum hirundinaceum*   10cm
It is one of Australia's most widespread and familiar birds. It is found wherever mistletoe grows, in rainforest, mangrove or desert. Its digestive system, in which its stomach is supplemented by a duct, enables it to pass large quantities of berries in a short time, thus further spreading the seeds of the berries on which the species mainly relies. It takes the fruit of other plants too, and some insects. It flies swiftly on narrow wings and calls in flight. Breeds October-March. Suspended purse-shaped nest.
Immatures: *like females.*
Voice: *warbling song with mimicry; also short-high-pitched note in flight.*   40D&MT, 43BL

41, 44   SPOTTED PARDALOTE *Pardalotus punctatus*   9cm
This spectacular little bird is often seen in tree-lined city streets, gardens, parks and golf courses as well as in forest and woodland. It feeds on insects in eucalypts and wattle. Usually sedentary, but with mome movement from south to north in autumn. It sometimes gathers in flocks in winter. Breeds June-January. Nests mainly in earth bank. Endemic.
Immatures: *upperparts yellow-green, underparts yellow.*
Voice: *a distinctive bell-like three-syllable 'slee-p ba-bee'. Sometimes called a 'bellbird' in error.*   41GC, 44FP/ANT

42   STRIATED PARDALOTE *Pardalotus striatus ornatus*   17cm
An orange-red spot and narrow white stripe on the wings distinguish this race. It frequents wattle scrub and mulga and other low trees. Its habits are similar to *striatus* to which it is closely related and of which it is sometimes regarded as a hybrid. In winter, it may form travelling flocks with *substriatus* in the west, and with *melanocephalus* in the north. Breeds August-December. Nests mostly in earth banks. Endemic.
Adults and immatures: *see nominate race.*
Voice: *'wit-e-cheu'.*   GW

45   STRIATED PARDALOTE *Pardalotus striatus substriatus*   11cm
A red spot and broad white stripe on the wings distinguish this widespread race. In winter it gathers in travelling flocks; in Western Australia some birds from the south-west move to winter in drier northern areas. Breeds August-December. Nests in earth hole; in Western Australia in tree holes or hollows, rarely in building crevices. Endemic.
Adults and immatures: *see nominate race.*
Voice: *'wit-e-cheu'; in WA 'wit-a-witta', 'be quick', or 'pick-wick'.*   JF

46   **FORTY-SPOTTED PARDALOTE** *Pardalotus quadragintus*   10cm
Endemic to Tasmania, its numbers have declined alarmingly this century. With a total population estimated at only 850 birds in 1982 it has become an endangered species. Competition for nesting sites from the Spotted and Striated (yellow-tipped) Pardalotes is believed to be one of the major reasons for its decline. It frequents the foliage of eucalypts. Breeds August-January. Nests in tree hollow to 20m.
Recognition: *plain crown and uniformly pale yellow face.*
Sexes: *alike.*
Immatures: *face, undertail and coverts paler.*
Voice: *double-noted whistle, second note lower.*   DM/NPI

47   **SPOTTED PARDALOTE** *Pardalotus punctatus xanthopygus*   10cm
Also known as the Yellow-rumped Pardalote. Its distribution, which spans the Nullarbor Plain, links the split populations of the Spotted Pardalote to which it is closely related. It frequents mallee and nearby taller eucalypt woodland, and feeds on insects. Usually sedentary but, in winter, feeding flocks may wander some distance. Breeds July-December. Nests in sloping tunnel dug into flat ground, with entrance extremely difficult to spot. Endemic. **Recognition:** *lemon yellow rump.*
Female: *duller, throat off-white.*
Immatures: *duller, crown grey.*
Voice: *resonant repeated 'ti-i-ing'.*   R&DK

48   **STRIATED PARDALOTE** *Pardalotus striatus striatus*   11cm
This, the nominate race, is distinguished by a yellow spot and narrow white strip on the wings. After the breeding season, most birds are believed to migrate to the mainland to overwinter. Singly, in pairs or family parties, it feeds high in foliage on insects. Breeds August-December. Nests mostly in a hole in an earth bank. Endemic.
Female: *duller.*
Immatures: *grey-black unstreaked crown.*
Voice: *'pick-it-up' or 'will-you'.*   TW

15 Bowerbirds

1, 4   SATIN BOWERBIRD *Ptilonorhynchus violaceus*   27-33cm
The violet-eyed Satin Bowerbird has two main populations, race *violaceus* in the south and the smaller race *minor* of the Atherton Tablelands. During the breeding season, the species lives in rainforest, wet eucalypt forest and adjacent woodland, and moves out, often in large flocks, to gardens and orchards in winter. It eats fruits throughout the year but feeds more on leaves and flowers in winter and insects in summer. Each breeding season, an adult male builds and maintains an avenue bower of two vertical, parallel walls of twigs, usually running north-south, on a mat base perhaps a metre or more in diameter. It is decorated with a great diversity of both natural and man-made objects and more than 300 items have been counted at a single bower. Blue objects predominate, but they are often yellow and brown and are mostly placed on the northern platform. A male will raid and flatten a neighbour's bower and steal ornaments. During the breeding season the bower is attended daily and the inside avenue walls are painted with charcoal or vegetable matter and saliva. A female visitor triggers a striking visual and vocal display by the male. He holds an ornament in his bill and performs a routine of strutting, bowing and flinging open his wings as he dashes back and forth across the avenue entrance uttering rhythmic buzzing and rattling notes and quiet mimicry. He mates in or near the avenue, and may mate with five or more females in a season. Immature males can become sexually active before attaining full adult plumage in the seventh year. There may be more than 20 bowers in an area and these are dispersed evenly far apart. The same bower territories tend to be occupied year after year by the same or a different male. Breeds September-February. Nests up to 35m in a tree as close as 24m from the nearest bower. Endemic.
Immatures: *like adult female until the fourth-year male undergoes changes in throat and bill colour.*
Voice: *drawn out whistle, harsh churrs, ringing advertising calls, buzzing and rattling.*   PG

2, 5   REGENT BOWERBIRD *Sericulus chrysocephalus*   24-28cm
The Regent Bowerbird inhabits wet forests and scrub, particularly rainforest. It forages from ground level to the canopy and feeds primarily on fruits, but also on leaves, insects and spiders. It may be found in the same rainforest as Satin Bowerbirds and Green Catbirds and sometimes all three species can be seen feeding simultaneously in a fig tree. In the non-breeding season, it visits gardens and orchards and forages singly and in small groups. Mostly solitary and sedentary in the breeding season. The striking plumage of the adult male is attained at 4-6 years although females may breed when 3 years old. The adult male builds an avenue bower similar to that of the Satin Bowerbird, but it is smaller. Many bowers are concealed by a thick vine layer directly above the bower, and hence they are seldom found. Male Regents sparsely decorate their bowers with brown small shells, blue, red or black berries, fresh leaves and sometimes flowers and man-made objects. Unlike the Satin Bowerbird, ornaments are placed mostly within the avenue. The male paints the inside avenue walls. An adult male at its bower holds an ornament in its bill and performs strutting, head-bobbing, bowing and wing-opening to a visiting female or immature male. Quiet chattering, twittering and mimicry, only audible a metre or so from the bower, occur throughout display. Like the Satin Bowerbird, immature males display on platforms and rudimentary bowers to females and immatures males. Breeds October-January. Nests up to 10m. Endemic.
Sexes: *distinctly different.*
Immatures: *like adult female but sub-adult males have yellow bill.*
Voice: *metallic, te-aar, chattering and mimicry, no loud advertising calls.*   2PG, 5T&PG

3, 6   GOLDEN BOWERBIRD *Prionodura newtoniana*   23-35cm
The species lives in tropical rainforest above 900m and has a restricted distribution in north-east Queensland from near Cooktown to the Seaview Range, north of Townsville. It is the smallest of the bowerbirds, yet the male builds a massive 1-3m high maypole bower comprising two pyramids of sticks built around two saplings about a metre apart. These structures are fused together with fungus and bridged by a horizontal perch on which the male displays to visiting females. The male festoons the display perch and nearby parts of the bower with grey-green lichen, fruits and dried cream flowers with black seeds attached. Bowers are built on sloping hillsides and are dispersed evenly throughout suitable habitat. An adult male maintains and defends one bower, but a single bower may be attended by several female-plumaged males. This bowerbird occurs singly and in small groups, and feeds predominantly on fruits, but also takes beetles and cicadas. Breeds September-February. Female nests in tree crevices up to 15m above ground. Endemic.
Immatures: *first year plumage like adult female, then plumage of immature male becomes washed with yellow before assuming the adult male plumage.*
Voice: *croaks, rattles, mimicry.*   3NC, 6H&JB

7   GREAT BOWERBIRD *Chlamydera nuchalis*   32-37cm
The Great Bowerbird is Australia's largest bowerbird, and is quite common. It inhabits rainforest, eucalypt forest, riverine vegetation, dry woodland, mangroves and urban gardens. An adult male builds and maintains one large avenue bower. Its ornamentation is very like that of the Spotted Bowerbird, but the Great Bowerbird also collects red objects. The male's bower display is similar to that of the Spotted Bowerbird. It also has a brilliant nape patch. Normally hidden, its lustrous rose-lilac feathers suddenly opens into a beautiful fan when displaying. It occurs singly and in small groups, and feeds on fruits, insects and spiders. Breeds August-February. Female nests to 10m. Endemic.
Sexes: *alike, but female smaller, sometimes paler; lilac neck patch reduced or absent.* **Immatures:** *paler than adults, lack neck patch.*
Voice: *like Spotted Bowerbird.*
                                                                              H&JB

8   WESTERN BOWERBIRD *Chlamydera guttata*   25-31cm
The Western Bowerbird is closely related to the Spotted Bowerbird, and there are similarities in its plumage, habits, breeding and voice. Also similar are the bower ornaments, display and the painting of the inside avenue walls. It frequents vegetation in the rocky ranges of the dry inland particularly where the native fig occurs, and visits homestead gardens. The diet is predominantly native figs but includes other fruits, seeds, nectar, insects and spiders. It occurs singly and in small groups and forms winter foraging flocks. It has a band of lustrous lilac-pink plumes on the nape which it exposes when displaying. Breeds August-February. Rainfall regulates the start of breeding. Endemic.
Female: *nape patch duller and smaller.*
Immatures: *paler body plumage than adults.*
Voice: *likeSpotted Bowerbird.*
                                                                              B&BW

9   SPOTTED BOWERBIRD *Chlamydera maculata*   25-31cm
The Spotted Bowerbird, more common in the north of its range, inhabits dry, open woodland, inland riverine vegetation, and visits homestead gardens. The male builds an avenue bower of twigs and grasses and places hundreds of display objects on the platform and in the avenue. Ornaments (preferably white, green, amber and mauve) include bones, pebbles, shells, fruits and man-made glass and metallic objects. In display at the bower the male turns its hindneck towards the female to expose a nape fan of iridescent lilac-pink plumes. Mates in the avenue or on the bower platform. Breeds October-January. Nests from 2-15m in tree branches or mistletoe clumps.
Female: *nape plume smaller or absent.*
Immatures: *lack plume.*
Voice: *renowned for mimicry of natural and mechanical sounds; ringing metallic advertising calls; harsh grindings, hissing and clicking.*
                                                                              CC

10   FAWN-BREASTED BOWERBIRD *Chlamydera cerviniventris*   25-30cm
The Australian range of the Fawn-breasted Bowerbird is restricted to Cape York Peninsula. It lives in coastal woodlands, forest edge, riverine vegetation and mangroves. The drab coloured adult male builds the most elaborate, ornately decorated of the two-walled avenue bowers. One end of the platform and the tops of both avenue walls are decorated profusely with many fresh green fruits, particularly bunches of green berries. The male paints the inside walls with vegetable matter. The twigs are green when freshly painted and turn a dull grey and red-brown when dry. Occurs singly and in small groups. Mainly breeds September-December. Nests to 10m.
Sexes: *alike.*
Immatures: *like adults, but forehead more streaked greyish.*
Voice: *like Spotted Bowerbird.*
                                                                              EZ

11   SPOTTED CATBIRD *Ailuroedus melanotis*   26-30cm
Sedentary in tropical upland rainforest in north-east Queensland. Males do not build bowers or courts. Monogamous breeding pairs hold year-round territories and defend them in the breeding season by song and chasing. Noted for their strange wailing notes uttered throughout the day particularly at the onset of breeding. Females build the nest and incubate the eggs and both sexes feed the young. They occur in small foraging flocks in the non-breeding season and singly or in pairs at any time of the year. Feeds chiefly on fruits, but also leaves, flowers, seeds, insects and nestling birds. Forages from ground level to the canopy. Breeds September-March. Nests to 15m.
Sexes: *alike.*
Immatures: *head greener and less mottled; upper parts duller.*
Voice: *repertoire includes loud cat-like wailing notes; baby cries; single or double high pitched squeak or 'chip'.*
                                                                              R&DK

15

12   GREEN CATBIRD *Ailuroedus crassirostris*   28-33cm
Monogamous breeding pairs occupy year-round territories in rainforest. Males do not build bowers or courts. Quiet in the non-breeding season but can be located by their 'chip' call. In the nesting season, neighbouring territorial males engage in singing bouts throughout the day. Male and female members of a pair have different songs and sing a duet against neighbouring pairs. Females build the nest and incubate the eggs and both sexes feed the young. The diet is primarily fruits, especially figs, and includes flowers, leaves, seeds, frogs, insects, millipedes and nestling birds. Forages from ground level to the canopy but mostly in the middle and upper vegetation levels. Breeds September-February. Nests to 18m. Endemic.
Sexes: *alike.*
Immatures: *duller than adults and less distinctly streaked.*
Voice: *like Spotted Catbird; song dialects vary throughout its range.*   GC

13   TOOTH-BILLED BOWERBIRD *Scenopoeetes dentirostris*   24-27cm
The Tooth-billed Bowerbird lives in tropical rainforest between 600 and 1400m. Around September, the male clears a display court on the forest floor and decorates it with fresh leaves placed with the under-surfaces uppermost. Throughout the breeding season, males perch above their courts and the forest rings with their loud calls as neighbouring males sing and counter-sing against each other to advertise their presence and attract mates. Fruits predominate in the diet, which includes insects and leaves. The species gets its name from its bill serrations which are used primarily for tearing and eating leaves but also for snipping off leaves for the display court. Breeds November-February. Female nests up to 27m. Endemic.
Sexes: *alike.*
Immatures: *like adults, but browner above and paler below.*
Voice: *loud and varied repertoire including mimicry; harsh 'chuck'.*   PG

Orioles and Figbirds

14   OLIVE-BACKED ORIOLE *Oriolus sagittatus*   25-28cm
Northern populations of the widespread Olive-backed Oriole are sedentary. South-eastern populations migrate north in the non-breeding season. The species lives in eucalypt forest and woodland and adjacent rainforest, visits parks and gardens, and feeds on fruit and insects. Monogamous breeding pairs hold nesting territories. Both sexes feed the young and vigorously attack and chase potential avian predators from the nest area. Breeds September-January. Suspends nest in fork of outer foliage up to 20m high.
Sexes: *slightly different; male greener and female greyer.*
Immatures: *duller than adults, greyish upperparts, wing and tail feathers edged rufous, bill and eye blackish.*
Voice: *loud, clear, rollicking song resembling 'olly-olly-ole'; mimicry.*   JP

15   YELLOW ORIOLE *Oriolus flavocinctus*   25-30cm
The Yellow Oriole inhabits wet tropical forests and woodlands, mangroves, parks and gardens. It is noted for its melodious, incessant song delivered for up to 2 hours at a time from perches within tree foliage. It feeds on fruit and insects and mostly occurs singly and in pairs, but small groups visit fruiting trees. Breeds August-January. Nests to 15m.
Sexes: *similar, but female paler.*
Immatures: *upperparts paler than adults; body more heavily streaked; bill dark.*
Voice: *loud, repetitive, liquid bubbling notes, harsh scolding.*   H&JB

16, 17, 18   FIGBIRD *Sphecotheres viridis*   27-29cm
Figbirds are arboreal and frequent rainforest edge, eucalypt forest, woodland and urban parks and gardens. They feed on many kinds of native and cultivated fruits but, as the name suggests, they specialise in eating fig fruits. Locally nomadic when searching for fruiting trees. Unlike orioles, figbirds forage in large, noisy flocks of 100 or more in the non-breeding season. In the breeding season they form monogamous pairs, and both sexes feed the young. The facial skin patch of the male sometimes flushes red.
Females: *like immatures.*
Voice: *chattering and chirping, squeaks and short, sharp yelps.*

16, 17 Northern race *flaviventris* YELLOW FIGBIRD Frequents tropical woodlands and gardens. It hybridises and intergrades with the green southern race where their ranges meet around
Townsville. Breeds September-March and nests to 20m high.   16D&MT, 17GC
18 Southern race *vieilloti* GREEN FIGBIRD Breeds October-February. Nests to 20m.
Female: *(similar to female of race* flaviventris).   K&BR

338

Birds of Paradise

19, 22   VICTORIA'S RIFLEBIRD *Ptiloris victoriae*   23-25cm
Named in honour of Queen Victoria in 1850 by John Gould. This riflebird, restricted to north-east
Queensland and adjacent offshore islands, lives in tropical rainforest and frequents woodland and gallery
forest. It forages like treecreepers up tree trunks to the canopy and uses its stout decurved bill to search
and probe for insects and spiders in arboreal epiphytic ferns and orchids. It also feeds on fruits. The
species is promiscuous and, in the breeding season, solitary adult males deliver advertising calls and display their plumage to attract females for mating. Display sites include the tops of tree stumps and high
exposed tree perches. Each adult male may have more than one display site within its territory. In
response to a visiting female, a displaying male adopts an upright posture with tail raised, opens and fans
its wings so the wing tips extend above the head and moves its head from side to side. In a display
between adult and immature male, the two males face each other and almost touch. Each bird in turn
extends its opened wings forward, throws back its head and opens its bill wide. The tail is then spread
and the two birds sway from side to side with their wing tips meeting out from the breast. In flight, the
wings of the male make an audible, rustling sound. Breeds October-January. Female nests in tree or palm
foliage to 5m. Sometimes the nest rim is decorated with a sloughed snake-skin. Endemic.
Immatures: *like adult females until immature male develops black feathers and wing rustling.*
Voice: *single rasping 'yaas'; female less vocal.*   H&JB

20, 23   MAGNIFICENT RIFLEBIRD *Ptiloris magnificus*   †28-33cm ‡26-28cm
In Australia, the Magnificent Riflebird is restricted to the tropical rainforest of Cape York Peninsula.
Like a treecreeper, it forages singly up tree trunks and along branches in the middle and upper vegetation levels in search of insects and spiders, it also feeds on fruits. The species is promiscuous and, in
the breeding season, solitary adult males call from high exposed branches to advertise their presence
and attract mates. When a female visits the display perch, the male spreads open both wings, stretches
the head back and swings it from side to side to expose the metallic iridescent throat and breast shield.
A displaying male may relax its wings then snap them back to produce a rustling sound in unison with
its swaying head. No vocal sounds accompany the display. Breeds October-February. Nests from 2-12m
in palms or dense tree foliage. Sometimes the outer nest rim is decorated with a sloughed snake-skin
Sexes: *distinctly different.*
Immatures: *like adult female.*
Voice: *loud reverberating wee-hoo whistle by adult male; female whistles are more
    subdued.*   20BP, 23D&MT

21   PARADISE RIFLEBIRD *Ptiloris paradiseus*   25-30cm
The Paradise Riflebird lives in rainforest and disperses to adjacent eucalypt woodland and forest in the
non-breeding season. It mostly forages singly in trees and feeds on fruit and insects, and can be located by showers of debris from above. Its wings rustle in flight. In the breeding season, solitary adult
males deliver advertising calls from high display perches. On the approach of a female, the promiscuous male opens and fans its wings, cocks the tail, points the bill up and exposes the lime-green gape.
The male encloses the female with its outstretched rustling wings, claps its wing tips together and performs mating. Breeds October-January. Nests up to 25m. Endemic.
Male: *similar in coloration to the male Victoria's and Magnificent Riflebirds.*
Immatures: *like females.*
Voice: *double, sometimes single, harsh, loud explosive 'yaas'.*   T&PG

24   TRUMPET MANUCODE *Manucodia keraudrenii*   27-32cm
The loud trumpet-like blast of the male, which gives the species its name, is produced by modified
coiled windpipes. It lives in rainforests in Cape York Peninsula. Monogamous breeding pairs hold a territory and specialise in feeding on figs. The female of a pair builds the nest and incubates the eggs and
both sexes feed the young. Adults feed on fruit and insects and usually forage singly, in pairs or in mixed
species flocks in the middle to upper levels of the forest. Breeds October-January. Nests to 20m.
Sexes: *similar.*
Immatures: *like adults, but less glossy.*
Voice: *drawn out, far carrying trumpet-like call.*   BP

16 Mostly Black-and-white Birds

AUSTRALIAN MAGPIE *Gymnorhina tibicen*

1   Western form *race G.t.dorsalis*   37-43cm
Confined to southwestern WA. Habits and voice as for the Black-backed Magpie.
Male: *closely resembles the White-backed Magpie.*
Female: *(illustrated) black mottled on the back with white edged feathers.*   JD

2   Black-backed form *G.t.tibicen* Nominate race   38-44cm
Widely spread and common throughout Australia, the magpies live in all types of open woodland, and is
equally at home in parks and suburban gardens. Although it can become tame, it will not hesitate to swoop
down viciously on any bird or person deemed to be a threat to its nest. Inland, it is wary of humans. Adult
magpies congregate in well-defined groups dominated by polygamous males. The female builds the nest,
usually in a tree up to 20m high, sometimes on a pole. The brood is fed by both parents until they are able
to fly. Even then they will continue to pester any adult to beg with incessant plaintive piping. Magpies feed
on insects and other invertebrates taken on the ground or levered from likely crevices. Birds not yet of
breeding age often form large flocks with other unattached birds. Breeds July-March.
Male: *illustrated.*
Female: *nape mottled dusky grey.*
Immatures: *like dull female - black plumage greyer.*
Voice: *a variety of carolling and warbling notes - often in duet or chorus with other birds - especially at dawn and dusk. One of the most familiar and evocative of all Australian
bird sounds.*   PG

3   White-backed form *G.t leuconota*   38-44cm
Habits and voice as for the Black-backed Magpie.
Male: *illustrated.*
Female: *white back indistinctly mottled.*
Immatures: *like dull female - black plumage greyer.*   T&PG

Many hybrid forms occur where populations overlap - ranging from fully black-backed to fully white-
backed birds. Sometimes, the change from black-backed to white-backed can be abrupt - with fully
black and fully white backed birds living in adjacent territories.

Others: Tasmanian form *G.t.hypoleuca*   43cm
Male and female similar to mainland White-backed races

4   BLACK BUTCHERBIRD *Cracticus quoyi*   32-45cm
There are two forms of this the largest of the butcherbirds. More northerly populations are larger, have a nar-
rower bill and are wholly black; those south of Cooktown are smaller with a broader bill, and go through a
rufous phase from immaturity. Sedentary, it frequents all levels of forest and mangroves and feeds on small
animals, eggs, crustaceans and fruit. Breeds September-February. Nests to 10m or in lower mangrove tree.
Female: *smaller.*
Immatures: *generally - dull black washed brown; north-eastern Queensland only - mostly rufous.*
Voice: *beautiful bubbling or yodelling 'ah-oo-ah'.*   T&PG

5   BLACK CURRAWONG *Strepera fuliginosa*   47cm
Confined to Tasmania and islands of the Bass Strait, and widespread. It frequents the wetter forest and high-
er tablelands in ones and twos in summer and forms large flocks in winter. Some birds descend to lower
altitudes during this period, and become nomadic. Breeds August-December. Nests to 20m. Endemic.
Recognition: *(cf Grey Currawong): blacker; white tail and wing tips almost absent.*
Sexes: *alike.*
Immatures: *like adults except for yellow gape.*
Voice: *loud ringing 'kar-week week-kar'.*   GW

6   PIED CURRAWONG *Strepera graculina*   46cm
The aggressive Pied Currawong is one of eastern Australia's most conspicuous birds. It lives mainly
in wooded country and is often seen and heard in suburban parks and gardens. High country popula-
tions tend to descend to lower altitudes in winter, and may gather in large flocks. It feeds on insects,
nestlings and eggs, carrion and berries. Nests to 20m. Endemic but extends to Lord Howe Island.
Sexes: *alike.*
Immatures: *grey-brown.*
Voice: *ringing 'cur-ra-wong' and wolf-whistles.*   D&MT

7   PIED BUTCHERBIRD *Cracticus nigrogularis*   32-35cm
In pairs, small parties and family groups, the Pied Butcherbird lives in open woodland or timbered pastoral land and is widespread across its range except in desert areas. In the south-west it is slowly extending its range southwards as forests are cleared. Family groups sing in a superb alternating chorus. It feeds on nestlings, insects, mice, snakes and lizards. Breeds August-December. Nests high. Endemic.
Sexes: *alike.*
Immatures: *brown-grey where adult plumage is black.*
Voice: *outstandingly beautiful song of loud mellifluous notes, sometimes by moonlight; some mimicry.*   D&MT

GREY CURRAWONG *Strepera versicolor*

8   Western race *S.v.plumbea*   46-55cm
Dark grey to brownish black. White markings as for nominate race. Range: York & Eyre Peninsulas, central and western Australia.   GC

9   Eastern race *S.v.versicolor (nominate)*   45-51cm
The palest grey of the race. White tip to wing and tailquills, white under tail coverts - and white patch under wing (visible in flight).Range: Victoria and NSW.   CG

Other races:-
    Black-winged race *S.v.melanoptera*   45-51cm
The darkest mainland race. Range: Southeast of South Australia and the Murray Mallee
    Tasmanian race *S.v.arguta*   47cm
Plumage similar to *melanoptera.*

10   GREY BUTCHERBIRD Silver-backed race *Cracticus torquatus argenteus*   28cm
Two silver-backed races of the Grey Butcherbird occur in north-west Australia - *argenteus* (illustrated) in the Northern Territory, and *latens*, a slightly different form in the Kimberley. They closely resemble the Grey Butcherbird in behaviour. Breeds July-January. Nests 1-7m from the ground. Endemic.
Female: *brown wash on crown.*
Immatures: *browner, white parts duller.*
Voice: *melodious rollicking whistling, often in duet; mimicry.*   T&PG

11   GREY BUTCHERBIRD *Cracticus torquatus*   28-32cm
Its pre-eminently lovely song is one of the hallmarks of this familiar bird. It is equally well-known for impaling nestlings and other prey to be eaten later. In any timbered areas it may be seen singly, in pairs or family parties. Being sedentary, it may become relatively tame in gardens but is fearless in defence of the nest. Tasmanian birds are larger. Breeds July-January. Nests 1-7m high. Endemic.
Female: *brown wash on crown.*
Immatures: *browner, white parts duller.*
Voice: *loud melodious rollicking whistling, often in duet; some mimicry.*   D&MT

12   BLACK-BACKED BUTCHERBIRD *Cracticus mentalis*   25cm
This Cape York-dwelling bird is a tropical variant of the other butcherbirds. In forest or woodland, and around any settlement, it is seen singly or in pairs. It forages in trees and shrubs for insects, lizards, small birds and nestlings, and eats some seeds. Breeds October-December. Nests high in tree fork.
Recognition: *(cf Pied Butcherbird): the differences are mainly its white instead of black throat and smaller size.*
Sexes: *alike.*
Immatures: *duller.*
Voice: *euphonious carolling, softer than Grey Butcherbird; some mimicry.*   EW/NPI

13   SPANGLED DRONGO *Dicrurus bracteatus*   30cm
Singly, in pairs or parties, this bird, distinguished by its forked 'fishtail', frequents forest fringes, open woodland, mangrove, parks and gardens. It feeds mainly on insects snapped up in the air, or gleaned from foliage; also nectar. Eastern birds are partly migratory after breeding, some moving northwards as far as New Guinea, others southwards. Breeds September-March. Nests on horizontal fork to 15m high.
Female: *smaller.*
Immatures: *head dull black spangled blue, spotted white below, brown eye.*
Voice: *harsh twanging and tearing sounds, chattering, creaky whistle.*   HP

14, 15 MAGPIE-LARK (Peewee) *Grallina cyanoleuca*   26-30cm
All over Australia, except in Tasmania where it only occurs as a vagrant, the widespread Magpie-lark lives most-ly in open timbered country, always near water for the mud needed to construct the nest, and is frequently seen in wooded suburbia and city parks. It is bravely combative and noisy in defence of its territory and chases off much larger birds. While readily accepting the presence of humans, it may unexpectedly attack them in the breeding season. It sometimes also attacks its own image in reflective surfaces like windows, or even a car wind-screen. It feeds on small invertebrates and insects, also aquatic creatures. When foraging on the ground, its head bobs pigeon-like as it walks. Established pairs are generally sedentary, but non-breeding birds form nomadic flocks that can reach several thousand. Breeds all months in response to rain. Builds mud nest plastered to a tree, pole or building. Endemic, but recently recorded in New Guinea.
Female: *similar, but throat white encircled with black band, no white eyebrow.*
Immatures: *white eyebrow and throat.*
Voice: *mainly strident 'pee-o-whit' or 'pee-o-whee', and a liquid 'orch-id'.*   D&MT

16   COMMON MYNA *Acridotheres tristis*   24cm
Not to be confused with the native Noisy Miner, this bird, a native of India, was originally introduced to Melbourne in 1860 and subsequently released in Sydney and parts of Queensland, including the canefields to combat insects, but without success. It has become one of Australia's worst avian pests, and many bemoan the way its aggressive territorialism has driven off much-loved native birds. It lives in pairs and family groups and roosts communally in park and street trees, under bridges and elsewhere. Any source of food is exploited. Breeds October-March.
Sexes: *alike.*
Immatures: *duller.*
Voice: *strident rollicking chatter; accomplished mimic.*   D&MT

17   COMMON STARLING *Sturnus vulgaris*   21cm
A native of Europe, the Common Starling, introduced into Victoria in the mid-19th century, has since spread extensively through urban areas, cleared land and native bush. Although it usefully preys on insect pests, it displaces native birds, damages fruit crops, and becomes a nuisance by nesting in house roofs. Declared a pest in Western and South Australia and vagrants are shot on sight. It feeds on fruit and insects. It gathers in very large flocks in autumn and winter and thousands may settle for the night in communal roosts.
Sexes: *alike.*
Immatures: *grey-brown upperparts, paler below.*
Voice: *nasal 'nark-nark-nark' and warbling calls.*   D&MT

18   METALLIC STARLING *Aplonis metallica*   24cm
Also known as the Shining Starling. This highly sociable bird arrives from New Guinea to breed in north-eastern Queensland in August and departs in March. Huge breeding colonies take over large rainforest trees in which to roost and nest and hundreds of their large untidy nests may festoon a sin-gle tree. Fruit is the main diet and dense feeding flocks may crowd a fruiting tree, with birds dashing continuously between the feeding and nesting areas. The noise set up by a colony can be deafening.
Sexes: *alike.*
Immatures: *duller, white underparts streaked black.*
Voice: *incessant medley of brassy chattering and whistling.*   H&JB

19   WHITE-WINGED CHOUGH *Corcorax melanorhamphos*   47cm
The White-winged Chough lives in forest, woodland and mallee, always near water. It forages mainly on the ground, often at roadsides and is usually seen in parties of up to 20 methodically turning over litter in search of insects, small animals and seeds. Feeding groups of up to 100 are not uncommon in winter. Breeds June-March. Builds mud nest in tree up to 10m. Endemic.
Recognition: *(cf Currawongs): white wing window visible mostly in flight. smaller down-curved bill; red eye and longer tail.*
Sexes: *alike.*
Immatures: *smaller, tail shorter, eye brown.*
Voice: *plaintive whistling and mournful piping, strident alarm call.*   KV/BOC

20   LITTLE CROW *Corvus bennetti*   48cm
Familiar in country towns and outback stations. Highly nomadic when conditions are bad inland and may travel great distances in large flocks after breeding. Mainly eats insects, also grain and carrion. Performs spectacular aerobatics in flight. Breeds in spring or after rain in desert regions. Nests in loose colonies in scrubby trees and on poles. Endemic.
Recognition: *flips wings up and tail down in time with each 'nark'; no throat hackles.*
Sexes: *alike.*
Immatures: *underparts sooty brown, eye brown.*
Voice: *nasal 'nark-nark-nark' and warbling calls.*   GC

21   TORRESIAN CROW *Corvus orru*   50cm
This mainly tropical corvid lives a mostly sedentary existence in farmland, woodland and along timbered inland water courses. It feeds on insects, crops and carrion. Immatures form flocks until 2 years old. Breeding season varies across range. Nests high in eucalypts and among pylons.
Recognition: *(c/f Australian Raven) voices differ; repeatedly shuffles the wings on landing; does not flip them when calling; throat hackles inconspicuous.*
Sexes: *similar.*
Immature: *brown tinge to feathers, brown eye.*
Voice: *repeated nasal, high-pitched, clipped notes 'uk-uk-uk-uk' or 'ok-ok-ok-ok'.*   GC

22   FOREST RAVEN *Corvus tasmanicus*   52cm
The only corvid in Tasmania. Small isolated populations also live on the mainland where they frequent dense forest within the ranges of the Australian and Little Ravens. Widespread in Tasmania where it frequents all types of habitats from dense forest in the high country to coastal woodlands. Nomadic flocks form in the non-breeding winter months. Breeds August-November. Nests high in tree. Endemic.
Recognition: *short and indistinct throat hackles; shorter tail and larger bill than other ravens.*
Sexes: *alike.*
Immatures: *underparts sooty brown, eye brown.*
Voice: *loud very deep 'kor-kor-kor-r-r'.*   TW

23   LITTLE RAVEN *Corvus mellori*   50cm
The Little Raven lives in open alpine woodlands, inland plains and well watered pastoral areas. Often in nomadic flocks, it feeds on large insects, carrion and spilt grain. Inland birds migrate in large flocks south-east during summer heat, and alpine birds descend to lower levels to winter. Breeds August-December; later in alpine regions. Nests in trees, also on poles or in low bushes inland. Endemic.
Recognition: *shuffles or flicks wings above back when calling; throat hackles inconspicuous.*
Sexes: *alike.*
Immatures: *underparts sooty brown, eye brown.*
Voice: *clipped 'kar-kar-kar'.*   T&PG

24   AUSTRALIAN RAVEN *Corvus coronoides*   56cm
Largest of the corvids, and common in most wooded habitats and well watered pastoral areas. Often wary and difficult to approach. Usually in pairs or small flocks of immatures. Feeds on large carrion, including dead or dying lambs, also insects and grain. Breeds July-September. Nests high in tall tree. Endemic.
Recognition: *calls with head lowered and tail nearly horizontal - seldom flicks wings; long conspicuous hackles on bulging throat; bare skin on sides of chin.*
Female: *slightly smaller.*
Immatures: *brown wash on underparts, eye brown.*
Voice: *drawn out 'ahh-ahh-ahh-r-r-r' including in flight.*   GC

WATER BIRDS

BIRDS OF THE INLAND WATERS, SHORE AND OCEAN

SECTIONS 17 TO 21

SPECIES NOTES

17 Long-legged Waterbirds

1, 2   CATTLE EGRET *Ardea ibis*   53cm
The Cattle Egret's invasion of Australia was first reported in 1948. Since then the species has spread
rapidly and continues to do so. The birds are usually seen in flocks in the vicinity of grazing cattle and
other farm animals, feeding on the insects they disturb. They sometimes perch on the animal's back.
Breeds all months depending on food availability. Nests in colonies in trees with other water birds.
Recognition: *bill and neck shorter and thicker than other egrets. (Breeding) orange-buff head, breast and back
with nuptial plumes especially on back; reddish-orange bill, face and eyes; dark legs. (Non-breeding) yellow
bill, face and eyes; dark legs lighter above knee.*
Adults and immatures: *alike.*
Voice: *low croaks and guttural sounds.*   1LS, 2AMcG

3   INTERMEDIATE EGRET *Ardea intermedia*   63cm
The spectacular nuptial plumes of this bird fall in a cascade of delicately-fringed aigrettes to form a
mantle over its back which sweeps well beyond the tail - hence its popular name of Plumed Egret.
Solitary or in groups, its behaviour and general appearance is akin to that of the Great and Little Egrets.
Breeds throughout the year when food is plentiful. Nests in colonies often with other water birds.
Recognition: *(Breeding) bill orange-red; eyes yellow, facial skin blue-green, upper legs red, feet black. (Non-
breeding) bill yellow, legs yellowish.*
Immatures: *as winter adult.*
Voice: *croaks and growling sounds.*   GW

4   GREAT-BILLED HERON *Ardea sumatrana*   1.5m
This giant heron is wary and secretive and spends most of the day skulking in mangrove swamps bor-
dering tidal rivers and estuaries. It flies out from its deep seclusion on the receding tide, especially at
dusk, to feed on the mudflats and in shallow waters. Its prey includes quite large fish. Sedentary.
Breeds in all months. Nests in a tree over water. **Sexes:** *alike.*
Immatures: *rusty brown.*
Voice: *harsh croaks and said to 'roar like an angry bull'.*   AH

5   WHITE-NECKED HERON *Ardea pacifica*   90cm
Also known as the Pacific Heron, Australia is the stronghold of this stately heron, but it is occasionally seen in New
Guinea and New Zealand. It is fairly widely distributed inland, less so towards the coast, and lives in mainly shal-
low fresh water areas and wet paddocks. It seldom frequents salt or brackish waters. Usually alone, it stalks through
wet grass or wades in shallow waters hunting for frogs, insects, crustacea and fish. It is strongly nomadic and large
eruptions may occur in an area after good rains. Breeds all months. Nests in tree usually in or over water, often in
small colonies.
Sexes: *alike out of breeding season.*
Immatures: *grey neck spotted with black.*
Voice: *deep croaks.*   ES

6   GREAT EGRET *Ardea alba*   91cm
The largest of the white egrets in Australia it is distributed worldwide in warm and temperate areas
and is probably known by more English names than any other bird, including Large Egret (Australia),
Great White Egret (Europe), Common Egret (America), Great Egret (Japan and Australia) and White
Heron (New Zealand). It is usually seen stalking alone in shallow inland and coastal waters ready to
strike with its long bill to seize a fish or other aquatic prey. Breeds at anytime according to food sup-
ply but mainly October-March. Nests in colonies in tree-tops usually with other water birds.
Recognition: *(Breeding) nuptial plumes on back extend well beyond tail; bill black, eyes yellow, face green-
ish, legs dark below paler above. (Non-breeding) bill, face and eyes yellow, legs blackish.*
Adults and immatures: *similar.*
Voice: *deep croaking and cawing notes at breeding colony.*   D&MT

7, 8   EASTERN REEF EGRET *Egretta sacra*   61-66cm

Reef Egrets, also known as Reef Herons, are essentially coastal birds and are found all around the coast-line and offshore islands of Australia - though rarely in Tasmania. The Australian birds can be either grey or white. White birds exceed grey in the north and vice versa in the south - with only grey birds in south-ern Australia. Both forms interbreed and grey and white nestlings often hatch in the same brood. The Reef Egret is usually seen alone patrolling tidelines and reefs in search of small fish and other marine creatures. It breeds all months, but mostly September-January, and nests in loose colonies in trees or on rock ledges.

Recognition: *the white form is distinguishable from other white egrets by its shorter and thicker legs and crouching hunting gait.*

Adults and immatures: *similar. Immatures of the grey form are brown.*

Voice: *loud croaks.*   D&MT

9   LITTLE EGRET *Egretta garzetta*   56cm

Usually seen singly in shallow water actively 'puddling' to dislodge prey from the bottom. Breeds all months depending on the food supply, and nests in colonies in trees often with other water birds.

Recognition: *(Breeding) two ribbon-like nuptial plumes on head and others on back and breast; black upper mandible, legs and feet; yellow face, eyes and soles. (Non-breeding) similar except for absence of plumes.*

Adults and immatures: *alike.*

Voice: *croaks and growling sounds.*   H&JB

10   WHITE-FACED HERON *Egretta novaehollandiae*   68cm

Familiar in estuaries, inland lakes, swamps and wet grasslands across the continent, it is probably Australia's best known heron. It waits and watches in shallow water for prey, sometimes puddling with its feet to disturb aquatic animals, and also stalks for reptiles, young birds, frogs, rodents and insects. It often feeds in associated flocks. Sedentary or nomadic in search of food. Breeds all months. Nests high in a tree, sometimes well away from water.

Sexes: *alike.*

Immatures: *lack white on head and cinnamon on breast.*

Voice: *harsh croak.*   D&MT

11, 12   PIED HERON *Ardea picata*   48cm

This heron of the tropics, frequents salt and freshwater swamps and nearby grasslands usually in loose feeding flocks of 30 or more. It feeds on fish and small invertebrates and sometimes scavenges at garbage dumps in search of food. Large flocks of several hundreds may gather around feeding areas in times of drought. It is aggressive towards other species to the point of stealing their prey or forcing them to disgorge. Sedentary, migratory or nomadic. Breeds September-November. It nests in large colonies in trees.

Sexes: *alike.*

Immatures: *head white without a crest.*

Voice: *loud 'ohrk', soft coo.*   H&JB

13, 14, 15   STRIATED HERON *Butorides striatus*   43-51cm

Also known as the Mangrove Heron, this species is found extensively throughout the tropical and sub-tropical regions of the world and belongs to a group of some thirty races sometimes referred to as the 'greens herons'. In Australia, there are two forms: a greenish grey-backed form, which is commonly seen all along the northern and eastern coasts; and a rufous form, which occurs in north-western Australia, and sporadically on the Queensland coast and elsewhere. It is characterised by short legs and stumpy body, and skulks looking more like a bittern than a heron. It mostly frequents mangrove swamps, tidal estuaries and mudflats. It roosts when the tide is in among the mangroves, and moves out onto the mudflats as it recedes. It usually hunts alone crouching low on the mud, sometimes wait-ing and watching absolutely still and at other times stalking stealthily along, poised to jab at its prey. It feeds on crustaceans, fish, molluscs, insects and particularly mud-skippers. Very wary, it freezes if disturbed or flies off low. Breeds September-December. Nests in dense foliage over water.

Sexes: *alike.*

Immature: *(see illustration).*

Voice: *squawks, explosive 'hoo'.*   T&PG

17

16, 17 NANKEEN NIGHT HERON *Nycticorax caledonicus*   56-65cm
This bird usually has two long head plumes throughout the year and is essentially nocturnal in habits.
It is widespread across the continent in a varied habitat which includes swamps, lagoons, river margins
and mangrove estuaries. It roosts communally by day, sometimes in large colonies, in leafy trees usual-
ly near water and takes wing at dusk in slow silent flight to the feeding grounds. It feeds mainly on
fish, but also takes a variety of other aquatic prey, insects, and even mice. Breeds September-
March/April. Nests in a tree or shrub up to 25m high above water; also on ground on treeless islands.
Sexes: *alike.*
Immatures:*(see illustration).*
Voice: *loud guttural 'kwak'.*   T&PG

18 AUSTRALASIAN BITTERN *Botaurus poiciloptilus*   66-76cm
This is the biggest of the Australian bitterns. It lives in dense reed beds fringing rivers and
swamps. It is most active at dusk and during the night and hunts alone. If approached, it silently
fades away and is rarely seen. Its food includes yabbies, eels, fish and small mammals and
insects. Seems to be nomadic. Breeds October-January. Nests sometimes colonially in reeds.
Recognition: *c/f illustration of immature Nankeen Night Heron if in doubt.*
Sexes: *alike.*
Immatures: *paler.*
Voice: *legend has it that its weird loud booming at night is the call of the fabled bunyip.*   H&JB

19 BLACK BITTERN *Ixobrychus flavicollis*   54-66cm
The Black Bittern lives in thick vegetation along rivers, creeks and mangroves, sometimes in rain-
forest near water, and is more inclined to show itself in the open than other bitterns. By day, it roosts
in a tree, at night it forages singly or in pairs for fish, frogs or crustaceans. Probably sedentary.
Breeds September-January. Nests semi-colonially in trees over water.
Female: *upperparts browner, less streaked below.*
Immatures: *duller, breast brown streaked yellow.*
Voice: *long drawn-out croaking, soft 'coo-oorh'.*   PM

20 LITTLE BITTERN *Ixobrychus minutus*   30cm
The extremely secretive and elusive Little Bittern lives in thickly vegetated swamps, lakes and rivers and
is believed to be nocturnal. It freezes at the slightest provocation, rarely takes flight, and steals away if
approached. Usually solitary, it feeds on small fish, insects and frogs. Probably migratory. Breeds October-
December. Nests on a platform of rushes and reeds in swamp vegetation or on tree branch over water.
Female: *crown and back brown, underparts streaked brown.*
Immatures: *browner, heavily streaked.*
Voice: *deep croaking monotonously repeated.*   RG

21 GLOSSY IBIS *Plegadis falcinellus*   52cm
This, the smallest of the ibises in Australia, frequents mostly inland fresh shallow waters including wet
grasslands, swamps and lagoons. It is gregarious and generally feeds in flocks on a variety of insects,
molluscs, and crustaceans; sometimes rice seeds. As it is strongly nomadic, its distribution is patchy and
variable. Breeds variably in response to rainfall. Nests in colonies in low vegetation standing in water,
mostly with other waterbirds.
Adults: *glossier, brighter in colour, head less streaked, bill more curved. Female: bill shorter.*
Voice: *croaks and grunts.*   D&MT

22 AUSTRALIAN WHITE IBIS *Threskiornis molucca*   70cm
Previously known as the Sacred Ibis. Common and locally abundant - flocks of over 10 000 have been
recorded in Victoria. It lives in swamps, margins of streams and lakes, adjoining grasslands, and city
parks where it can become tame. It feeds variously on aquatic creatures, insects such as grasshoppers and
garbage. Breeds August-November in south, February-May in north. Nests in mixed colonies over water
or in swamp vegetation.
Sexes: *similar but bill of female shorter.*
Immatures: *head and neck feathered.*
Voice: *grunts.*   D&MT

23   STRAW-NECKED IBIS *Threskiornis spinicollis*   70cm
The most numerous of the ibises in Australia - over 200 000 breeding birds have been recorded in South Australia. In pairs and flocks it frequents swamps and the margins of lakes and streams, also dry pastures, and feeds on frogs, small reptiles, mammals and, usefully, locusts and grasshoppers. It is highly nomadic, and odd birds stray as far as New Guinea; otherwise it is an endemic species. Breeds variably, depending on rain. Nests colonially in swamp vegetation and trees.
Female: *bill shorter.*
Immatures: *lacks neck plumes, feathered to crown, neck shorter.*
Voice: *grunts and croaks.*   T&PG

24   ROYAL SPOONBILL *Platalea regia*   75cm
The Royal Spoonbill is distinguished by its black bill and legs, and a spectacular crest of head plumes in the breeding season. It is frequently seen wading singly or in small parties, sometimes in flocks in shallow coastal and inland waters, and feeding by sweeping its long spoon-shaped bill from side to side. It is partial to shrimps and also takes fish and molluscs. Sometimes flies at great heights. Breeds October-May. Nests in colonies in tall trees over water.
Female: *bill shorter.*
Immatures: *bill shorter, flight feathers tipped black.*
Voice: *low grunting and croaking; bill clapping.*   D&MT

25, 28   BLACK-NECKED STORK (Jabiru) *Ephippiorhynchus asiaticus*   1.29-1.70m
The Black-necked Stork is better known in the north than in the south but it is nowhere common. It mostly frequents freshwater lagoons, estuary mudflats, mangrove swamps, swampy ground and flooded pastures, and quietly paces through the shallows probing for fish, amphibians, and crustaceans. Except when breeding it is usually seen alone. It is wary and flies off if approached. It labours to become airborne and its flight is ponderous. Sometimes soars to great heights. It is partly nomadic. Breeds March-June. Nests at or near the top of a tree or a large bush up to 25m.
Sexes: *female - eye yellow, male - eye black.*
Immatures: *like adults but black is brown and white is dusky.*
Voice: *almost mute, claps bill at nest.*   25KI, 28JF

26   YELLOW-BILLED SPOONBILL *Platalea flavipes*   89cm
When breeding, this spoonbill grows long nuptial breast plumes instead of a crest. It is the more abundant of the two spoonbills, and more often seen inland and in small areas of water, such as farm dams. It feeds on fish, aquatic insects and molluscs. It sweeps methodically with its flat bill and stirs the bottom to dislodge prey. It is highly nomadic with an erratic distribution. Breeds September-January or according to conditions. Nests in colonies or in tree in or near water. Endemic.
Sexes: *male's bill longer than female's.*
Immatures: *face not outlined black.*
Voice: *feeble grunts, bill claps.*   T&PG

27   SARUS CRANE *Grus antigone*   1.3-1.4m
The existence of the Sarus Crane in Australia was not known until about 20 of them were spotted on the Normanton River in North Queensland in 1966. It is distinguished from the Brolga by an extension of the bare red facial skin downwards to form a distinct collar on the neck, and by its pink legs instead of grey. Its habits are similar. It disperses after breeding and forms large, loose feeding flocks. Breeds mainly January-March. Like the Brolga it nests on a platform of vegetation just above water level.
Sexes: *alike, female smaller.*
Immatures: *like Brolga.*
Voice: *wild trumpeting usually in duet.*   D&MT

29 **BEACH STONE-CURLEW** *Esacus magnirostris* 53-58cm
The Beach Stone-curlew, alone and in pairs, frequents quiet sandy beaches and mudflats of northern and eastern Australia and around coastal islands. It is sedentary and sightings are usually far between. During high tide it shelters in mangroves or foreshore trees, emerging as the water recedes to feed on crabs crustaceans and insects. It is active at night. Breeds October-February. Nests in a scrape in the sand.
Sexes: *alike.*
Immatures: *similar but duller.*
Voice: *banshee wail higher pitched than Bush Stone-curlew.* GC

30 **BROLGA** *Grus rubicunda* 1.25m
The Brolga, one of the world's largest cranes, is famed for its graceful mutual dancing display rituals performed during courtship and socialising, when the birds bow, advance and retreat, trumpet and fling objects into the air. It lives near swamps, shallow lakes, wet grasslands and pastures, and has a varied diet of vegetable matter, insects, cereal grains and sedge tubers. Sometimes seen in very large flocks in the north of its range during the drier months, and it is nomadic. Breeds October-April. Nests on mound in shallow water.
Sexes: *similar.*
Immatures: *facial skin paler pink.*
Voice: *various trumpetings and hoarse croaks.* JMcC

31 **BUSH STONE-CURLEW** *Burhinus magnirostris* 50-58cm
The Bush Stone-curlew lives in open woodland, edges of forest, and along inland watercourses. It is still abundant in parts of the tropical north but is approaching extinction in pastoral areas in the south where once it was common. It is wary, and may crouch near ground if approached rather than fly away. It is mostly active nocturnally and emerges at dusk sometimes in groups to fly perhaps some distance to a feeding area to forage for insects, spiders and fruits. Sedentary. Breeds August-January. Nests in a scrape on the ground. Endemic.
Sexes: *alike.*
Immatures: *paler.*
Voice: *loud wailing 'wee-loo', often at night.* PJ

1 BLACK SWAN *Cygnus atratus*   1.17-1.42m
Native to Australia, the Black Swan is most often seen on extensive shallow stretches of permanent water where it can reach to the bottom to feed, and occasionally on brackish or even salt water. It flies with neck outstretched in V-formations. After breeding, enormous flocks, sometimes of many thousands, gather to moult. Breeds variably from February to September. Nest is a heap of vegetable matter in water..
Sexes: *males, larger; females, bill and iris lighter.*
Cygnets: *grey-brown.*
Voice: *high-pitched 'creaky-gate' bugles, including in flight.*   PR

2 MUTE SWAN *Cygnus olor*   1.27-1.56m
The graceful Mute Swan, bigger than the Black Swan, was introduced progressively into Australia from the late 1800s for release on ornamental lakes, but not always successfully. Small breeding colonies survive, such as at Northam, WA and Lake Leake, Tasmania. It can be very tame, although extremely aggressive when breeding. It eats aquatic plants, frogs, fish and small birds. Breeds mostly in late winter or spring. Nests on floating vegetation.
Sexes: *alike.*
Cygnets: *brown-grey.*
Voice: *mostly silent, completely so in flight, but hisses and grunts savagely when breeding.*   PG

3 CAPE BARREN GOOSE *Cereopsis novaehollandiae*   1m
The Cape Barren Goose breeds on small islands off the southern coast of Australia vegetated with tussock grassland and heath, from the Furneaux Group in the east to the Recherche Archipelago in the west. After breeding many birds disperse to adjacent mainland and northern Tasmania. It grazes on grasses and herbage. Pairs probably mate for life and are exceptionally belligerent in defence of their breeding territories. Breeds May-August. Nests in trees, on rocky ledges or on the ground. It was hunted to near extinction in earlier days. Endemic.
Sexes: *similar.*
Immatures: *paler.*
Voice: *honking and grunting.*   T&PG

4 WANDERING WHISTLING-DUCK *Dendrocygna arcuata*   60cm
Rarely seen away from water, and frequents deep tropical lagoons and swamps, where it feeds almost exclusively, diving deep for aquatic vegetation. It is usually seen in closely-knit flocks either on the water or roosting on the bank and is very watchful and wary. During the wet season it disperses inland and vagrants may appear in the south. Breeding is linked with rainfall. Nests in long grass.
Sexes: *alike.*
Immatures: *duller.*
Voice: *high whistles and twitters.*   T&PG

5 AUSTRALIAN WOOD DUCK *Chenonetta jubata*   48cm
Also known as the Maned Goose. A mane of elongated black neck feathers characterise this duck, and a small pointed bill and long neck give it a rather goose-like appearance. It has claws on its feet which provide purchase for climbing and perching in trees. It lives mostly on land in country near water, and grazes on grass and plants, including at night. It gathers in large flocks after breeding. Locally nomadic. Breeds in spring or after heavy rains. Nests in tree hollow. Ducklings jump out to calling parents below soon after hatching. Endemic.
Immatures: *paler.*
Voice: *'mew' or 'mmwarp'.*   GC

6 MAGPIE GOOSE *Anseranas semipalmata*   ♂75-92 ♀71-81cm
Normally in flocks of several thousand, it frequents swamps and marshy margins of rivers and lagoons of the tropical north, and feeds on aquatic vegetation. Now almost entirely absent in the south where formerly abundant. Unlike other waterfowl, it has half-webbed feet, a prominent head knob, and a hooked bill; and it moults progressively without becoming flightless. Nomadic after breeding. Breeds during the Wet and nests on a floating platform of vegetation.
Sexes: *similar, but male's head knob sometimes larger (also larger in older birds).*
Immatures: *mottled brown-grey.*
Voice: *resonant honking.*   JF

7   PLUMED WHISTLING-DUCK *Dendrocygna eytoni*   61cm
Rarely swims and never dives, and is most commonly seen in very large flocks, feeding widely on open grass plains, paddocks and lagoon edges. Often seen perching in trees. Flocks leave their day-time camps near a water source to feed at night on seeds, legumes and vegetable material. On return-ing to the daytime camp, birds land on water and immediately swim ashore to roost. They disperse inland in the wet season in the north. Breeding is related to rainfall. Nests in long grass. Endemic, but vagrant in New Guinea. **Sexes:** *alike.*
Immatures: *paler.*
Voice: *high-pitched whistling and twittering.*   B&BW

8   GREEN PYGMY-GOOSE *Nettapus pulchellus*   36cm
More often seen than the Cotton Pygmy-Goose, this bird lives in pairs and small flocks in the tropics amongst the blue waterlilies, on dams, lagoons and lakes. It is exceptionally aggressive, and males often fiercely attack each other. It only rarely leaves the water and walks on land with difficulty. It dives deep for water plants or seeds, or takes water-lily buds. Sedentary; sometimes nomadic. Breeds during the wet season. Nests in tree hole.
Female: *neck not solid green all round, faint white eye-stripe.*
Immatures: *like females.*
Voice: *whistles and trills.*   D&MT

9   COTTON PYGMY-GOOSE *Nettapus coromandelianus*   38cm
This uncommon duck is entirely aquatic and seldom leaves water. Usually in pairs or small flocks, it fre-quents deep lagoons and freshwater lakes and feeds on aquatic plants and their seeds during the evening and night. It is shy and retiring and hides by day far out among the waterlilies. Sedentary. Breeds January-March. Nests in tree hollow usually over water.
Female: *less green on back, no black collar.*
Immatures: *like females.*
Voice: *staccato cackles, quacks.*   D&MT

10   FRECKLED DUCK *Stictonetta naevosa*   59cm
This rare and vulnerable duck is most often seen in small family parties in permanent heavily-vege-tated swamps and creeks. By day it retires to dense cover in deep water, then flies to the shallows at dusk to feed. Its diet of algae, seeds and weeds is obtained by a filtering action, most often while wad-ing on the shore line. It is sedentary but wanders inland in flocks, during drought. Breeding relat-ed to climatic conditions. Nests at water level. Endemic.
Sexes: *non-breeding male and female lack red bill saddle.*   GC

11   RADJAH SHELDUCK *Tadorna radjah*   55cm
Also known as the Burdekin Duck and White-headed Shelduck. Because of its tameness and slow flight it is an easy target for shooters and has disappeared from the east coast. Usually in pairs and small parties it frequents shallow brackish water, mudflats and mangroves near the coast. It roosts by day near cover at the water's edge and moves out to feed in the shallows for small aquatic animals, algae and sedge. Some movement further inland in wet season. Breeds April-July. Nests near water in large hollow limbs.
Sexes: *alike.*
Immatures: *white parts flecked brown.*
Voice: *loud hoarse whistling.*   ES

12   AUSTRALIAN SHELDUCK *Tadorna tadornoides*   72cm
As this bird is most abundant at sea level and on the coast, its alternative name Mountain Duck has been described as a 'piece of ingenious folklore'. Its other alternative name, the Chestnut-breasted Shelduck aptly describes the bird. Shy and wary and keeps well out on shallow lakes and marshes. Rafts of per-haps 10 000 birds gather to moult in summer after breeding. It feeds mostly on grass and herbage. Seldom dives. It forms strong pair bonds for life. Breeds in winter. Nests in tree to 25m high. Endemic.
Male: *in eclipse is paler on breast and white neck ring shrinks.*
Immatures: *duller.*
Voice: *deep honking.*   KI

13   PACIFIC BLACK DUCK Anas superciliosa   50-61cm
Widespread and probably the most numerous and familiar duck in Australia. Singly, in pairs and flocks it is seen wherever there are stretches of water. Becomes tame in city parks. A typical dabbling duck, it feeds by dredging mud by up-ending, and filtering seeds from the surface. Nomadic. Breeds usually July-October south; March-May north. Nests on ground, in grass or tree hole.
Sexes: *similar.*
Immatures: *black above, underparts yellow.*
Voice: *female, quacks, male loud courtship peeps.*   D&MT

14   MALLARD *Anas platyrhynchos*   55-68cm
Introduced from Europe, the Mallard has settled well into its Australian habitat. Too well, perhaps, for it interbreeds with the closely-related native Black Duck and, being the dominant strain, it is feared that it may overwhelm those characteristics with which the Black Duck survives the rigours of the Australian climate. Familiar in urban parks and environs. Breeds throughout the year. Nests on the ground or in tree holes. Male in eclipse is similar to female but the bill is dull green.
Immatures: *black above, yellow wing and underparts.*
Voice: *quacks similar to Pacific Black Duck.*   E&DH

15   CHESTNUT TEAL *Anas castanea*   48cm
Usually in pairs or small groups, it mostly frequents saltwater and brackish lakes and swamps of the coastal areas, and is abundant in Tasmania. When seen together with the Grey Teal, the females are difficult to separate. Dabbles mostly for aquatic plant material and insects. Usually sedentary. Breeds June-December. Nests on the ground or in crevices. Both parents stay with the ducklings. Endemic. Recognition: female is darker than Grey Teal and lacks the latter's white throat patch.
Immatures: *paler.*
Voice: *female loud quack, male peep or whistle. (Male left, female right)*   PG

16   AUSTRALASIAN SHOVELER *Anas rhynchotis*   45-53cm
The shoveler's broad, shovel-like bill is fringed with larger lamellae than the other dabbling ducks and is specially adapted for sieving small aquatic organisms from the water surface. It lives in thickly-vegetated swamps, usually well out in small parties often amongst other flocking ducks - sometimes foraging communally in a V-shaped formation. Very wary. It has a habit of rising into the air with a clap of the wings. Sedentary. Breeds August-December or after flooding. Nests mainly on the ground. Male in eclipse plumage resembles female. Endemic.
Immatures: *paler.*
Voice: *occasional 'took-took' but mostly silent.*   GC

17, 20   HARDHEAD *Aythya australis*   42-58cm
Also known as the White-eyed Duck. In pairs or flocks, sometimes very large, the Hardhead lives in pools and streams. Seldom ashore, it is a bird of deep water, a particularly strong swimmer and at home even in swiftly-flowing turbulent water. It dives deep for plant material, small animals and fish. If alarmed, it rises vertically with loudly whirring wings. Perhaps the fastest flyer of all Australian ducks. Breeds October-December, but variable. Nests mainly in swamp vegetation, or tree hollow over water. **Sexes:** *similar, but male's eye is white.*
Immatures: *golden-brown.*
Voice: *soft croaks and whistles, but usually silent.*   17GC, 20B&BW

18

18   GREY TEAL *Anas gracilis*   47cm

The ubiquitous Grey Teal is often seen in immense flocks and is highly nomadic in adapting to Australia's erratic rainfall. It mainly lives on inland swamps and tree-lined rivers in winter, and moves to the coast as these dry up in summer. All types of water, whether salt, brackish or fresh, offer it a home. It is a typical dabbling duck and feeds on seeds of land and water plants, small crustaceans, insects and their larvae. Breeds throughout the year according to water levels. Nests on the ground, in crevices and tree holes.

Sexes: *alike.*
Immatures: *paler.*
Voice: *female quacks, male peeps.*   D&MT

19   BLUE-BILLED DUCK *Oxyura australis*   44cm

The diving Blue-billed Duck lives entirely on water in thickly-vegetated swamps singly or in pairs; or in very large flocks on open lakes in winter. It is completely helpless on land, and labours in take-off to become airborne. It is secretive and wary; and usually keeps distant from the shore. It dives at once if alarmed and may travel far before resurfacing. Breeds September-March. Nests in dense reeds. Endemic.

Male: *blue bill only when breeding; plumage duller in eclipse;* **Female:** *freckled brown overall; resembles a small Freckled Duck with a stiff tail.*
Immatures: *paler.*
Voice: *low quacks, seldom heard.*   T&PG

21   PINK-EARED DUCK *Malacorhynchus membranaceus*   38-45cm

This duck is distinguished by its remarkable bill. Usually in pairs and small groups, it frequents mainly shallow lakes and swamps. It is extremely nomadic in response to rainfall and its numbers sometimes erupt after flooding. It feeds in shallow water for small organisms and often swims in circles in pairs to stir up mud. Breeds variably according to rainfall. Nests on a log, or in a bush or tree hole to 10m. Endemic.

Sexes: *alike.*
Immatures: *paler, pink ear patch less distinct.*
Voice: *several pleasant trilling or chirruping notes.*   LS

22   MUSK DUCK *Biziura lobata*   60-72cm

This bird frequents swamps and inlets singly or in companies, and dives for food and when seeking cover if approached. It is seldom seen on land. The polygamous male has a variety of lures to attract females during the breeding season; it secretes an oil which emits a powerful musky smell; it inflates its large pendulous bag below the bill during display and erects its tail feathers in a fan while kicking back 2m jets of water. Breeds September-December, but variable. Nests in dense reeds. Endemic.

Female: *reduced bill lobe.*
Immatures: *like females.*
Voice: *sometimes shrill whistle or 'plonk' sound.*   GC

1   GREAT CRESTED GREBE *Podiceps cristatus*   61cm

Widespread in many parts of the world, this is one of the most intensively studied of all birds, in part due to its unusual appearance; in part to its extraordinary and intricate courtship display of several phases culminating in a spectacular 'weed dance'. In Australia it is found in the vegetated margins of large expanses of still water, usually in pairs. Swims and dives, submerges, and patters over water when taking off in flight. Sedentary or migratory. Breeds November-January. Nests on floating vegetation.

Sexes: *alike.*
Immatures: *lack ear tufts and ruff.*
Voice: *variety of discordant calls.*   GC

2   HOARY-HEADED GREBE *Poliocephalus poliocephalus*   31cm

The male has two plumage phases: after breeding it loses the buff breast and the white lines on the head, but can usually be identified then by the broad black bar down the nape. Usually in pairs, sometimes several of these together when breeding, feeding on aquatic plants and insects in marine or muddy estuaries. Sedentary or nomadic. Breeds November-January or after rain. Nests in clump of weeds in shallow lightly vegetated inland waters or swamps. Endemic, but has spread sparingly to New Zealand.

Sexes: *similar.*
Immatures: *like non-breeding adult.*
Voice: *low notes, mostly silent.*   JE

3   AUSTRALASIAN GREBE *Tachybaptus novaehollandiae*   26cm

Also known as the Little Grebe. Familiar on any vegetated stretches of water, this species is somewhat similar in appearance to the Hoary-headed Grebe with which it often associates, although in the breeding season the male Australasian Grebe has rather brighter plumage and a creamy patch between eye and bill. It is less ready than the Hoary-headed Grebe to take to flight when alarmed. Undertakes nomadic flights, mostly at night. Breeds September-January. Nests on floating vegetation.

Sexes: *alike.*
Immatures: *like non-breeding adult.*
Voice: *rattling trill; noisier than the Hoary-headed Grebe.*   GC

4   CHESTNUT RAIL *Eulabeornis castaneoventris*   52cm

Living as it does in remote tropical mangroves, and being wary, shy and difficult to flush, the Chestnut Rail is rarely observed. It is more confident when at low tide it emerges into the open, searching the exposed mudflats for crustaceans. Characteristically, it flicks its tail when walking. It is seen singly or in family parties. Sedentary. Breeds October-February. Energetically defends the nest which is in mangrove roots or tree to 3m high. **Sexes:** *alike.*

Immatures: *not recorded.*
Voice: *repeated harsh screech, grunting.*   TH

5   LEWIN'S RAIL *Rallus pectoralis*   23cm

Shy and elusive and infrequently observed in its habitat of dense reedy sections of swamps and lakes. When flushed, it prefers running to flying. Its long slender beak is used in probing for crustaceans and insects. Throughout its range there is a size variation, south-eastern birds being the smallest. The larger south-western race is possibly extinct. Solitary and sedentary. Breeds August-December. Nests in or near water.

Sexes: *alike.*
Immatures: *grey faintly barred white.*
Voice: *'cree-ek', 'jik-jik-jik'; grunting.*   JP

6   BUFF-BANDED RAIL *Rallus philippensis*   31cm
The Buff-banded Rail is not uncommon in well-vegetated coastal areas including the margins of mangroves and inland habitats near water. Sometimes visits settled areas, forages for insects, small animals, seeds and aquatic plants. It is timid and runs away swiftly with tail flicking when danger threatens, infrequently resorting to flight. Solitary or in pairs. Birds in the west tend to be darker , those on Cape York Peninsula smaller. Some are nomadic and wander to New Guinea and islands to the north and west. Breeds mostly September-March. Nests low in grassy cover.
Sexes: *alike.*
Immatures: *duller.*
Voice: *creaky squeak.*   D&MT

7   RED-NECKED CRAKE *Rallina tricolor*   30cm
The Red-necked Crake lives in the obscurity of a remote habitat in the dense rainforest and watercourse vegetation of northern Queensland, and is mainly nocturnal. Especially secretive in habits, it always keeps to cover. It walks, swims underwater, flits silently, or flies in an ungainly fashion. It eats insects and freshwater animals. Solitary or in small family parties. Sedentary. Breeds November-April. Nests on or near ground.
Sexes: *alike.*
Immatures: *duller, belly barred chestnut.*
Voice: *shrill 'tare', sharp 'tok' mostly at night.*   H&JB

8   AUSTRALIAN SPOTTED CRAKE *Porzana fluminea*   20cm
The Australian Spotted Crake is not as timid as its relatives, and resorts less to dense cover. It lives in the vegetated margins of fresh, brackish or salt water, and feeds on aquatic plants, molluscs and insects and is seen singly, in pairs or companies. Breeds August-February. Nests in vegetation in shallow water. Endemic.
Female: *paler.*
Immatures: *upper parts browner.*
Voice: *harsh 'crake'; various chatterings.*   K&BR

9   SPOTLESS CRAKE *Porzana tabuensis*   20cm
A somewhat plain and timid bird with red legs. It frequents dense thickets around fresh water and salt swamps, and mangroves; also beaches and off-shore islands. It feeds on insects, molluscs and aquatic plants. Sedentary or nomadic. Breeds September-January. nests well hidden in vegetation in shallow water.
Sexes: *alike.*
Immatures: *duller, throat dull white.*
Voice: *accelerating 'kop-kop', 'croo'.*   GC

10   BAILLON'S CRAKE *Porzana pusilla*   16cm
Also known as the Marsh Crake. A widespread species, its long toes enable it to walk over water plants; it also swims and dives, and may roost in nearby trees. Its diet is composed of molluscs, seeds and green matter. Shy and secretive. Nomadic or migratory. Breeds September-February. Nests in a clump in shallow water.
Sexes: *alike.*
Immatures: *paler, less distinct markings.*
Voice: *squeaky 'chut', 'crak'; alarm calls.*   B&BW

11   WHITE-BROWED CRAKE *Porzana cinerea*   18cm
This long-toed crake runs about on water-lily pads or other floating vegetation amongst coastal swamps, lakes and mangroves of northern Australia. Besides seeds and swamp plants, it feeds on insects often taken on the wing. Walks with tail flicking and flies weakly with legs trailing. Not over-timid or shy of observers. Sedentary or nomadic. Breeds September-May. Nests in swamp vegetation or rice fields.
Sexes: *alike.*
Immatures: *crown brown.*
Voice: *often in concert at dusk, repeated 'crake', chattering and churring.* FJ

12   BUSH-HEN *Amaurornis olivaceus*   26cm
The mainly nocturnal Bush-hen lives in restricted habitats of wet grassy vegetation along creeks, in lantana thickets, rainforest margins, or swamps of north-eastern Australia. It calls frequently, sometimes incessantly, by day or night, especially in the wet season; were it not for this calling it would be difficult to find, for it is a reclusive bird. Seen singly, in pairs or family parties. Feeds terrestrially on insects, seeds and leaves. Sedentary or migratory. Breeds October-April. Nests low in grass.
Female: *smaller.*
Immatures: *duller, head black.*
Voice: *single 'tok', drawn-out 'nee-you'.*   LR

13   PURPLE SWAMPHEN *Porphyrio porphyrio*   45cm
In the south-west, the purple of the neck, shoulder edge and breast is replaced by blue; in Tasmania by purple-blue and Tasmanian birds are larger. Seen singly, in pairs or loose groups, it lives among reeds in swamps, river margins and lakes including in public parks. Flicks tail when walking and swimming, exposing white under-tail coverts. It eats green shoots. Shy, but becomes tame in parks, but if alarmed will promptly take wing. Sedentary. Breeds variably. Nests on platform in reeds.
Sexes: *alike.*
Immatures: *duller.*
Voice: *mostly silent, some metallic cackling.*   D&MT

14   TASMANIAN NATIVE-HEN *Gallinula mortierii*   45cm
Found only in Tasmania, this bird is flightless, and almost twice the size of its mainland relative, the Black-tailed Native-Hen. It is often seen in open grassy areas along creeks and swamps, and pastures, from sea level to 1 100m. It runs swiftly, flicking its tail when disturbed. It lives in pairs or family groups in clearly defined and jealously guarded territories, and feeds on vegetable matter. Sedentary, with little or no wandering. Breeds June-January. Nests in low grass near water. Endemic.
Sexes: *alike.*
Immatures: *duller, washed grey.*
Voice: *harsh 'see-saw' uttered as a duet.*   TW

15   EURASIAN COOT *Fulica atra*   38cm
The Coot is distributed from Europe across the Old World to Australia and New Zealand. The distinctive white frontal plate is its familiar feature. It frequents fresh and brackish swamps, floodwaters and artificial lakes, forming large rafts on open water. It dives for vegetable matter and feeds on land on green shoots and takes scraps of food tossed to it in public parks. Usually gregarious, it may be belligerent during breeding August-February. Sedentary or migratory. Nests low near water.
Sexes: *alike.*
Immatures: *paler, throat whitish.*
Voice: *sharp, shrill calls.*   D&MT

16   BLACK-TAILED NATIVE-HEN *Gallinula ventralis*   35cm
Unlike the flightless Tasmanian Native-Hen, this bird is a strong flier. It is highly nomadic and can appear almost anywhere quite suddenly. Singly or in pairs, but more often in large flocks, it frequents margins of swamps, lakes, and rivers and irrigated pastures. It feeds on green shoots of grasses, herbs and weeds. It walks and runs with tail cocked or fanned. Breeds variably depending on rainfall. Nests on or close to the ground near water. Endemic.
Sexes: *alike.*
Immatures: *duller.*
Voice: *mostly silent; metallic cackling.*   B&BW

17   COMB-CRESTED JACANA *Irediparra gallinacea*   24cm
Also known as the Lotusbird, this bird has distinctive toes and claws which help it walk over plants growing in still waters. It used to breed as far south as Sydney until about 1976. It flies well, using the feet as a rudder, and may roost in trees. The comb colour changes from red to yellow in moments of excitement. Sedentary or nomadic. Nests on a small platform of floating vegetation.
Sexes: *alike.*
Immatures: *breast white.*
Voice: *shrill alarm call, squeaking.*   KI

19

18   DUSKY MOORHEN *Gallinula tenebrosa*   38cm
It is distinguished by a bright red frontal plate and white-edged tail, and lives as happily on artificial city ponds and lakes as on outback permanent swamps and rivers. It looks duck-like, especially when it up-ends to feed on underwater vegetation. Gregarious out of breeding season, August-February. Nests among rushes or at foot of tree growing in water.
Sexes: *alike.*
Immatures: *browner.*
Voice: *strident 'kerk', shrieks.*   LS

19   BANDED STILT *Cladorhynchus leucocephalus*   41cm
The first breeding colony was only recorded in 1930. It lives in salt lakes, estuaries and inlets, sometimes in great flocks. It feeds mainly on brine shrimps, and rafts of several hundred sometimes crowd togeth-er in shallow water to corner prey. It is seasonally nomadic over great distances, with movement away from the interior towards the coast in summer. Breeds in immense colonies mainly May-December, on large inland salt lakes. Nests on a scrape in the ground or on floating vegetation. Endemic.
Sexes: *alike.*
Immatures: *head, neck, back white, no breastband.*
Voice: *yelping and wheezing.*   B&BW

20   PAINTED SNIPE *Rostratula benghalensis*   ♂22cm ♀25cm
The Painted Snipe lives in marshy areas generally with ample cover, in pairs and small parties. The male incu-bates the eggs and rears the chicks and puts on an aggressive defence display. Somewhat nocturnal, secretive and solitary. Breeds October-December (south), March-May (north). Nests in mud depression, in small colonies.
Recognition: *(cf Latham's Snipe): conspicuous pale 'horse collar'; broad whitish eye ring, flight clumsy with dangling legs, shows black mark across underwings.*
Female: *brighter.*
Immatures: *like male but lacking black breast band.*
Voice: *clicking sounds.*   TL

21   LATHAM'S SNIPE *Gallinago hardwickii*   26cm
Nesting in the northern islands of Japan, this strong, swift-flying snipe migrates southwards, arriving in Australia during August, and is also known as the Japanese Snipe. Over the next month others arrive in greater numbers to reach the south-eastern and Tasmanian coastal areas and disperse into wet pad-docks, irrigated areas, mangroves, lake margins and swamp edges. It feeds mainly at night on worms, aquatic larvae and seeds. Extremely wary; when alarmed it will burst up in zigzagging flight before dropping back into cover some distance away. Return flights begin February/April.
Sexes and immatures: *alike.*
Voice: *single loud 'crek' in flight.*   JP

22   BLACK-WINGED STILT *Himantopus himantopus*   38cm
The word stilt is aptly descriptive of this long-legged but graceful bird. It frequents both saline and shallow fresh waters of lakes, estuaries, swamps or sewage ponds, and normally forms smaller flocks than the Banded Stilt. It gathers its food usually by wading. Nomadic according to seasonal conditions. Breeds August-December. Nests colonially on the ground adjacent to shallow water.
Sexes: *alike.*
Immatures: *crown, nape and eye patch grey.*
Voice: *high-pitched puppy-like yapping or yelping.*   CC

23   RED-NECKED AVOCET *Recurvirostra novaehollandiae*   46cm
Sweeping its long upcurved bill rhythmically from side to side, the Red-necked Avocet sweeps shallow water or mud for aquatic insects, crustaceans and plant matter. Like the Banded Stilt, with whom it often associ-ates, it will also submerge and swim readily. It is seen in small groups or large flocks, mostly in salty or brack-ish swamps rather than on freshwater, but occasionally appearing at tidal inlets. Sedentary or nomadic in response to rainfall. Breeds August-December. Nests colonially on the ground or in shallow water. Endemic.
Sexes: *alike.*
Immatures: *paler markings.*
Voice: *yelps, yaps and wheezes.*   KI

Migratory and Resident Waders 20

1, 4   MASKED LAPWING *Vanellus miles*
(A) Race *miles* Masked Lapwing   36cm
(B) Race *novaehollandiae* Spur-winged Lapwing   38cm
Both races carry sharp-pointed shoulder spurs on the wings. The rounded wing-tips and erratic wing-beats help to identify it in flight. The populations meet at about Mackay, Queensland, where some hybridise. Black 'lapels' and full black cap readily distinguish the southern birds and the very large facial wattles the northern. The Lapwing is common and widespread in open wetlands, most pastures and estuaries, and often seen on golf courses and parks. It has benefited from land clearance. It characteristically stalks with shoulders hunched, to dart head down at insects, worms and crustaceans. Seeds also are sometimes eaten. It wanders locally including at night in pairs and small flocks - sometimes in hundreds when not breeding. It is very wary and signals danger with its calls at the slightest provocation. It retreats to cover in shallow waters to roost. Breeds June-January in the south, variably in the north. Nest is a depression in open country and it is boldly aggressive in its defence.
Sexes: *alike.*
Immatures: *spotted on crown and back.*
Voice: *rapid 'keeks' also at night.*   1ES, 4H&JB

2   GREY PLOVER *Pluvialis squatarola*   29cm
Breeds in the high Arctic regions during the northern summer. It visits Australia between August and March/April and frequents the seashore and grassy mudflats fairly well around the coast but it is uncommon. It is rarely seen inland. It is timid and wary. It is seen singly, in small parties or large congregations, and mainly keeps aloof from other species. It may assume its striking full breeding plumage of black underparts and patch part-black upperparts before departure.
Sexes: *alike.*
Immatures: *paler grey-buff.*
Voice: *poignant 'pee-o-wee'.*   T&PG

3, 6   PACIFIC GOLDEN PLOVER *Pluvialis fulva*   25cm
Less shy and more erect in stance than the Grey Plover, the Pacific Golden Plover is also more commonly seen in Australia, August-April, after breeding in Alaska and Siberia. In Australia it frequents rocky coasts, beaches and sandflats, occasionally inland swamps and grassy paddocks and even grassy airstrips and golf courses. Often in large companies, most birds are in white and buff-mottled non-breeding plumage, but some may be patchy, just losing, or beginning to attain, the handsome plumage of black dappled on the upperparts with gold spots.
Sexes and immatures: *alike in non-breeding plumage.*
Voice: *piping 'too-weet'.*   3D&MT, 6MC/AA

5   BANDED LAPWING *Vanellus tricolor*   28cm
The Banded Lapwing often lives in short grass in inland habitats and will travel long distances during hot periods to find shade. Seen in small parties or winter flocks, it is nomadic, wary, and actively defensive at the nest, swooping on intruders or putting on distraction displays. It feeds on insects and tiny animals, seeds and shoots, often loosely raking the ground with one foot to flush prey. Breeds June-November. Nests in ground depression. Endemic.
Sexes: *alike.*
Immatures: *mottling on crown and breast.*
Voice: *harsh 'kew-kew', often at night; chiming 'a-chee-chee'.*   ES

7   RED-KNEED DOTTEREL *Erythrogonys cinctus*   18cm
The endemic Red-kneed Dotterel lives on the edges of swamps and vegetated lagoons in all but the most arid or most humid of regions, and is widespread throughout mainland Australia. It is commonly seen darting about in the mud, singly, in pairs or companies, probing with jerky head-bobbing for small creatures in mud or water. Sedentary or nomadic during dry conditions. Breeds September-December. Nests in ground depression close to water.
Sexes: *alike.*
Immatures: *upperparts brown, white below.*
Voice: *'chet-chet', trilling.*   D&MT

8   BLACK-FRONTED DOTTEREL *Elseyornis melanops*   15cm
Usually in pairs or family parties, this small wader frequents dry river beds, swamps and lagoon edges and feeds on small aquatic animals and insects. It runs rapidly and bobs its head when at rest. Sedentary or nomadic in dry conditions. Breeds August-January. Nests in ground depression or among stones in a stream bed.
Sexes: *alike.*
Immatures: *lack breastband and black forehead.*
Voice: *rapid churring.*   H&JB

9   RED-CAPPED PLOVER *Charadrius ruficapillus*   15cm
Native to Australia, the Red-capped Plover is distributed widely inland, as well as around the coast, and is often seen in pairs or flocks on beaches, rivers and margins of lakes. It scurries quickly with sudden pauses. If approached, it flies off a short distance to resume running. It eats insects and small crustaceans. Disperses in flocks after breeding September-January. nests in scrape in the ground.
Female: *lacks black markings, paler, legs greenish.*
Immatures: *paler than adult female, upperparts mottled.*
Voice: *'tik' or 'tink', trilling and churring.*   GC

10   INLAND DOTTEREL *Charadrius australis*   20cm
Australia's Inland Dotterel is a bird of the open plains, and is adapted to living in gibber country and semi-arid places where it may frequent the margins of lakes and streams. It has spread throughout much of the WA wheatbelt. Though not timid, it flies well away if flushed. During the heat of the day it covers its eggs with soil, and takes shelter in the shade. Becomes active after sunset. Eats insects and seeds. Some birds are nomadic. Breeds April-October. Nests in scrape on ground. Endemic.
Sexes: *similar.*
Immatures: *lack black markings, back dappled.*
Voice: *'quik', alarm note 'kr-oot'.*   GC

11   HOODED PLOVER *Thinornis rubricollis*   20cm
The endemic Hooded Plover is most abundant in Tasmania, coastal areas of southern Australia and around inland salt lakes in the south-west. In pairs, family parties or small flocks, it frequents open stretches of beach with grassy sand dunes. It is usually seen running along the water's edge or among jetsam. It is shy and easily disturbed. Breeds August-February. Nests in a ground depression.
Sexes: *alike.*
Immatures: *brown above, white below, no black markings.*
Voice: *short piping notes and barking 'kew-kew'.*   RL

12   ORIENTAL PLOVER *Charadrius veredus*   25cm
The Oriental Plover is a non-breeding visitor to Australia, arriving from its breeding grounds in China in September and departing in March. It is mainly seen in the north, on the seashore, swamps on inland plains, ploughed paddocks, or other little-disturbed stretches of grass. Its flight is swift and characterised by erratic zigzags. At rest it stands upright and motionless. Seen singly, in pairs and small flocks. Extremely wary.
Sexes and immatures: *alike in non-breeding plumage; breeding male has chestnut and black breastband.*
Voice: *sharp whistling note.*   EZ

13   DOUBLE-BANDED PLOVER *Charadrius bicinctus*   18cm
The Double-banded Plover is a trans-Tasman migrant arriving in February from breeding grounds in New Zealand and nearby islands. It leaves Australia in September or October by which time the non-breeding plumage of only a faintly-marked brownish breastband is giving way to a clearly-defined breastband and a black collar around the lower throat. It is seen on the seashore, mudflats and salt marshes, also inland on swamps and in ploughed paddocks, taking its food from the mud by probing.
Sexes: *alike.*
Immatures: *like non-breeding adults.*
Voice: *piping whistle 'chip-chip', musical trilling.*   AF

14   LESSER SAND PLOVER *Charadrius mongolus*   20cm
Also known as the Mongolian Dotterel. A non-breeding visitor from breeding grounds in Central Asia
arriving during September and departing in April. Commonly seen around the coast, particularly in the
north and east in estuaries, mangroves, mudflats and sandy beaches, usually in small parties or flocks.
Often associates with Double-banded and Greater Sand Plovers. Occasionally inland. It runs swiftly
and probes in wet sand or mud for food.
Sexes: *alike; in breeding plumage breast-band is rufous-red, lores black, underparts and forehead white.*
Immatures: *upperparts lightly scalloped.*
Voice: *short penetrating 'drrit'.*
                                                                                 D&MT

15   GREATER SAND PLOVER *Charadrius leschenaultii*   23cm
A non-breeding visitor from northern Asia arriving in October and departing in March,
and found throughout most of the coastal areas feeding on tidal sand and mudflats, singly
and in flocks. It is less often seen than the Lesser Sand Plover, except in the west. If dis-
turbed it usually flies up without moving far away and returns to the same spot.
Recognition: *(cf Lesser Sand Plover): larger, paler, longer legs and thicker bill.*
Sexes: *alike in non-breeding plumage.*
Immatures: *upperparts scalloped lighter.*
Voice: *trilling; louder than Lesser Sand Plover.*
                                                                                 D&MT

16   RINGED PLOVER *Charadrius hiaticula*   19cm
A rare summer vagrant to Australia from its breeding grounds in northern Europe and Asia. It frequents
muddy and sandy shores, sometimes with other plovers and stints. It feeds on small crustaceans,
worms and insects and their larvae.
Female: *similar, but black markings are duller.*
Voice: *pleasant two-note call.*
                                                                                 BC

17   RED-NECKED STINT *Calidris ruficollis*   15cm
One of the smallest and most-commonly seen of the waders regularly to visit Australia, migrating from north
eastern Siberia or Alaska. The salmon-pink colouring about the head and neck which gives it its name occurs
only in the breeding plumage, so is not usually seen here. Flying in tightly-packed wheeling flocks over a
large part of the continent, it visits beaches, mudflats, estuaries and swamp margins. It feeds busily, probing
wet sand or mud with a quick jabbing action, often in company with other waders. It frequently overwinters.
Sexes: *alike.*
Immatures: *browner.*
Voice: *'chit-chit'.*
                                                                                 D&MT

18   LONG-TOED STINT *Calidris subminuta*   14-15cm
First recorded in Australia in 1886, but accepted as a regular summer visitor only in 1960 from breeding grounds in Siberia. Its distribution in Australia is patchy and it is far less often seen than the Red-
necked Stint. Frequents fresh water habitats rather than tidal flats. It feeds with darting runs and
freezes if disturbed. In Australia September to April. Recognition (cf Red-necked Stint): taller and
slimmer stance, darker upper parts, legs greenish-yellow and longer.
Sexes: *alike in non-breeding plumage; breeding plumage darker above, crown rufous streaked darker.*
Voice: *chirruping trilling; 'chee-chee'.*
                                                                                 B&BW

19   SANDERLING *Calidris alba*   18cm
The Sanderling breeds in the Arctic Circle, and is seen as a non-breeding visitor along most
Australian coasts from September to April, though not commonly. It feeds on beaches with dart-
ing movements at the water's edge, running after receding waves to pick its prey from the wet
sand, sometimes taking to the air to avoid the incoming flow. Reluctant to fly far if disturbed.
Recognition: distinctive white under-parts contrasting with the black of the legs and feet.
Sexes: *alike in non-breeding plumage; male in breeding plumage is mostly cinnamon streaked black.*
Voice: *soft twittering and chattering.*
                                                                                 GC

20

20, 21   CURLEW SANDPIPER *Calidris ferruginea*   21cm
Among the most common of the migratory waders, it reaches Australia from its northern Siberian breeding grounds north of the Arctic Circle in September and departs in April - but some overwinter here, many of which are probably immatures. It frequents a wide range of habitats, both coastal and inland, often in company with other waders. It frequently submerges its head in shallow water when probing for worms, crustaceans and insects with its long curved bill. It makes an imposing sight when massed in dense compact whirling flocks that can be numbered in thousands.
Sexes: *alike; non-breeding males have less rufous on the head, neck and underparts than the breeding males.*
Voice: *chirruping.*   D&MT

22   BROAD-BILLED SANDPIPER *Limicola falcinellus*   18cm
Somewhat rare in Australia except on northern coasts, the Broad-billed Sandpiper is an inconspicuous non-breeding summer visitor from north Siberia, often seen in small flocks with Red-necked Stints. Mostly frequents tidal mudflats, it feeds with a deliberate up-and-down drilling movement, with the head and neck often submerging.
Recognition: *(cf Red-necked Stint): long sickle-shaped bill, and a branching white eye stripe.*
Sexes: *alike in non-breeding plumage; breeding plumage has upperparts darker with tawny markings, breast heavily streaked.*
Immatures: *slightly darker.*
Voice: *chattering and trilling.*   EZ

23   SHARP-TAILED SANDPIPER *Calidris acuminata*   23cm
A visitor from Siberia, the Sharp-tailed Sandpiper is perhaps the most abundant of the migratory waders. Numbers are at their peak from August to April but very few stay throughout the year. Flocks of up to 1 000 have been recorded in the south. It frequents a wide variety of habitats, including swamps, mudflats, irrigation areas, and mangroves, and feeds in shallow water on aquatic creatures and vegetation, often with other waders.
Sexes: *similar but females smaller.*
Immatures: *on arrival, similar to breeding adults with pink-rufous plumage.*
Voice: *soft metallic 'pleep', shrill piping notes.*   KI

24   PECTORAL SANDPIPER *Calidris melanotos*   23cm
Breeds in Siberia, Alaska and Canada and a rare but regular summer visitor to Australia. In behaviour, habitat and appearance it is similar to its Sharp-tailed relative.
Recognition: *(cf Sharp-tailed Sandpiper): abrupt change from brown breast to white belly, short tail, yellow legs and slightly longer and more decurved bill. Different calls.*
Female: *smaller, otherwise similar to non-breeding male; breeding male is more intensely coloured.*
Immatures: *more buff.*
Voice: *rasping chatter, twittering.*   BJC

25   GREAT KNOT *Calidris tenuirostris*   28-30cm
This, the largest of the sandpipers, breeds in Siberia, and vast numbers overwinter in northern Australia as non-breeding migrants from August to March. A concentration of over 100 000 was recorded between Broome and Port Hedland WA in September 1982. It is often seen in company with godwits, but the numbers thin out towards the south. It frequents mainly estuaries and tidal mudflats, occasionally inland lakes. Some stay all year.
Sexes: *alike in non-breeding plumage; breeding male is darkly striped on head and neck, breast black-grey.*
Immatures: *darker and more mottled than non-breeding adults.*
Voice: *'knut-knut'.*   T&PG

26   RED KNOT *Calidris canutus*   25cm
After breeding in the Arctic Circle between August and April, it visits Australian shores in large numbers and frequents coastal sand flats, the margins of estuaries and rivers. Sporadically seen inland. It feeds in close-packed flocks that move in unison. The scientific name comes from its King Canute-like action in running out in the wake of retreating waves.
Recognition: *(cf Great Knot): shorter bill, less boldly mottled, squatter posture.*
Sexes: *alike in non-breeding plumage. Breeding males are deep chestnut red on breast and below (rarely seen in Australia).*
Immatures: *browner.*
Voice: *'knut-knut'.*   D&MT

27   TEREK SANDPIPER *Xenus cinereus*   25cm
The very long slightly upcurved bill, bright orange part-webbed feet, and crouching stance while foraging, are distinctive features of the Terek Sandpiper. It also characteristically dashes about actively, teeters, and bobs its head. Singly and in small flocks, occasionally in large concentrations, it is seen on estuaries, mudflats and coastal brackish swamps. It breeds in northern Eurasia and is in Australia August to April, some overwintering.
Sexes and immatures: *alike in non-breeding plumage; breeding male is more mottled and brown.*
Voice: *piping trill.*   D&MT

28   WOOD SANDPIPER *Tringa glareola*   23cm
A somewhat uncommon non-breeding migrant from northern Europe and Asia. It begins arriving in small numbers on northern Australian coasts in August and spreads southwards to all States. Singly or in small flocks, it frequents shallow stretches of fresh or brackish water, more usually inland, and often fringed with river red gums. Feeds on shellfish and insects. It swims well, and perches in trees.
Sexes and immatures: *alike in non-breeding plumage; breeding plumage is more boldly marked.*
Voice: *'chif-chif', whistling.*   E&DH

29   MARSH SANDPIPER *Tringa stagnatilis*   23cm
Often called the Little Greenshank, the Marsh Sandpiper is a generally uncommon summer visitor to Australia, although sometimes seen locally in quite large numbers. Mostly solitary or in small groups, it frequents both salt marshes and fresh water, mainly inland. It forages in shallow water, sometimes swims with head held high. It breeds in Eurasia.
Sexes: *alike in non-breeding plumage; breeding male is darker, spotted on throat and breast.*
Immatures: *like non-breeding adults.*
Voice: *subdued 'tee-oo', sharp alarm 'tchik-tchik'.*   DE/A

30   COMMON SANDPIPER *Actitis hypoleucos*   20cm
The Common Sandpiper, a non-breeding migrant from Europe and northern Asia, is commonly seen in the north, less so in the south, between July and May. Singly, or only in very small parties, it haunts rocky coastal streams, beaches, inlets and small inland bodies of water including stock dams. Often perches on rocks or posts. It is characterised by constant nervous up and down teetering and rapid flight close to water with down-arched, rapid flicking wingbeats.
Sexes: *alike in non-breeding plumage; breeding male has upperparts and breast markings darker.*
Immatures: *similar to non-breeding adults.*
Voice: *piping 'twee-wee-wee'.*   TH

31   WANDERING TATTLER *Heteroscelus incanus*   28-29cm
The Wandering Tattler, a summer non-breeding migrant from Alaska, is comparatively rare in Australia, and has only been recorded on the east coast, chiefly on rocky areas. Its flight is swift and graceful
Recognition: *(cf Grey-tailed Tattler): slightly larger, darker, longer nasal groove extending to three-quarters length of bill; also different habitat and voice.*
Sexes and immatures: *alike in non-breeding plumage; breeding birds have strongly barred underparts.*
Voice: *rapidly repeated 'whee-we-we' and fluting notes.*   T&PG

32   COMMON GREENSHANK *Tringa nebularia*   34cm
The distinctive Greenshank is widespread, mainly in coastal regions, but also common in some of the wetlands in the interior. Restlessly wary. Usually alone or in small parties, it is sometimes seen in large flocks. It is more common in the north. It feeds by wading in shallow water. Breeding in Eurasia, it is in Australia September to April.
Sexes: *alike in non-breeding plumage; breeding males are darker, spotted brown on neck front and breast.*
Voice: *staccato whistling, fluting.*   GC

33   GREY-TAILED TATTLER *Heteroscelus brevipes*   26-27cm
Breeds in far north of eastern Siberia and one of the commonest of the migratory waders in Australia between September and April. It mostly frequents tidal mudflats and mangrove-fringed shores, singly, in small groups and larger flocks. At high tide it roosts in trees or on rocks, or on the roof of any handy building. Habitually bobs the head and flicks the rear end.
Sexes: *alike in non-breeding plumage; male in breeding plumage is finely barred on throat, breast and flanks.*
Immatures: *pale edges to wing feathers.*
Voice: *variations on 'troo-eet'.*   D&MT

34   RED-NECKED PHALAROPE *Phalaropus lobatus*   17-20cm
This wader breeds across northern Europe and Asia and winters at sea, mainly in the eastern Pacific. It was first sighted in Australia near Melbourne in 1962, and later on swamps and lakes on or close to the coast. It feeds while swimming in shallow water, picking water insects from the surface, and characteristically spins rapidly around to disturb prey from the bottom. It is very buoyant and sits high in the water.
Female: *larger and brighter in breeding plumage than the male, a rufous band reaching from the eye round the neck.*
Immatures: *darker.*
Voice: *'chick'.*   WW/A

35   ORIENTAL PRATINCOLE *Glareola maldivarum*   23cm
A regular non-breeding migrant from eastern Asia, arriving October in flocks numbering hundreds or even thousands in north-western Australia. It spreads mainly across the north, but stragglers sometimes reach southern areas. It frequents edges of swamps and lagoons, claypans and airfields often in mixed flocks with Australian Pratincoles. Its deeply-forked tail gives it a swallow-like appearance in flight and much of its insect food is hawked on the wing.
Sexes: *alike in non-breeding plumage; breeding male has buff throat bordered black.*
Immatures: *paler.*
Voice: *'chick-chick'.*   KF/A

36   AUSTRALIAN PRATINCOLE *Stiltia isabella*   24cm
The Australian Pratincole lives and breeds mainly in Australia, but many migrate to overwinter in New Guinea and Indonesia. It frequents dry open coastal and inland plains in the vicinity of water. It is partly nomadic and able to cope with conditions of extreme heat. It characteristically bobs up and down and runs rapidly It flies gracefully and frequent zig-zagging. Its tail is shorter and less deeply forked than that of the Oriental Pratincole. Breeds October-January. Nests among stones on the ground, in colonies.
Sexes: *alike.*
Immatures: *browner and mottled.*
Voice: *whistled 'weeteet'.*   H&JB

37   EASTERN CURLEW *Numenius madagascariensis*   60cm
The long-billed Eastern Curlew breeds in eastern Siberia and is seen all around the coasts of Australia between September and April/May as a non-breeding migrant. A few stay all year. Common along northern and eastern coasts, it is usually alone or in small numbers, seldom in large flocks, on beaches and muddy estuaries. Wary. Probes for crabs and worms. Often it roosts in mangrove trees at high tide.
Sexes and immatures: *alike in non-breeding plumage; breeding male is tinged cinnamon above.*
Voice: *'ker-loo' or 'kor-lew' including in flight.*   D&MT

38   WHIMBREL *Numenius phaeopus*   46cm
Breeds all around the high Arctic latitudes and overwinters in Australia from September to March/April. It is seen more often along the northern and eastern coasts than in the south and west. It frequents muddy estuaries, sandflats, salt marshes and coral cays, alone or in small flocks, often with other waders. Normally wary but has become quite tame at some Great Barrier Reef resorts. Some may remain all year in northern Australia.
Sexes and immatures: *alike.*
Voice: *high clear repeated whistles.*   D&MT

39   LITTLE CURLEW *Numenius minutus*   35cm
A non-breeding visitor from north-eastern Siberia and seen sometimes in very large flocks in the north west of the continent from September to May but rarely south of the Tropic of Capricorn. Usually in small groups, it frequents paddocks playing fields, airfields and flood plains; and feeds on insects, their larvae, and possibly seeds. Individual birds or small flocks may move southwards to avoid especially heavy monsoonal rains. 'Freezes' when flushed. May become tame near habitation.
Sexes and immatures: *alike.*
Voice: *variations on 'chee-chee'.*   T&PG

40   BLACK-TAILED GODWIT *Limosa limosa*   36-43cm
An uncommon non-breeding visitor from northern Europe and Asia, arriving in Australia during September and departing in May. Solitary, in small flocks, sometimes in hundreds, it frequents coastal tidal estuaries, fresh and brackish lagoons and swamps often with Bar-tailed Godwits. Most common along northern and north-eastern coasts. Flight is swift, sometimes spectacularly acrobatic.
Recognition: *(cf Bar-tailed): smaller, less mottled, broad black tip to tail on white rump, white underwing, bill usually straight.*
Sexes: *alike; breeding plumage striking red-brown.*
Immatures: *some wing coverts edged with buff.*
Voice: *sharp 'witta-wit' and 'kip-kip'.*   EZ

41, 42   BAR-TAILED GODWIT *Limosa lapponica*   ♂38-42cm ♀42-45cm
The Bar-tailed Godwit arrives in great numbers in August/September from its breeding grounds in north-east Siberia and spreads right around the coast for its summer visit until take-off time for breeding in April/May. Concentrations of tens of thousands have been recorded on Eighty Mile Beach between Broome and Port Hedland in WA. It is seen on coastal sandy shores, mud-flats and marshes, probing, sweeping and jabbing into mud or sand between the tides for small crustaceans and worms. Large flocks may form to fly swiftly in tight wheeling formation. Departing birds fatten for their long trans-world journey and may have assumed their breeding plumage before leaving. Many birds remain behind to overwinter.
Recognition: *(cf Black-tailed Godwit): bill usually slightly up-curved, plumage lighter and more mottled.*
Female: *larger.*
Immatures: *more buff edging on feathers.*
Voice: *variations on 'witta-wit', 'ki-kip'.*   D&MT

43, 44   RUDDY TURNSTONE *Arenaria interpres*   23cm
The Turnstone visits Australian coastal regions from September to April, from its breeding grounds in eastern Siberia and Alaska. It reaches Tasmania and is especially abundant in the north of the continent. Some birds, probably non-breeding immatures, stay to overwinter. It frequents rocky shores, shingly beaches, estuaries and coral cays, and characteristically runs about overturning stones, shells and beach debris, or pushing up heaps of seaweed to expose small prey with its sharp short bill. It also skilfully uses it to open hard-shelled mussels and barnacles. At high tide it roosts on exposed rocks, or retreats to sand-spits with other waders. In flight it shows a panel of white in the wing, and a black-barred undertail
Sexes: *male brighter than female.*
Immatures: *more buff edging to feathers.*
Voice: *'kut' or kitititit'.*   43T&PG, 44RV/A

45   RUFF *Philomachus pugnax*   23-30cm
The Ruff takes its name from the very large ruff fluffed up by the male in courtship and territorial displays (but not likely to be seen in Australia). The female of the species is known as a Reeve. It was only in the early 1960s that the Ruff was first noted here, possibly because it had previously been over-looked as a Sharp-tailed Sandpiper, which the female somewhat resembles. It frequents swamps, lagoons, sewage farms and tidal mudflats, often with other waders, but it remains as yet a rare summer visitor. Breeds in Eurasia.
Female: *smaller.*
Immatures: *buff wash, neck darker.*
Voice: *normally silent; very rarely muted notes.*   E&DH

21 Seabirds

1, 2 BLACK-BROWED ALBATROSS
Diomedea melanophris   83-93cm Wingspan c 230cm

The circumpolar range of the Black-browed Albatross spans the oceans from the Antarctic pack ice to the equator, and it is possibly the most abundant and widespread of the albatrosses. It is the albatross most often seen in southern Australian waters, especially from May to November after dispersing from its breeding islands in the sub-Antarctic. The Falklands are its stronghold with a breeding population estimated from 500 000 to 3 million. It readily follows ships and gathers in large numbers around trawlers. It forages inshore and in harbours, and feeds on fish, squid and cuttlefish. Recognition: bright yellow-orange bill; underwing blackish.

Sexes: *alike.*

Immatures: *dusky about head and narrow breastband; bill dark grey-green with black tip.*

Voice: *mostly silent, harsh grunting.*   1 AR, 2 PGR

3 SHY ALBATROSS *Diomedea cauta*   100cm Wingspan c 198-256cm

Also known as the White-capped Albatross. The only albatross to breed in Australia, with nesting colonies on Albatross Island off the north-west tip of Tasmania, and on two of the Maatsuyker Islands off its south coast. It also breeds on islands around New Zealand's subantarctic where two subspecies also occur. The Albatross Island colony was discovered by Flinders and Bass during their circumnavigation of Tasmania in 1798. This colony was subsequently decimated by sealers but has largely recovered. Tends to avoid inshore waters and follows ships less than other species, hence the name 'shy'. Mostly seen in Australian seas between July and October. Breeds from September.

Recognition: *the underwing is mainly white with a small black patch at its root.*

Sexes: *alike.*

Immatures: *dusky head and breastband.*

Voice: *cackling and gurgling.*   H&JB

4 WANDERING ALBATROSS *Diomedea exulans* 107-135cm Wingspan c 340cm

The wingspan, sometimes over 3.5 metres, exceeds that of all other living birds. Its gliding flight is effortless and graceful, and it may follow even the fastest of ships for days and nights on end ready to drop on scraps thrown overboard. It is a true wanderer and its feats of flight over enormous distances around the globe are legendary. It is seen all through the year in Australian waters but mostly in winter on leaving its breeding islands in the southern oceans. Up to 500 birds have been seen feeding at Sydney's sewage outlet at Malabar, but population numbers have declined alarmingly in recent years, the cause thought to be drowning of birds caught during long-line fishing operations.

Recognition: *(cf Royal Albatross): difficult to separate, but at close range black in tail of the Wandering is one clue.*

Sexes: *similar.*

Immatures: *brown with white face. Adult plumage reached in 9 years.*

Voice: *deep throaty 'bleats', mainly silent at sea.*   BA

5 SOOTY ALBATROSS *Phoebetria fusca*   84-89cm Wingspan c 203cm

The dark-plumaged Sooty Albatross has a distinctive tapered tail, and glides on constantly-adjusted long slender wings. It has the reputation of being the most accomplished and graceful flier of all seabirds. It is a regular follower of ships for long periods, and ancient seafarers believed that the souls of men drowned overboard passed into this bird. Some think that this was the 'pious bird of good omen' shot by the Ancient Mariner in Coleridge's famous tale. It visits Australian waters in winter, chiefly along the southern coasts and Tasmania. Breeds on various sub-Antarctic and Atlantic Ocean islands.

Recognition: *wholly sooty-brown.*

Sexes: *alike.*

Immatures: *bill stripe paler.*

Voice: *sad screaming 'pee-ooo' at the nest.*   GJ

6   LIGHT-MANTLED SOOTY ALBATROSS
Phoebetria palpebrata   79-89cm Wingspan l.83-2.18m
The name is descriptive of this bird's elegant two-toned plumage which sets it apart from the wholly brown, closely-related Sooty Albatross. Its flight is equally impressive in ease, grace and manoeuverability - it is able to hang motionless in mid-air beside a cliff edge and land on a ship's masthead in a gale. Its range is circumpolar and extends to the Antarctic pack-ice. It is highly pelagic, and less often seen in Australian waters than the Sooty Albatross. Nests on sub-Antarctic islands, including Macquarie Island, in summer.
Recognition: *distinctive light-grey mantle on back.*
Sexes: *alike.*
Immatures: *browner; no blue line on bill.*
Voice: *'peee-arr' at nest, trumpeting at sea.*   BW/AAD

7.   YELLOW-NOSED ALBATROSS
Diomedea chlororhynchos   71-81cm Wingspan 180-200cm
It is common, and frequents warmer waters than other albatrosses, sometimes as far north as the Tropic of Capricorn. It frequents Australian seas throughout the year, but is most numerous from May to October. Shy, and follows ships only occasionally, but congregates around fishing boats. It feeds at night on the surface. Breeds on various sub-Antarctic islands.
Recognition: *underwings are mostly white, with narrow black margins.*
Sexes: *alike.*
Immatures: *bill all black.*
Voice: *shrill bleating laugh.*

8.   GREY-HEADED ALBATROSS   AR
Diamedea chrysostoma   c 81cm Wingspan c220cm
The Grey-headed Albatross, with a range extending southwards to the ice pack, frequents colder waters than other albatrosses. Visits to Australian waters are at their peak between May and November, and it is then fairly common off the Western Australian coast and Tasmania, but it is rarely seen off the east coast. It breeds on various sub-Antarctic islands including Macquarie Island.
Recognition: *relatively broad black band along leading underwing edge.*
Sexes: *alike.*
Immatures: *browner and darker.* **Voice:** *braying sounds.*   GJ/AAD

9   NORTHERN GIANT-PETREL
Macronectes halli   81-94cm Wingspan 183-218cm
The Northern Giant-Petrel has only in recent years been recognised as a separate species distinct from the Southern, but the two are extremely difficult to distinguish. The habits are very similar but the Northern Giant-Petrel forages and breeds on more northerly islands. It is a winter visitor to Australia's southern waters, and arrives up to two months ahead of the Southern Giant-Petrel. Breeds on various sub-Antarctic islands July to February.
Recognition: (cf Southern Giant-Petrel): *reddish-tipped bill throughout life; crown and upperparts always darker.*
Sexes: *alike.*
Immatures: *all brown-black.*
Voice: *like Southern Giant-Petrel.*   GJ

10-11.   SOUTHERN GIANT PETREL
Macronectes giganteus.   86-99 cm. Wingspan 185-205 cm
A large, pale bill, stouter body, and a less greaceful flight distinguish the giant petrels from the albatrosses. About one in ten birds of this species fledge white and remain so for life. It ranges widely over the southern oceans and is regularly seen off southern Australia, especially in winter. Frequently follows ships. Like all fulmars, it will eject an evil smelling stomach oil when approached. They also have a persistent musty smell. Giant petrels are the only petrels to come ashore to feed, where they are aggressive scavengers of carrion, eggs and chicks. At sea they eat fish, molluscs and plankton. The species breeds October-November on various sub-Antarctic islands including Macquarie Island.
Recognition: (cf Northern Giant Petrel): *green tipped bill; adults pale head; only the Southern Giant Petrel is seen in white plumage.*
Sexes: *alike* **Voice:** *whinnying and squawking.*

12   WHITE-CHINNED PETREL *Procellaria aequinoctialis*   51-58cm Wingspan c 340cm
The largest of other all-dark petrels (Black and Westland), but extremely difficult to separate, except for
its white chin - but some birds lack this feature. The species is essentially circumpolar in range, but is only
occasionally seen in Australian waters. It follows ships and is aggressive when feeding around fishing trawlers.
Breeds on various sub-Antarctic islands generally November-January.
Sexes: *alike.*
Immatures: *similar to adults.*
Voice: *croaking and screaming at the nest.*   MFS

13   CAPE PETREL *Daption capense*   41cm
The chequered Cape Petrel is commonly seen in Australian waters from late summer to early spring. It is
also widely known as Pintados (meaning painted - the scientific name *daption* is an anagram of pintado), or
as Cape Pigeon, perhaps from its habit of pecking food from the water. It floats in large aggressive feeding
flocks with much squabbling over food. It often follows ships and also dives shallowly for small sea creatures. Nests in Antarctica and nearby islands.
Sexes and immatures: *alike.*
Voice: *rasping and rattling sounds.*   TH

14   GREAT-WINGED PETREL *Pterodroma macroptera*   c 44cm
This long, slender-winged petrel flies at great speed in wild undulations, shooting upwards to 30 metres or
more and diving steeply on swept-back wings. Nearly circumpolar in range and highly pelagic, seldom visiting offshore waters except when breeding. Usually solitary, and mainly a nocturnal feeder. Rarely follows
ships. Breeds January-September. It nests in a burrow or on the ground on islands off the coast of WA; also
in southern latitudes.
Recognition: *stocky build, short black bill; no distinctive markings.*
Sexes and immatures: *alike.*
Voice: *rapid 'kik-kik-', sibilant 'si-si-si', deep braying.*   NK

15   WHITE-HEADED PETREL *Pterodroma lessonii*   40-46cm
Seen usually alone in Australian waters all months, but uncommon except around Tasmania. Circumpolar
in range and highly pelagic. Closely related to the Great-winged Petrel, and its flight is equally spectacular.
Rarely follows ships. Breeds August-May in southern latitudes. Nests in burrows then disperses both north
and south.
Recognition: *head and underparts white; underwings dark.*
Sexes and immatures: *alike.*
Voice: *variations on 'wik-wik' and 'oooer' at sea.*   JW

16   PROVIDENCE PETREL *Pterodroma solandri*   41cm
In 1788 this bird saved the convict settlement on Norfolk Island from starvation - a recorded 170 000 being
harvested in only 3 months in 1790. Not surprisingly, the species became extinct there. Now it breeds only
on the forested slopes of Lord Howe Island, where it is abundant from February to November, before dispers-
ing in a limited area mainly in the north Pacific. It is common along the edge of the continental shelf off the
NSW coast from April to October.
Recognition: *dark grey-brown, dull white flash underwing.*
Sexes and immatures: *alike.*
Voice: *screeching 'kir-rer-rer kik-kik-kik' in flight.*   PF

17   GOULD'S PETREL *Pterodroma leucoptera*   c30cm
This small gadfly petrel breeds only at Cabbage Tree Island off Port Stephens on the NSW coast from Octo-
ber to April - with a total breeding population estimated at only 250-300 pairs. It stays at sea during the day
feeding and comes in to roost after dark. Nests are mainly in crevices between boulders amongst the cabbage
tree palms or Pisonia trees, whose sticky seeds are a hazard.
Recognition: *mainly white below; sooty black crown and darker above than related species.*
Sexes and immatures: *alike.*
Voice: *rapid high-pitched 'ki-ki-ki-ki'.*   AR

18   BLACK-WINGED PETREL *Pterodrama nigripennis*   c 30cm
Where the only known breeding ground was previously on the Kermadec Islands, new colonies are now being found off New Zealand, on Norfolk and Lord Howe Islands and elsewhere. It is regularly but not often seen off the eastern coast, including on Heron and Muttonbird Islands. It is migratory and approaches ships. Breeds November-May and nests in burrows.
Recognition: *mainly white below with narrow black margins on the wings.* **Sexes and immatures:** *alike.*
Voice: *'peet', 'pee-pee', or 'pee-ur'.*   T&PG

19   BROAD-BILLED PRION *Pachyptila vittata*   25-30cm
The Broad-billed Prion breeds on various islands of the southern oceans including around New Zealand, and disperses widely in winter. It is seldom seen in Australian waters but dead and dying birds are occasionally washed ashore along the southern coasts. It feeds on plankton by skimming the surface with head submerged or by flying under water.
Breeds: *September-January in burrows.*
Sexes and immatures: *alike.*
Voice: *chicken-like 'ku-aku-a-kuk'.*   MFS

20   SALVIN'S PRION *Pachyptila salvini*   25cm
Also called the Lesser Broad-billed Prion, but is exceedingly difficult to separate from the Broadbilled Prion even in museum specimens. It breeds in millions in the Indian Ocean on Marion, Prince Edward and Crozet Islands, and disperses widely in winter. It is a regular visitor to the seas off southern Australia but is most often recorded from casualties washed up on the beach after storms, especially in the southwest. Breeds October-January in colonies and nests in burrows.
Sexes and immatures: *alike.*   TP

21   ANTARCTIC PRION *Pachyptila desolata*   27-39cm
Also known as the Dove Prion, it ranges widely throughout the cooler waters of the Southern Ocean. It breeds in Antarctic islands including Macquarie Island in early summer. Dispersing widely over the southern oceans, it is one of the prions most commonly washed up as derelicts on the southern beaches. Breeds November-February and nests in burrows.
Sexes and immatures: *similar* **Voice:** *throaty cooing in flight*   MFS

22   FAIRY PRION *Pachyptila tartur*   34-38cm
The smallest of the prions, and the only one to breed in Australian waters, with large colonies on Bass Strait islands and around Tasmania. It also breeds on Marion Island and around New Zealand. Usually in flocks, it flies swiftly when foraging low over the waves. It deserts the nesting colony in March, returning in August, often to the same partner and nest. Breeds in summer. Nests in burrow or rocky crevice.
Sexes and immatures: *alike.*
Voice: *'kuk-kuk-kuk-oo-er'.*   GR

23   SOUTHERN FULMAR *Fulmarus glacialoides*   46-50cm
The Southern Fulmar lives and breeds mainly within the cold seas of the Antarctic Ocean and is only seen as a rare visitor in Australian waters off the southern coast in winter. It is similar in appearance and habits to its northern namesake of Arctic waters, including nesting on cliff ledges. It feeds on offal, carrion, plankton and fish and gathers in large squabbling flocks around trawlers and whaling stations. Occasionally follows ships. Breeds November-December.
Sexes and immatures: *alike.*
Voice: *cackling.*   BA

24   FLESH-FOOTED SHEARWATER *Puffinus carneipes*   41-45cm
Usually in flocks and common during summer in southern waters. Breeds on islands south-west of WA, also on Lord Howe Island and around New Zealand. After breeding it disperses widely, mainly in tropical waters. It dives and skims the surface on stiff wings when feeding mainly on small fish. Breeds November-March. Nests in colonies in burrows among rocks or low dense vegetation.
Recognition: *stocky; large pale bill; flesh-coloured legs and feet.* **Sexes and immatures:** *alike.*
Voice: *high pitched 'which-yew'.*   GR

25   WEDGE-TAILED SHEARWATER *Puffinus pacificus*   41-46cm
Widespread throughout the tropical Indian and Pacific Oceans, and breeds on Lord Howe Island and numerous islands off Australian coasts such as Heron Island on the Great Barrier Reef. The drama of the nightly return of clouds of birds to their breeding grounds, and the clamour of countless wailing voices during the night is unforgettable. Breeds September-May. Nests in colonies in burrows, rock crevices and on coral sand.
Recognition: *lazy gliding flight, wings inclined forward.*
Sexes and immatures: *alike.*
Voice: *wailing 'ka-koo-er' and catlike cries.*   ES

26   BULLER'S SHEARWATER *Puffinus bulleri*   c 46cm
Breeds only on Poorknights Islands off New Zealand's north island. Disperses extensively in the Pacific after breeding and is seen relatively frequently at sea off the coast of eastern Australia. Flight, mostly near the surface, is lazy and graceful. Breeds November-January. Nests in burrows and rock crevices.
Recognition: *dark head; distinctive grey and black upperwing with lateral M-mark; white below.*
Sexes and immatures: *alike.*
Voice: *mewing calls at nest.*   JW

27   SOOTY SHEARWATER *Puffinus griseus*   40-46cm
The Sooty Shearwater is the common muttonbird in New Zealand and breeds in millions on its numerous off-shore islands. It migrates over enormous distances and returns to its breeding grounds in November. Some breed on islands off the south-eastern coast and in Tasmania and are seen mostly in spring and early summer. Nests in burrows.
Recognition: (cf Short-tailed): *a little larger and darker; white underwing but difficult to separate.*
Sexes and immatures: *alike.* **Voice:** *wheezing, crooning and cackling.*   JW

28   SHORT-TAILED SHEARWATER *Puffinus tenuirostris*   40-43cm
Also known as the Muttonbird. It is the only petrel to breed solely in Australia with millions congregating each year on islands around Tasmania and off southern and south-eastern mainland coasts. Breeds November-March and nests in burrows. Dispersal after breeding begins in mid-April on a vast figure-of-eight 20 000 nautical mile migratory route of the Pacific to the Aleutian Islands and back via the central Pacific. It was an important source of food for the early sealers and has since been exploited commercially.
Recognition: *see Sooty Shearwater*
Sexes and immatures: *alike.*
Voice: *very noisy spluttering, wheezing and wailing.*   T&PG

29   FLUTTERING SHEARWATER *Puffinus gavia*   31-36cm
A common winter visitor to waters off south-eastern Australia after breeding on islands around New Zealand. Some remain throughout the year. Usually in flocks, sometimes large. Flight is characteristically low, direct, brisk and busy with bursts of rapid wingbeats. Dives for food. Breeds August-March. It is easily confused with Hutton's Shearwater and it is extremely difficult to distinguish the differences at sea.
Sexes and immatures: *alike.* **Voice:** *cackling sounds.*   MFS

30   HUTTON'S SHEARWATER *Puffinus huttoni*   c 38cm
This species breeds in New Zealand's south island and is an occasional visitor to Australian seas mainly off the south-eastern coast - sometimes in flocks. Breeds August-April.
Recognition: (cf Fluttering Shearwater): *much alike.* **Sexes and immatures:** *alike.*
Voice: *deeper than the Fluttering Shearwater, with repetitive cackling 'ko-wow-haw'.*   GH

31   LITTLE SHEARWATER *Puffinus assimilis*   25-30cm
This species occurs in the Atlantic, Pacific and Indian Oceans. In the Australaaian region, it breeds on Norfolk and Lord Howe Islands, and islands off the coast of Western Australia. It flies with rapid wingbeats, interspersed with short glides, close to the surface, and frequently dives for food. Relatively sedentary, absent from nesting sites only in November and December. Breeds in winter and nests in a burrow or under a rock.
Recognition: *the smallest black and white shearwater in Australian waters. Flight more flapping than close relatives.*
Sexes and immatures: *alike.*
Voice: *high-pitched wheezing and crooning.*   PF

32   WHITE-FACED STORM-PETREL *Pelagodroma marina*   21cm
The White-faced is the only storm-petrel to breed in Australian waters, and nests on many off-shore islands in the southeast and southwest - the best known colony being on Mud Island in Victoria. Also breeds around New Zealand and on islands in the North Atlantic. Visits nesting burrows after dark. Breeds October-February and spreads northwards, some as far as the Arabian Sea to over-winter. Mostly pelagic and seldom seen inshore except when breeding. In flight, it skips over surface with legs dangling.
Recognition: *white face and underparts.*
Sexes and immatures: *alike.*
Voice: *oft-repeated moaning 'pee-oo' at the nest.*   MFS

33   BLACK-BELLIED STORM-PETREL *Fregetta tropica*   22cm
An infrequent visitor to seas off the southern coast and Tasmania from breeding grounds on sub-Antarctic islands and New Zealand. Usually alone, sometimes in groups. Flies close to waves swiftly and erratically with legs dangling. Breeds in sub-Antarctic in summer.
Recognition: *white underparts and underwing (black belly often difficult to see).*
Sexes and immatures: *alike.*
Voice: *shrill piping in flight.*   JW

34   WHITE-BELLIED STORM-PETREL *Fregetta grallaria*   22cm
Only occasionally seen in Australian waters off the south-eastern coast as a rare visitor from breeding islands in the Atlantic and Pacific Oceans, including Lord Howe Island, where a dark form also occurs. Such black birds cannot easily be distinguished from the black-bellied species, and even the white-bellied form cannot be clearly discerned when the bird is in the water. Breeds December-May dispersing northwards to the tropics. It follows ships.
Recognition: *black except for white rump and underparts (but some dark below).*
Sexes and immatures: *alike.*
Voice: *shrill whistling.*   BJC, PF, JdeSD/NPI

35   GREY-BACKED STORM-PETREL *Garrodia nereis*   19cm
An infrequent but regular winter visitor to Bass Strait and the Tasman Sea from breeding grounds in Antarctic and sub-Antarctic seas. Little is known of its behaviour and movements. It feeds on plankton and is attracted to the lights of ships and lighthouses.
Recognition: *black head, white underparts, grey rump.*
Sexes and immatures: *alike.*
Voice: *twittering at the nest site.*   PF

36   WILSON'S STORM-PETREL *Oceanites oceanicus*   19cm
Breeds on Antarctic and sub-Antarctic islands and is possibly the world's most abundant bird. It is widespread as a winter migrant in all oceans. Common in Australian seas, including inshore, from April-June, especially off the east and west coasts. It skips and flutters close to the waves while feeding, with legs dangling as though walking on water. Breeds in Antarctica in summer.
Recognition: *conspicuous white rump, square-cut tail.*
Sexes and immatures: *alike.*
Voice: *sparrowlike chattering while feeding at sea.*   TH

37   ARCTIC JAEGER *Stercorarius parasiticus*   (including tail) 67cm
Breeds in the Arctic tundra and a regular transequatorial summer migrant. It is seen in Australian inshore waters mainly from September to April, more commonly in the east. It has several plumage phases ranging from light to dark. It lives on fish, molluscs, carrion, scraps from ships, and pirates food and eggs from other birds.
Recognition: *long pointed tail feathers (absent in moulting birds as often seen in the Southern Hemisphere).*
Sexes: *alike.*
Immatures: *similar to non-breeding adults.*
Voice: *gull-like shrieks, shrill staccato calls.*   CK/A

38   LONG-TAILED JAEGER *Stercorarius longicaudus*   (including tail) 58cm
Breeds in the Arctic tundra and a regular transequatorial summer migrant. It is the most pelagic of the Jaegers and is rarely seen in Australian waters. Like other skuas, it is a piratical feeder. The long tail feathers, held cocked when the bird is on the water, are distinctive.
Recognition: (cf Arctic Jaeger): *smaller and slimmer less conspicuous white wing flashes.*
Sexes: *alike.*
Immatures: *mottled and barred.*
Voice: *shrill yelping.*   GRJ/A

39   POMARINE JAEGER *Stercorarius pomarinus*   (including tail) 78cm
Breeds in the Arctic tundra and is a regular transcontinental migrant to overwinter in the southern waters from September to April. More frequently seen off south-eastern Australian coasts than elsewhere, but tends to prefer off-shore waters. Groups of 40 or 50 may follow ships. Plumage very variable, the species occurring in light, intermediate and dark forms. Often harasses gulls and terns to take their food.
Recognition: *in non-breeding plumage, the twisted tail feathers form blunt 'spoon'.*
Sexes: *alike.*
Immatures: *buff mottling and blotching.*
Voice: *squeaking, harsh chattering.*   TL

40, 41   PACIFIC GULL *Larus pacificus*   66cm
The endemic Pacific Gull is the largest of the gulls found in Australia, and its massive bill is the largest of any gull. It is usually seen singly, in pairs or sometimes loose groups patrolling the water's edge. It is an aggressive feeder, sometimes killing young birds up to the size of a Muttonbird, and eating nestlings and eggs. Occasionally dives for food. There is a belief, though not universally held, that Pacific and Kelp Gulls break open the shells of hard-shelled prey, such as molluscs, crabs and sea-urchins, by dropping them onto rocks from a height - often using the same 'anvil' continually and creating a midden of broken shells. Rarely seen inland, its habitat is on headlands and high places or low sandy spits on the coast and on offshore islands. Adults are sedentary, young birds disperse widely. Breeds August-November.
Recognition: (cf Kelp Gull): *larger size and bigger bill; clack band on white tail.*
Sexes: *alike.*
Voice: *harsh 'kiaw' and variants of 'ow-ow'and 'yow-yow'.*   D&MT

42.   KELP GULL *Larus dominicanus.*   59 cm
A recent colonist, perhaps from New Zealand, the Kelp Gull was first noted in Australia at Botany Bay in 1943 and later found breeding on Moon Island, NSW, in 1958. It is now most common in Tasmania and Bass Strait. It frequents beaches, reefs, and jetties, feeding on fish, small birds and eggs, shellfish and carrion, and may harry terns. Sedentary or dispersive after breeding September-December; nests on the ground.
Sexes: *alike*
Voice: *hoarse 'gorah', sobbing staccato sounds.*

43.   SOUTH POLAR SKUA *Catharacta maccormickii*   53cm
This skua, which lives and breeds on the Antarctic Continent was once seen by Scott within 150 miles (c 240km) of the South Pole during his epic and tragic expedition of 1912. It regularly migrates across the equator to the high northern latitudes of the Pacific, Indian and Atlantic oceans and has even been recorded in Greenland. Only rarely seen in Australian waters. Attracted to fishing trawlers.
Recognition: (cf Great Skua): *smaller; variable plumage from almost white-bodied to blackish.*   GJ/
AAD

44.   GREAT SKUA *Catharacta skua*   61cm
A marauding, quarrelsome, fearless and fearless scavenger which breeds on sub-Antarctic islands (including Macquarie). It is a regular winter visitor to southern Australian seas. Sometimes visits harbours and follows ships. It eats other birds, rats, mice, rabbits, carrion and offal as well as piratical feeding. Aggressive, particularly at the nest.
Sexes and immatures: *alike.*
Voice: *shrieking and crowing.*   GJ

45   SILVER GULL *Larus novaehollandiae*   43cm
The familiar and ubiquitous Silver Gull lives right around the coast in a variety of habitats, and is also found inland where there are lakes and rivers - sometimes in large flocks. It feeds naturally on small fish and other aquatic life, but will readily gather to scavenge for offal jettisoned by fishing boats, sewage outfalls and refuse dumps. Breeds in colonies usually on small islands, sometimes on headlands or lakes. Also breeds in New Zealand and New Caledonia.
Sexes: *alike.*
Immatures: *bill and legs grey.*
Voice: *raucous cries.*   D&MT

46   COMMON DIVING-PETREL *Pelecanoides urinatrix*   26cm
This small and stocky petrel is the most widespread of all diving petrels and is fairly common in southern Australian waters. It is seen singly or in small loose flocks resting on the surface or diving to feed submerged on small fish and other marine life. It breeds on islands in the Bass Strait and south of Tasmania, also in New Zealand and on various sub-Antarctic islands, including Macquarie, and nests in burrows. Relatively sedentary.
Sexes and immatures: *alike.*
Voice: *variations on 'ku-ku-ah'.*   JW

47   LITTLE PENGUIN *Eudyptula minor*   43cm
The smallest of the penguins and the only one to breed in Australia, with substantial rookeries all along the southern and Tasmanian coasts and islands. Also breeds in New Zealand. It goes to sea before dawn and returns after dark, a spectacle watched by thousands of people every year at Phillip Island near Melbourne, as the colony tumbles out of the surf to roost. It remains ashore without food for two-three weeks when moulting, living on its fat reserves. Breeds July-March. nests in a rock crevice or burrow underneath tussock-grass or other vegetation.
Sexes: *alike.* **Immatures:** *bill smaller.*
Voice: *'yap-yap' calls.*   R&DK

48   ROCKHOPPER PENGUIN *Eudyptes chrysocome*   60cm
The Rockhopper Penguin breeds on sub-Antarctic islands, including Macquarie Island, and is a rare non-breeding visitor to the most southerly of Australia's shores during winter. They are aptly named as they hop with great agility over rocks with feet together, and jump into the sea feet first instead of diving like other penguins. Breeds spring to early summer. Nests in rocky areas.
Sexes: *similar.*
Immatures: *similar but duller.*
Voice: *barking and growling.*   MFS

49, 50   WHITE-WINGED BLACK TERN *Chlidonias leucopterus*   23cm
A regular non-breeding summer visitor to northern Australia from Asia and southern Europe, with occasional incursions southwards (with stragglers reaching Tasmania and South Australia. Most of the birds seen in Australia are in various stages of mottled non-breeding plumage. It frequents swamps, estuaries and coastal lagoons. It often associates with Whiskered Terns in hovering flocks over shallow water, and they are not unalike when both are in non-breeding plumage. It takes insects on the wing or from the surface.
Immatures: *similar to non-breeding adults.*
Voice: *harsh 'kreek'.*   49BJC, 50GC

51   ARCTIC TERN *Sterna paradisaea*   38cm
Breeds in the Arctic and sub-Arctic, and makes a remarkable migratory flight across the world, southwards to the Antarctic pack ice. By moving with the summer between the two hemispheres, it experiences more hours of daylight than any other bird. It is a rare visitor to Australia, mainly in the south-west and south-east, from September to May.
Recognition: (cf Common Tern): *shorter bill, smaller head and long tail streamers.*
Sexes: *alike.*
Immatures: *forehead white, crown white instead of all black.*
Voice: *like Common Tern.*   E&DH

52   BRIDLED TERN *Sterna anaethetus*   42cm
Widespread in tropical seas and also breeds in Australia. Usually in flocks, it frequents islands off the northern coasts. It roosts on the ground and in trees or bushes, and feeds at sea by plunging and dipping, often nocturnally. Northern birds are probably sedentary, southern ones migrate northwards after breeding. Breeds September-January. Nests colonially on off-shore islands on sand, shingle and rock ledges unusually under cover.
Recognition: (cf Sooty Tern): smaller, browner plumage and white eyebrow line continues past and behind eye.
Sexes and immatures*: alike.*
Voice: *'yap-yapping'.*   *GC*

53   BLACK-NAPED TERN *Sterna sumatrana*   36cm
Distributed widely in tropical waters of the Indian and Pacific Oceans, the Black-naped Tern also frequents the coral cays and shallow lagoons of coastal and inshore waters of north-eastern Australia. It roosts and nests colonially on sand cays of the Great Barrier Reef, and fishes in large flocks, sometimes with other terns and noddies by diving or hovering to pluck prey from the surface. Breeds September-December.
Sexes: *alike.*
Immatures: *similar to non-breeding adults.*
Voice: *barking and sharp shrill chattering.*   *T&PG*

54   COMMON TERN *Sterna hirundo*   38cm
A regular non-breeding visitor from northern Asia. It migrates as far south as Antarctica and is seen in Australia, usually in flocks, between October and March. Frequents coastal estuaries, reefs, bays and salt-fields. It fishes by skimming the surface with bill down, sometimes submerging.
Recognition (cf Arctic Tern): *bill black or red with black tip.*
Sexes: *alike.*
Immatures: *similar to non-breeding adults.*
Voice: *grating 'keee-uh' or 'kik-kik'.*   *GC*

55   CASPIAN TERN *Sterna caspia*   56cm
Of worldwide distribution, and the largest of the terns. It frequents coastal habitats, inshore islands, rivers and lakes, but though widespread, it is generally uncommon. It fishes by hovering and by high spectacular dives. Unsociable and aggressive. Breeds October-February (south), all months (north). Nests singly and in colonies on sandy beaches, shingle and headlands.
Sexes: *alike.*
Immatures: *similar to non-breeding adults.*
Voice: *crow-like 'kraa-uh'.*   *H&JB*

56   WHITE-FRONTED TERN *Sterna striata*   42cm
The White-fronted Tern breeds in New Zealand and crosses the Tasman Sea to Australian waters, as young birds. It is seen mostly in the summer off the south-east coast and around Tasmania, where there have been some recent breeding records. It is mainly coastal, and takes fish in the surf. Sometimes follows fishing boats. Often seen in flocks, sometimes in the company of Crested Terns.
Recognition: (cf Common Tern): *almost white underwing.*
Sexes: *alike.*
Immatures: *similar to non-breeding adults.*
Voice: *whistling 'tsit', and 'kee-uk'.*   *GC*

57   ROSEATE TERN *Sterna dougallii*   41cm
The subtle rose-coloured tinge usually present on the breast and underparts gives this graceful tern its name. Usually in flocks, it breeds in colonies on several sand cays and off-shore islands on the Great Barrier Reef and off the west coast of Australia but is generally uncommon. Widespread in the northern hemisphere, and non-breeding birds reach northern Australia. Breeds September-May.
Recognition: (cf Common Tern): *tail streamers extend well beyond folded wings.*
Sexes: *alike.*
Immatures: *similar to non-breeding adults.*
Voice: *rattling and rasping.*   *T&PG*

58   GULL-BILLED TERN *Sterna nilotica*   43cm
Found throughout the world, and widespread in Australia both inland and around the coast. It frequents swamps, lakes and estuaries, also ploughed land. It eats fish and small reptiles, and skims above the surface hawking for insects. Breeds October-March (May in the north-west). Nests on the ground in colonies.
Recognition: *stout black bill and longer thicker legs than other terns.*
Sexes: *alike.*
Immatures: *similar to non-breeding adult.*
Voice: *harsh cries.*
                                                                                GC

59   CRESTED TERN *Sterna bergii*   48cm
The Crested Tern raises its shaggy crown plumes when it is excited or alarmed, and is one of the largest of the terns. It is the commonest tern in Australia, and is found in coastal and near-coastal waters. It dives for fish and may flock around shoals; occasionally takes young turtles and eggs. Sedentary, but young birds disperse. Breeds March-December. Nests in large colonies on off-shore islands. Widespread in the Indian and Pacific Oceans.
Sexes: *alike.*
Immatures: *dusky, crown mottled.*
Voice: *cawing and 'wep-wep'.*
                                                                                D&MT

60   LESSER CRESTED TERN *Sterna bengalensis*   42cm
Found mainly in northern tropical waters, it is less common than the Crested Tern. It is noisy and restless and dives for fish in deep sea as well as in shallower waters. Often harried by frigatebirds. Sedentary, but young birds may disperse. Breeds May-November. Nests colonially on off-shore islands. Widespread from the Mediterranean to the Southern Hemisphere.
Recognition: (cf Crested Tern): *smaller, black forehead (breeding) and deeper yellow bill.*
Sexes: *alike.*
Immatures: *bill grey-yellow.*
Voice: *like Crested Tern.*
                                                                                GC

61   WHITE TERN *Gygis alba*   36cm
This pure white bird breeds in colonies in tropical and subtropical seas - on islands which include Norfolk and Lord Howe - and has only been seen rarely in Australian waters off the coast of NSW. A surface feeder on small fish. Its flight is light and its outstretched wings appear to be translucent when seen from below. Breeds in colonies October-March. Nests in a tree fork in pine groves on Norfolk Island.
Sexes and immatures: *alike.*
Voice: *soft resonating 'tung', quiet chatter.*
                                                                                T&PG

62   LITTLE TERN *Sterna albifrons*   25cm
Worldwide distribution. Breeds in Australia along much of the coast except in the west and south-west. Frequents coastal inlets, beaches and islands. Dives for fish. Aggressive during nesting, with diving attacks on intruders. Breeds October-January. Nests on sandy beaches on coasts and islands close inshore.
Sexes: *alike.*
Immatures: *similar to non-breeding adults.*
Voice: *high-pitched rasping.*
                                                                                T&PG

63   FAIRY TERN *Sterna nereis*   27cm
The Fairy Tern, whose scientific name means water nymph, breeds in Australia and is common along much of Australia's southern coast where the Little Tern is absent. Also breeds in New Zealand and New Caledonia. In shallow coastal waters and estuaries it dives for fish and crustaceans in noisy and sometimes very large flocks. Breeds November-February. Nests colonially on offshore islands and sandy coasts.
Recognition (cf Little Tern): *slightly larger, paler above, less black before eye, bright yellow bill without black tip.*
Sexes: *alike.*
Immatures: *crown mottled.*
Voice: *high-pitched alarm calls.*
                                                                                GC

64, 65 SOOTY TERN *Sterna fuscata*   47cm
Immense colonies of this tern are to be seen on islands of the Great Barrier Reef, Torres Strait and off the
northern and north-western coasts of Australia. It is also widespread in tropical and sub-tropical seas of the
Atlantic, Indian and Pacific oceans, including Lord Howe and Norfolk Islands, and is perhaps the most
pelagic of all the terns. It feeds by snatching food from just below the surface. In Australia it breeds in spring
in the south and in autumn in the north and nests on a scrape of sandy ground or under a bush. A mass of
wheeling and screaming Sooties returning to their breeding islands makes an unforgettable spectacle.
Recognition: (cf Bridled Tern): *slightly larger, forehead patch all forward of the eye, blacker plumage above.*
Sexes: *alike. Immatures: upper parts speckled.*
Voice: *calls like 'wideawake'; barking and growling.*   64H&JB, 65R&DK

66   WHISKERED TERN *Chlidonias hybridus*   26cm
Breeds from the Mediterranean through Indonesia to Australia, also in Africa. In Australia it is widespread across the continent, particularly in freshwater lakes and rivers, usually in flocks; rarely on the
coast. It hawks for insects over water, scoops fish and other aquatic prey from the surface, or partly submerges. Migratory northwards to winter. Breeds October-December. Nests in colonies in water vegetation, sometimes with other waterbirds.
Sexes: *alike. (Non-breeding plumage like non-breeding White-winged Tern).*
Immatures: *similar to adults in winter.*
Voice: *harsh piping.*   KI

67   LESSER FRIGATEBIRD *Fregata ariel*   71-81cm
Widespread in tropical seas and overlaps the range of the Great Frigatebird. Breeds in the Coral
Sea, on the Great Barrier Reef and along the northern coasts. Piratical, and often robs boobies of
their catches. The adult preens a great deal. During stormy weather, it may shelter in mangroves
and spread its wings on the leaves to dry. Breeds May-December. Nests on the ground or in trees.
Recognition: *male all black with white flank; female has black chin.*
Immatures: *similar to adults, breast mottled.*
Voice: *'kukukuk'.*   GR

68   GREAT FRIGATEBIRD *Fregata minor*   86-100cm
Widespread in the tropical seas of the Atlantic, Indian and Pacific oceans. Breeds on islands
in the Coral Sea, and a regular non-breeding visitor to northern and eastern coasts. During the
day it is usually seen soaring above its breeding island, often at a great height where it is only
a speck. Its flight is swift and graceful. It dives on other seabirds to snatch prey and it also
takes flying fish, young turtles and squid from the surface, but does not swim or walk.
Recognition: *adult male entirely black; female has white chin and throat.*
Voice: *gurgling and chuckling.*   VS

69   WHITE-TAILED TROPICBIRD *Phaethon lepturus*   82cm including tail
Known to sailors as the Bos'nbird. Widespread in the world's tropical seas except eastern Pacific. Closest
breeding is on Cocos Island (where an apricot race occurs) and Walpole Island, a coral islet 240km south-
east of New Caledonia. A rare but regular visitor to eastern coasts, most sightings being of young birds
including casualties after storms. A vagrant elsewhere. Follows ships. Food includes flying fish.
Sexes: *alike.*
Immatures: *lack streamers, upperparts barred black.*
Voice: *harsh screams.*   AH

70   BLACK NODDY *Anous minutus*   36cm
Usually seen in large flocks on islands and reefs of the Great Barrier Reef, Torres Strait and
the Coral Sea and widespread in tropical Pacific and Atlantic Oceans. It is also known as the
White-capped Noddy.. It roosts in trees at night and flies to open sea beyond the reefs at day-
break. Sedentary. Breeds September-December. Nests in leafy trees.
Recognition: (cf Common Noddy): *blacker, smaller, slighter tail, whiter cap, longer bill.*
Sexes and immatures: *alike.*
Voice: *'krik-krik-krik'.*   KA

71   LESSER NODDY *Anous tenuirostris*   34cm
Breeds only on the Seychelles in the western Indian Ocean and the Abrolhos group of Islands off the coast of WA in large numbers. In the morning it flies out to sea to feed, and takes fish near the surface. It returns in the late afternoon to roost and nest in mangroves. Immature birds gather in 'creches' on the beach. Breeds September-December. Nests in vast colonies in mangroves.
Sexes: *alike.*
Immatures: *similar to adults, but crown may be whiter.*
Voice: *rattling, piping, whispering.*   B&BW

72   RED-TAILED TROPICBIRD *Phaethon rubricaudus*   86cm including tail
Widespread in the Pacific and Indian Oceans. Breeding areas include Norfolk and Lord Howe Islands and Raine Island off Australia's east coast and Rottnest Island off the west coast, and ranges far out sea. It dives for fish and squid. Rarely follows ships. Breeds mainly September-December in Australia. In pairs or loose colonies, nests in rock crevice or under a bush.
Recognition: (cf White-tailed Tropicbird): *pure white wings lacking black markings.*
Sexes: *alike.*
Immatures: *upperparts mottled, no tail streamers.*
Voice: *harsh clanging rattle.*   GC

73   GREY NODDY *Procelsterna cerulea*   30cm
This small noddy breeds on various islands in the South Pacific, including Norfolk and Lord Howe. A vagrant to eastern Australia from December to May, most often in January. A fairy-like flight. It paddles in the water and feeds on small fish and crustaceans picked from the surface.
Sexes and immatures: *alike.*
Voice: *continuous purring note.*   GR

74   COMMON NODDY *Anous stolidus*   40-45cm
This large, heavily-built brown noddy is widespread in tropical and temperate seas, and breeds in huge colonies on islands around the shores of northern Australia. It settles on the water in densely-packed rafts, and rests on any convenient floating perch, including the backs of turtles and even other larger birds. Feeds on fish mainly from surface beyond reefs. Roosts at night ashore. Breeds July-January. nests on the ground or low bush.
Recognition: *sharp separation of white cap from black lores.*
Sexes: *alike.*
Immatures: *cap absent or indistinct.*
Voice: *'kraa-kraa-kraa'.*   EZ

75   RED-FOOTED BOOBY *Sula sula*   75cm
The smallest booby. Distributed in tropical seas around the world, but seen in Australian waters only off the Queensland and WA coasts. It breeds in colonies on islands in the Coral Sea, on Raine Island and on the Ashmore Reef WA. Often roosts and nests in trees, and feeds mostly at night. Breeds May-September. Nests in bush well off the ground, sometimes with frigatebirds.
Recognition: *bewildering plumage variations from white to grey-brown. Red legs; sometimes long white tail.*
Sexes: *alike.*
Immatures: *similar to adults.*
Voice: *'krerk' or 'kronk'.*   GR

76, 77   MASKED BOOBY *Sula dactylatra*   86cm
Widely distributed in tropical oceans. Breeds on islands of the Great Barrier Reef, Torres Strait, Coral Sea, Lord Howe, Norfolk, Adele and Bedout (WA) Islands. Highly pelagic like all boobies and forages far out to sea - diving mainly for flying fish and squid. Seen only sporadically inshore around the coastline. Its reaction to human intruders at the nest is only rather mildly intimidatory, with side-to-side pecking movements, bill-lunging, or flicking bits of stick or coral. Boobies are so-called by sailors because of their reputation for stupidity of allowing themselves to be easily captured while perched on ships. Disperses widely after breeding. Breeding is continuous, but mostly July-December. Nests on ground in small colonies.
Recognition: *head pure white, tail black.*
Sexes: *similar.*
Voice: *male, 'pseep-pseep'; female 'kerk-kerk'.*   T&PG

78   BROWN BOOBY *Sula leucogaster*   75cm
Widespread in all tropical oceans. Least pelagic of boobies and commonly seen around Australia's
northern coasts and at numerous off-shore breeding islands. Large breeding colonies have been
recorded on Raine Island Qld, and Middle Island in the Lacepede Group, WA. It is seen around har-
bours and river mouths, and loafs on marker buoys. Breeds all months; nests mostly on the ground.
Recognition: *deep plain brown above, white below. (Beware of confusion with Red-footed in dark phase).*
Sexes: *similar.*
Immatures: *similar to adults; underparts brownish.*
Voice: *male, wheezing or hissing; female, sonorous 'kruk-kruk'.*   CW

79   AUSTRALASIAN GANNET *Morus serrator*   92cm
Widespread in summer in the coastal and offshore waters of southern Australia, Tasmania and New Zealand. In
Australia, it ranges further northward to winter. Its breeding colonies here are on islands in Bass Strait, on
Lawrence Rock (Vic) and around Tasmania. Most birds seen around the continent come from breeding colonies
in New Zealand. Singly, in small groups or large flocks, it feeds by plunge-diving. Breeds October-December.
Nests on a mound on the ground.
Sexes: *alike.*
Immatures: *speckled brown. Voice: variety of harsh loud notes.*   VS

80   BLACK-FACED CORMORANT *Phalacrocorax fuscescens*   69cm
The endemic Black-faced Cormorant lives entirely in a marine habitat along the offshore islands of
southern Australia and Tasmania. Usually singly or in flocks, but it sometimes forages in thousands.
Sedentary. Breeds in colonies mainly September-January. Nests on bare rock just above high water mark.
Recognition (cf Pied Cormorant): *black facial skin, less white on head. Head held low in flight.*
Sexes: *alike.*
Voice: *infrequent croaks.*   ES

81   LITTLE BLACK CORMORANT *Phalacrocorax sulcirostris*   64cm
Common and widespread, this small entirely black cormorant lives mainly on inland waters rather than on the
coast. It is sociable and often feeds in a large foraging mass. Nomadic. Breeds in colonies all months. Nests
very high in swamp trees with other cormorants and waterbirds. Range extends to Indonesia and New Zealand.
Recognition: *small and entirely black.*
Sexes: *alike.*
Immatures: *duller and browner.*
Voice: *croaking.*   H&JB

82   LITTLE PIED CORMORANT *Phalacrocorax melanoleucos*   64cm
Most familiar of the cormorants, and often seen close to habitation such as on stock dams and orna-
mental lakes in city parks, as well as on inland waters, streams, swamps, inlets and rocky islands. It
often forages alone, and eats small fish, yabbies, shrimps, tadpoles and larvae. Nomadic. Breeds all
months. Nests in colonies in bush or tree. Range extends to Malaysia and New Zealand.
Sexes: *alike.*
Immatures: *duller.*
Voice: *croaking.*   KI

83   PIED CORMORANT *Phalacrocorax varius*   66-81cm
Widespread on mainland except in most arid areas of interior; mostly coastal in south-west. Singly and
in flocks sometimes immense, it frequents mangroves, estuaries, rivers, lakes, swamps and rocky
islands. Rather uncommon. Breeds most months. Nests colonially on reefs, sand-banks and dead trees.
Also breeds in New Zealand. Recognition: conspicuous black trousers; bright orange spot in front of
eye.
Sexes: *alike.*
Voice: *threatening 'tok-tok'; other guttural noises and screaming.*   GC

84   GREAT CORMORANT *Phalacrocorax carbo*   92cm
The world's most widespread cormorant and the largest in Australia. It lives along the coast but more extensively inland on main waterways and freshwater lakes. Sociable and usually in groups, sometimes very large flocks. Often seen resting on sandbanks and mudflats or drying its wings on poles, snags and rocks. Breeds January-September. Usually nests colonially in trees and on ground.
Recognition: *all black (white flanks when breeding); yellowish chin.*
Sexes: *alike.*
Voice: *rather silent; some croaking at nest.*   T&PG

85   PIED OYSTERCATCHER *Haematopus longirostris*   48-52cm
The Pied Oystercatcher, common in Tasmania, is also found right around the Australian coast on islands, sandy beaches, mudflats and estuaries. Its stout bill, flattened at the sides, is used to dig into the sand for crustaceans and molluscs, and for opening hard-shelled bi-vales and prising limpets from the rocks. Wary. Sedentary. Breeds August-January. Nests in a scrape in the sand.
Sexes: *similar; female slightly larger.*
Immatures: *duller, bill and legs paler.*
Voice: *penetrating high-pitched 'kleep-kleep' or 'peepapeepapeep'.*   T&PG

86, 87 SOOTY OYSTERCATCHER *Haematopus fuliginosus*   48-52cm
          (A) Race *fulginosus* (southern form)
          (B) Race *ophthalmicus* (northern form)
For most of the year, the Sooty Oystercatcher, or Spectacled Oystercatcher in the north, lives close inshore on rocky coasts and coral reefs around the coast, but its distribution is patchy compared with that of the Pied Oystercatcher. Where they meet, they more or less keep to their different habitats, but may share nesting sites - though without interbreeding. The Sootys feed on crustaceans, sea worms and molluscs, opening them in the same way as the Pied Oystercatcher. Generally nests on islands, and does so in a shallow scrape in the sand, or in a rock cleft. Endemic.
Sexes: *similar; female slightly larger.*
Immatures: *wing coverts edged buff, legs grey.*   86T&PG, 87GC

88, 89 DARTER *Anhinga melanogaster*   94cm
Darters are found extensively in freshwater inland habitats of rivers, lakes, swamps and lagoons, particularly in the north. Generally solitary, but sometimes seen in loose parties resting, preening and drying wings (the feathers are not waterproof). Its body is usually submerged when it is swimming with its sinuous snakelike neck and head showing - hence its popular name Snakebird. It is wary and immediately sinks below the surface if approached, or it may dive and resurface well away. It slowly stalks prey underwater; its chief food being fish, speared with a sharp jab of the beak. In flight, it sometimes soars to great heights. Sedentary. Breeds irregularly but mostly October-March. Nests in a tree above water. Chicks over two weeks old will instinctively tumble out into the water if threatened - and scramble back when all is clear. Also found in tropical Asia, Africa and South America.
Immatures: *like females.*
Voice: *fearsome witchlike cackle.*   88PG, 89JF

90   AUSTRALIAN PELICAN *Pelecanus conspicillatus*   190cm
The familiar Australian Pelican is relatively common throughout the Australian mainland and Tasmania. It has spread to New Guinea in recent years and is sometimes seen as a vagrant in New Zealand, some Pacific islands and Indonesia. Mostly in flocks, it frequents estuaries, mudflats on the coast, rivers, large inland lakes and lagoons - and fishes in shallow water. Its main food is fish and crustaceans. It chooses remote and secluded sites for nesting. Large breeding colonies are found on the west coast on offshore islands and on the more extensive inland waterways in the east of the continent of which Lake Eyre is a notable example. It is highly nomadic and travels huge distances away from inland Australia in times of drought, as happened in 1977 after one of the most severe and widespread droughts of this century. It often soars at great heights floating on thermals. Its take-off to get airborne is long and involves much paddling and wing flapping. Breeds variably at any time after water levels are sufficient following rain. Nests on the ground or amongst water vegetation. Creches of hundreds of young birds are formed in the breeding colonies.
Sexes and immatures: *similar.*
Voice: *mostly silent, grunts or croaks at the nest.*   D&MT

ACKNOWLEDGEMENTS

We wish to reaffirm our indebtedness to the many people who contributed to the creation of our original work upon which much of this concise version is based - particularly the photographers. Without their continued co-operation and generosity, production of this Guide would not have been possible.

Credit is due to **Robeys Digital Pre-Press & Printing Services** of Canberra for converting the 815 colour separations to the smaller format, and combining them with new text and the distribution maps. Our thanks to **Allison Mortlock** for initiating the typesetting.

We are greatly indebted to **Bob Sneddon** for his advice on various production problems, and to **John Gooders** in the UK for his informative review of overseas trends in the design of bird guides.

Our appreciation is due to friends and acquaintances for the encouragement and help received, notably from **Graeme Chapman** and **Ederic Slater**, also to **Clare Lamberton** for her assistance in reading and checking text.

PHOTOGRAPHERS' CREDITS

The initials of the photographers listed on the following page are given at the end of each Species Note to identify who took the corresponding photograph(s).

THE PHOTOGRAPHERS

Dennis Avon.................DA
Barry M Allwright.......... A
Graham D. Anderson... GA
Kathie Atkinson .... KA
Douglass Baglin...........DB
J. Bell ....JB
Hans & Judy Beste.. H&JB
Harry Butler.................HB
Chris Cameron............ CC
John Carnemolla......JohnC
Norman Chaffer........... NC
Graeme Chapman.........GC
M.A.Chappell.............. MC
Brian Chudleigh........... BC
Brian J.Coates.............BJC
Jack Cupper..................JC
John Dart......................JD
Ron Dencio..................RD
John Disney.............JdeSD
Douglas D. Dow...........DD
Foch Dowling..............FD
Alistair Drake...............AD
Derek England............. DE
Johnny Estbergs.............JE
Kenneth Fink................ KF
Alan Foster...................AF
Jim Frazier.................... JF
Cliff Frith....................CF
Peter Fullagar.............. PF
Tom & Pam Gardner. T&PG
Ray Garstone...........RayG
Colin Gill................... CG
Robert Graves..............RG
John Gray..................... JG
Bob Green ....BG
Philip Green ....PG
Geoff Harrow.............. GH
Andrew Henley ....AH
Tony Hertog .... TH
David Hollands............ DH
E. & D. Hosking ....E&DH
Tony Howard ....TH
Keith Ireland.................KI
Fred James .... FJ

Gavin W. Johnstone.......GJ
G.R. Jones ....GRJ
Pat Jordan .... PJ
R. & D. Keller........R&DK
Peter Klapste ....PK
C.R. Knights ....CK
Peter Knowles ....PK
Nick Kolichis .... NK
Bill Labbett ....BL
Wayne Lawler ....WL
Ronald Legge ....RL
Fred Lewitzka .... FL
T.R. Lindsey ....TRL
Tom Lowe ....TL
Roy Mackay .... RM
Garth May .... GM
Ian McCann ....IMcC
John McCann .... JMcC
Arnold McGill .... AMcG
Ross McLennan ......RMcL
M.McNaughton. ....MMcN
Bob Miller .... BM
David Millege ....DM
M. & I. Morcombe.. M&IM
Ian L. Morgan ....ILM
Ian Morris .... IM
P.D. Munchenberg ....PM
Jim Napier ....JN
P. & J. Olsen........... P&JO
Frank Park ....FP
F.& B.Park ....F&BP
Steve Parish ....SP
Bill Peckover .... BP
Alwyn Pepper ....AP
Trevor Pescott .... TP
Harold Pollock ....HP
Jack Purnell .... JP
K. & B. Richards....K&BR
Paul G. Roach ....PGR
Peter Roberts .... PR
Graham Robertson....... GR
Len Robinson .... LR
Alan Rogers .... AR
Lyndon Schick .... LS

Vincent Serventy...........VS
Michael Seyfort .... MS
Ederic Slater ....ES
E.C.J.Smith .... ECS
Peter Soleness .... PS
Michael F. Soper........MFS
Chris Spiker .... CS
Frank Spolc .... FS
Gary Steer ....GS
Athal Tolhurst .... AT
D. & M. Trounson...D&MT
K. Vagg .... KV
Richard Vaughan .... RV
Trevor Waite ....TW
John Warham ....JW
John D. Waterhouse.... JDW
Brendan Watkins .... BW
Gary Weber .... GW
Cyril Webster ....CW
Harley Webster ....HW
Wardene Weisser ....WW
Bert & Babs Wells.. B&BW
Edgar Whitbourn.........EW
Michael Wright ....MW
Eric Zillmann ....EZ

Photographic Agencies

Animals, Animals, New
York............................ AA
Australian Antarctic
Division.....................AAD
Ardea London Limited... A
Australasian Nature Trans-
parencies....................ANT
Australian Picture Library
Pty Ltd.......................APL
Bird Observers Club..BOC
National Photographic
Index of Australian
Wildlife .... NPI
Photographic Library of
Australia ....PLA

SYSTEMATIC INDEX O[

ORDERS AND FAMILIES

PASSERINES